FM30
LESBIAN INSCRIPTIONS
IN
FRANCOPHONE SOCIETY AND CULTURE

Introduction

Renate Günther and Wendy Michallat

There have been a number of recent publications focusing on the representation of homosexuality in contemporary French culture. Key titles in this field include Lucille Cairns's *Lesbian Desire in Post-1968 French Literature* (Lampeter: Edwin Mellen, 2002) and two edited books: *Gay Signatures*, edited by Owen Heathcote, Alex Hughes and James S. Williams (Oxford: Berg, 1999) and *Gay and Lesbian Cultures in France*, edited by Lucille Cairns (Oxford: Peter Lang, 2002). The present volume both contributes to and extends this work with a collection of essays devoted exclusively to the study of lesbian inscriptions in Franco-phone society and culture. Spanning the period from the early nineteenth to the twenty-first century, this book explores a variety of lesbian discourses and representations, comprising chapters on poetry and the novel, contemporary film and television, art and architecture.

Within this wide-ranging chronology and interdisciplinary context, the essays in this collection inscribe a number of recurring themes which reflect the continuing reproduction of anti-lesbian myths and stereotypes across different historical periods. Representations of lesbian desire as a narcissistic drive towards fusional identification and the privileged image of lesbian motherhood thus alternate with a pathologising portrayal of lesbian sexuality and the Freudian notion that lesbianism is but a stage in a woman's development towards heterosexuality. However, some of the chapters in this book also discuss writers and film directors whose work attempts to create more positive lesbian inscriptions. Such cultural counter-discourses refute the portrayal of female homosexuality as narcissistic by subverting the hetero-normative construction of desire and identification as mutually exclusive positions. Countering the most common stereotypes, these discourses also construct a different image of lesbian subjectivity as both transgressive and empowering.

In the opening chapter, David Evans argues that lesbians in Baudelaire are the objects of neither the poet's usual misogynistic scorn, nor of the voyeuristic male gaze. Instead, Baudelaire expresses admiration and empathy for these transgressive figures. Through close readings of key poems and passages from the poet's own journals, Evans explores the Baudelairean lesbians' departure from conventional literary *topoi*, their restless quest for spiritual satisfaction and their transcendence of bourgeois morality. For Baudelaire, as Evans shows, lesbian desire exists outside the heterosexual cycle of reproduction and is thus revered as the pure, noble passion of glorious sterility. Yet, the 'chercheuses d'infini' are also acutely aware, like the poet himself, of a mysterious 'abîme béant'. Like a female equivalent of the Baudelairean dandy, the poet's lesbians mirror the tensions inherent in his own quest: the antagonism between his longing for the absolute and a melancholic sensitivity to the ultimate futility of this search.

Owen Heathcote, in chapter two, offers a comparative study exploring Honoré de Balzac's novel *La Fille aux yeux d'or* (1834–1835) and Chantal Akerman's film *La Captive* (2000). Although very different in period, tone and medium, both works portray the lesbian as a prisoner and behind a screen. Heathcote argues that, despite their apparently negative construction of the lesbian, Balzac and Akerman give an important new dimension to this figure. Firstly, both women in Balzac's novel and all the women in Akerman's film are lesbians. Lesbianism is thus shown to be not an exception, but the rule. Secondly, the lesbian figures in both works dominate the screens which are supposed to conceal and confine them. Compared to the male 'protagonists', the lesbians are the characters whose very elusiveness gives them an identity, an interest and a power which escapes their male companions, lovers and gaolers.

In the first of two chapters on images of the lesbian in contemporary French cinema, Lucille Cairns examines narratives of lesbian sex and sexuality in recent French and Francophone film (1990 to 2002). A key objective of her study is to ascertain the extent to which gendered differences may be discerned in the various representations of lesbo-eroticism. Starting with the hypothesis that the socially constructed cat-egories of men and women will tend to perceive and represent lesbian desire differently, Cairns explores this supposition through a close reading of selected texts. The national specificities of this representation are also examined, as Cairns asks whether metropolitan French, francophone Belgian, French Canadian and francophone African directors mediate differing perspectives on inter-female desire.

Sophie Bélot's study traces the work of French women filmmakers from the 1970s, a period in which they were engaged primarily in avant-garde cinema and concentrating on feminist issues such as abortion and rape. Subsequently, as Bélot shows, the number of women filmmakers in France has risen steadily, and common characteristics in the subject matter they tackle in their films can still be detected. While women film directors usually address issues such as family relationships, relations bet-ween men and women and female sexuality, they have tended to neglect the theme of female friendship. Bélot's chapter foregrounds this subject by focusing on the portrayal of relationships between women in a selection of French films from the early 1990s to 2000. It highlights representations of female friendship from a feminist perspective in films such as *Mina Tannenbaum* (Martine Dugowson, 1993), *Ainsi soient-elles* (Patrick and Lisa Alessandrin, 1995), *Gazon maudit* (Josiane Balasko, 1995) and *Baise-moi* (Coralie Trinh Thi and Virginie Despentes, 2000).

Brigitte Rollet's chapter analyses and evaluates fictional constructions of female homosexuality on French television, as she investigates images of the lesbian on both private and public channels. As her analysis shows, lesbian characters appear most frequently in the thriller genre which reinforces stereotypical images of lesbians as either victims or criminals whose very sexuality makes them look 'suspect' in the eyes of a hetero-normative society. This tendency to normalise female homosexuality is also evident in the pervasive portrayal of lesbians as 'feminine' characters or as mothers whose children are seen to compensate for their 'abnormal' relationships with other women. As lesbians become assimilated into dominant media discourses, the specificity of their identities and ex-periences is effectively erased.

Mireille Brioude opens the section on lesbians in twentieth-century French fiction and theory with an examination of the critical reception of Violette Leduc. Her chapter explores the reasons why the lesbian them-atic reigns preponderant in the reception of Leduc to the extent that the rest of her work, rich and diverse in both subject matter and style, is overlooked. Brioude looks at why commentators have simplified Leduc's work and reduced it to issues of sexuality, which occupied a relatively minor place in her *œuvre*, when her contemporaries Gide, Cocteau and Colette have maintained credibility as writers beyond such reductive definitions. The chapter traces both Anglo-Saxon and French press commentary of the period when Leduc was active as a writer and posthumous evaluations of her work in a critical analysis of the progressive constructions of her identity as a Lesbian writer.

Stephanie Schechner's study of the novels of Mireille Best opens with an examination of the pervasive negative inscriptions of the lesbian body in French literature. However, as Schechner shows, in the second half of the twentieth century a new generation of writers, including Mireille Best, attempted to illuminate lesbian subjects without destroying them and offered readers a more positive perspective on lesbian corporeality and sexuality. Schechner explores Best's representations of lesbian bodies in both sexual and non-sexual contexts. Her inquiry focuses on the question of how Best, even as she marks her work as similar to the projects of writers such as Monique Wittig and Hélène Cixous, opens up a new space for the representation of lesbian literary subjects in a way that accounts for their complexity and avoids narrow definitions of sexuality.

In a radical new reading of Simone de Beauvoir, Ursula Tidd draws on recent studies of female masculinities such as Judith Halberstam's *Female Masculinity* (Durham, N.C.: Duke University Press, 1998) to analyse the relationship between such masculinities and lesbian desire. Tidd argues for a re-evaluation of Beauvoir's novel *L'Invitée* as an exploration of the plurality of gender identities, including female masculinities. Lesbian desire in *L'Invitée* is represented not as a solipsistic desire for the self-same, but rather as a desire for authentic female difference, dramatised in an intense erotic encounter between the divergent female masculinities, deployed by the novel's female characters.

In the concluding section on the theme of space, Amanda Crawley-Jackson examines the spaces inhabited by lesbian inmates, as they have been represented in recent French prison narratives. Focusing on writings by Elisabeth Cons, Albertine Sarrazin, Danielle Huèges and others, her chapter suggests that the boundaries between open and closed, visible and hidden, in and 'out' are challenged in prison by lesbian practices. Traditional borders are transgressed in this otherwise most rigorously geo-metric moral and architectural space, as closeted becomes open, inside out, and as a sense of abjectness is experienced and narrated by authors for whom heterosexuality constitutes the very foundation of their 'normality' and identity. Crawley-Jackson's study demonstrates how topographical disruptions mirror the turbulence created by lesbian practices within an aggressively normative field.

Frances Hutchins' investigation of space explores two narratives centred around the discovery of queer space: Colette's *Ces plaisirs* (1932), also known as *Le Pur et l'Impur* after 1941, and photographer Brassaï's *Le Paris secret des années 30* (1976). Her chapter places these two texts in dialogue in order to determine what is at stake for each of these writers. *Le Paris secret* is the result of a series of nocturnal forays in which Brassaï explored, photographed and wrote about the secret places of Paris in the 1930s: the haunts of North African prostitutes and their pimps, gay and lesbian clubs and opium dens. As a photographer, especially in the age of the cumbersome camera, Brassaï's position as spectator and outsider would have been conspicuous. The Colette of *Ces plaisirs*, however, had the writer's privilege of unobtrusiveness. From her position as a 'nearly native informant', she insinuated herself into queer spaces that she did not necessarily claim for herself. As Hutchins shows, Colette's project, much like Brassaï's, exoticises the queer subject while implicating the author in this very exoticism.

In the final chapter, Sheila Crane discusses the architectural practices of American expatriates Elsie de Wolfe and Nathalie Clifford Barney. Crane argues that both women embraced elements of an aristocratic and thus deeply conservative eighteenth-century aesthetic, linked to Versailles in the careful re-appropriation and recreation of their own interior spaces. For Elsie de Wolfe, the architectural forms of Versailles were direct references in her renovation of the so-called Villa Trianon in 1903. For Barney, eighteenth-century traditions associated with *salon* culture and the picturesque garden provided the vocabulary for articulating her phil-osophy of friendship and amorous attachments. By examining the pro-cesses through which de Wolfe and Barney re-inscribed the buildings they inhabited, Crane traces the links between subjectivity, interiority and architectural space, while assessing the ideological and cultural significance of such a conservative tradition of female homoeroticism.

The articles in *Lesbian Inscriptions in Francophone Society and Culture* were developed from papers given at a conference of the same name held at the University of Sheffield in April 2004. Diminished in importance or simply ignored, lesbianism was routinely marginalised in critical work until relatively recently. It was a primary aim of the conference to demonstrate the presence of lesbian discourse and representation in a range of cultural expression over a broad chronological period. It was always the intention that papers from the conference should be published and in so doing we hope to have contributed in some measure to restoring the visibility of lesbian expression in Francophone cultural production.

Baudelaire, Lesbian Poet?
A Place for Women in *Les Fleurs du Mal*

David Evans
University of St Andrews

Only three of Baudelaire's poems deal specifically with lesbians: 'Lesbos', and the two 'Femmes damnées', one of which is subtitled 'Delphine et Hippolyte'. These poems were grouped consecutively as numbers eighty to eighty-two in the first edition of *Les Fleurs du Mal*, published on 21 June 1857. As early as 5 July that year, an article by Gustave Bourdin appears in *Le Figaro* accusing the author of blasphemy and salacious immorality in four poems, including these three:

> *Le Reniement de saint Pierre*, puis *Lesbos*, et deux qui ont pour titre les *Femmes damnées*, quatre chefs-d'œuvre de passion, d'art et de poésie; mais on peut le dire, il le faut, on le doit: si l'on comprend qu'à vingt ans l'imagination d'un poète puisse se laisser entraîner à traiter de semblables sujets, rien ne peut justifier un homme de plus de trente, d'avoir donné la publicité à de semblables monstruosités.[1]

An official report sent to the *Direction générale de la sûreté publique* refers to both 'Femmes damnées' poems as 'l'expression de la lubricité la plus révoltante', and so Baudelaire is prosecuted, as is well known, for his 'atteinte à la morale publique'.[2] On 20 August, during the trial, the court is warned of the 'Femmes damnées' and the details of 'les plus intimes mœurs des tribades' contained therein.[3] Since 'tribade', the official term

---

[1]   Baudelaire, *Œuvres complètes*, ed. Claude Pichois, 2 vols (Paris: Gallimard, coll. 'Bibliothèque de la Pléiade', 1975–1976), I, 1177 (hereafter O.C.).

[2]   Ibid., I, 1178.

[3]   Ibid., I, 1180.

for 'lesbian', is defined in *Littré* as a 'terme qu'on évite d'employer. Femme qui abuse de son sexe avec une autre femme', it is hardly surprising that, given Baudelaire's taste for provocation, we find amongst his lists of ideas for future projects the title 'Les Tribades'.[4] Although the cautious poet had added five apparently moralistic stanzas to 'Delphine et Hippolyte' just before publication, the court ordered that both this poem and 'Lesbos' be withdrawn from the volume, while the least explicit of the three texts, 'Femmes damnées', was allowed to remain.

The figure of the lesbian, featuring in only three poems of an initial hundred, might seem peripheral to Baudelaire's poetics, but he had originally planned to entitle his volume *Les Lesbiennes*, roughly between 1845 and 1847, when these three poems are thought to have been composed. Indeed, John E. Jackson sees this theme as so central to *Les Fleurs du Mal* that for the cover of his 1999 'Livre de poche' edition he chooses Gustave Courbet's *Le Sommeil*, a painting of two women entwined in apparently post-coital bliss, inspired by the poem 'Delphine et Hippolyte' itself and derided by Tamsin Wilton as nothing but 'pseudo-lesbian soft porn'.[5] Claude Pichois observes that nineteenth-century dictionaries do not attribute to the word 'lesbienne' the homosexual sense it carries today; the word appears neither in *Littré* nor in the *Dictionnaire général*, and the *Dictionnaire national* of 1847 informs us only that 'Les Lesbiennes sont célèbres par leurs débauches'.[6] The dictionaries, however, are slow to reflect contemporary usage, and in Baudelaire's *milieu*, the homosexual sense of the term would certainly be recognised. Before studying Baudelaire's treatment of his lesbians, the reader may be forgiven for fearing the worst: exploitative *tableaux*, perhaps, such as the titillating lesbian cat-fight which concludes Balzac's *La Fille aux cheveux d'or*, aimed squarely at the heterosexual male gaze? Or torrents of the misogynistic scorn which Baudelaire himself admits in one of several ardent love letters to Apollonie Sabatier: 'Vous voyez, ma bien belle chérie, que j'ai

---

d'odieux préjugés à l'endroit des femmes. — Bref, je n'ai pas *la foi*. — Vous avez l'âme belle, mais en somme, c'est une âme féminine'?[7]

The first point of note, however, is that Baudelaire's lesbians are objects neither of excited curiosity nor of cheap fantasy, whereas his representation of heterosexual woman, the satanic temptress, invites this sort of reading. In *Cutting the Body*, for example, Eliane DalMolin argues that 'Baudelaire scans the female body with the precision of a laser beam splicing her symbolic flesh'.[8] Thus, in 'Le Beau navire', the poet's predatory eye wanders over his mistress from one alluring body part to another, from the head, neck and shoulders to her bosom, nipples, legs and snake-like arms.[9] Similarly 'Les Bijoux', another banned poem, begins with an alluring hint of the nudity to come:

> La très chère était nue, et, connaissant mon cœur,
> Elle n'avait gardé que ses bijoux sonores [...].   (ll.1–2)

> Et son bras et sa jambe, et sa cuisse et ses reins,
> Polis comme de l'huile, onduleux comme un cygne,
> Passaient devant mes yeux [...].   (ll.17–19)

'Une Martyre' describes a painting of a headless female corpse propped on all fours on a bed, and in describing the 'cadavre impur' (l.49), Baudelaire is careful to include her stockings and garter:

> Un bas rosâtre, orné de coins d'or, à la jambe,
>   Comme un souvenir est resté;
> La jarretière, ainsi qu'un œil secret qui flambe,
>   Darde un regard diamanté.   (ll.25–28)

The lesbian poems, however, feature few of these sexually provocative descriptions. 'Lesbos' refers only to the women's 'baisers languissants' (l.2), and then to their caresses:

---

[7] Letter of 31 August 1857, *Corr.* I, 425; Baudelaire's italics.
[8] Ann Arbor: University of Michigan Press, 2000, 2.
[9] Ibid., 20.

Les filles aux yeux creux, de leurs corps amoureuses,
Caressent les fruits mûrs de leur nubilité.   (ll.18–19)

Here though, the hollow eyes suggest a mental torment akin to Baudelairean *spleen*, shifting the scene away from the simplistically provocative
towards the heart of Baudelaire's poetics, where the sexual experience,
like that of opium, hashisch, wine and music, represents a desperate and
doomed attempt to escape from the existential terror of the *gouffre*. Reinforcing this theme, Sappho's eye is described in similar terms in the same
poem: 'l'œil noir que tachette / Le cercle ténébreux tracé par les douleurs'
(ll.58–59). The suggestion of erotic flagellation in 'Femmes damnées'
('recélant un fouet sous leurs longs vêtements', l.18) also transcends the
gratuitously pornographic thanks to clear echoes of 'L'Héauton–
timorouménos', where pain inflicted either on himself or another provides
the poet with an outlet for spiritual anguish. 'Delphine et Hippolyte', one
might argue, features the most explicitly sexual imagery between two
women, from the 'caresses puissantes' (l.3) of the older, experienced ini-
tiator to the 'bras vaincus' (l.11) of the naïve child who exclaims:

Je veux m'anéantir dans ta gorge profonde,
Et trouver sur ton sein la fraîcheur des tombeaux!   (ll.83–84)

Yet of all three poems, this is the only detail which can be said to have
any real voyeuristic charge, and even here the eroticism lies rather in the
typically Baudelairean yearning for death and the preference for perfumes
over physical contact and visual stimulation. Indeed, in these texts the
poet concentrates on the future promise of ecstasy rather than the sexual
act itself, just as in his most successful love poems he lingers over the
stimulation of his imagination in order to delay the inevitable disappointment of the post-coital *vide* described in 'Une nuit que j'étais près
d'une affreuse Juive'. In 'Femmes damnées', therefore, the women are
not in contact, but rather, non-sexual body parts are pictured moving towards each other, but not touching: 'Et leurs pieds se cherchant et leurs
mains rapprochées' (l.3). Likewise, a reticent Hippolyte does not touch
her lover, although she senses that she soon will: 'je sens ma bouche aller

vers toi' (l.52), just as Delphine tempts her with some alluring future tenses:

Des plaisirs plus obscurs je lèverai les voiles,
Et je t'endormirai dans un rêve sans fin! (ll.39–40)

The lesbian characters, therefore, share the poet's understanding of the sensual strategies necessary to preserve a delicately unstable desire on the edge of fulfilment, and of the privileged role played by perfume. In both 'Parfum exotique' and 'La Chevelure', it is the heady scent alone which inspires the poet's reverie, and 'Delphine et Hippolyte' in particular exploits the erotic force of perfumes, with Hippolyte reclining 'Sur de profonds coussins tout imprégnés d'odeur' (l.2).

This notion of impregnation is central to Baudelaire's intellectual appreciation of lesbianism as a firm rejection of the reproductive cycle of nature. For Claude Pichois, 'l'amour lesbien répond [...] chez Baudelaire à son opposition morale et théologique à la nature, à la fécondation: Lesbos est la patrie de la contre-nature et de la stérilité.'[10] 'Delphine et Hippolyte' ends with a similar subversion of reproductive terms; as the poet imagines the women's descent into hell, he tells them how the putrid fumes 'pénètrent vos corps de leurs parfums affreux' (l.96). Thus both impregnation and penetration, characteristics of the heterosexual experience which Baudelaire abhors, are subverted, transposed to the level of the intangible 'odeurs' and 'parfums'. Thus the poetic value of the lesbian for Baudelaire is that she resists the perfidious way in which nature and heterosexual attraction conspire to keep man bound to its reproductive cycle, ensuring the survival of the species and condemning mankind forever to suffer *le Mal* and *le spleen*. In 'Tu mettrais l'univers...', Baudelaire tells womankind that 'la nature, grande en ses desseins cachés, / De toi se sert, ô femme, ô reine des péchés' (ll.15–16); in his *carnets*, he writes of heterosexual woman's inability to suppress her natural desires, in stark contrast to the dandy, who overcomes them in an expression of contempt for the natural order:

---

[10] O.C., I, 1061.

La femme est le contraire du Dandy.
Donc elle doit faire horreur.
La femme a faim et elle veut manger. Soif, et elle veut boire.
Elle est en rut et elle veut être foutue.
Le beau mérite!
La femme est *naturelle*, c'est-à-dire abominable.
Aussi est-elle toujours vulgaire, c'est-à-dire le contraire du Dandy.[11]

And so Baudelaire's lesbians share his aversion to the laws of nature. They rebel against society's blind conformity, 'De la réalité grands esprits contempteurs' ('Femmes damnées', l.22), and as such their symbolic value at the heart of *Les Fleurs du Mal* lies in their determined rejection of our fate.

Again, it is in 'Delphine et Hippolyte' that this point is most clearly made, as Delphine compares heterosexual union to a violent fertilisation of the soil:

[Les baisers] de ton amant creuseront leurs ornières
Comme des chariots ou des socs déchirants;

Ils passeront sur toi comme un lourd attelage
De chevaux et de bœufs aux sabots sans pitié…   (ll.31–34)

Whereas, Delphine warns, her kisses are 'légers' (l.29), those of a male lover will be 'cruels' (l.70); once Hippolyte offers him her 'cœur vierge', she will come running back, with her 'seins stigmatisés' (l.74), because by surrendering to the reproductive cycle she surrenders the hitherto sterile purity of her breast to its maternal function. And in 'Lesbos', Sappho's blasphemy of giving herself to a man is described as submission to fertility:

Elle fit son beau corps la pâture suprême
D'un brutal dont l'orgueil punit l'impiété.   (ll.67–68)

---

[11]   *Mon cœur mis à nu*, III, O.C., I, 677, Baudelaire's italics.

As Baudelaire makes clear in 'Avec ses vêtements…', it is precisely 'La froide majesté de la femme stérile' (l.14) which he values the most, admiring the sexually and spiritually alluring woman from afar without either of them succumbing to the temptations of lust, maintaining the necessary distance between them. Thus the young girls of Lesbos, admiring their own bodies in their mirror, are glorious symbols of sterility, which ensures that neither penetration nor impregnation takes place:

> Lesbos, terre des nuits chaudes et langoureuses,
> Qui font qu'à leurs miroirs, stérile volupté!
> Les filles aux yeux creux, de leurs corps amoureuses,
> Caressent les fruits mûrs de leur nubilité.   (ll.15–18)

The representation of homosexual desire as love of one's own mirror image might seem rather crude and all too obvious; yet of the mirror image in Mallarmé's 'Hérodiade', Bertrand Marchal suggests:

> Il y a dans la réflexion du miroir, mieux qu'un simple dédoublement, une opération spirituelle, une véritable transformation, l'identité […] ne passe pas par la destruction du double imaginaire sur la glace, mais par la négation de soi en face de ce double plus pur, si bien que cette identité idéale qu'elle proclame confine en fait à la pure absence.[12]

The girl in whom homosexual desire awakens, therefore, is seen to reject her impure material self, devoting her life to glorifying her idealised form in the mirror. An undated fragment, probably from the 1840s, entitled 'Le Goinfre', features a variant of this stanza and underlines the importance of the sterile reflection to Baudelaire's appreciation of the lesbian:

> Que cette canicule aux yeux pleins de lueurs […]
> Rend de leurs frêles Corps les filles amoureuses,
> Et les fait au miroir, stérile volupté,
> Contempler les fruits mûrs de leur virginité.   (ll.9–14)

---

[12]   *Lecture de Mallarmé* (Paris: José Corti, 1985), 44.

Reinforcing our suspicions, this fragment also transposes the notion of impregnation to the level of the intangible, non-reproductive: 'L'air imprégné d'une amoureuse rage' (l.25).

The lesbians' rejection of their procreative potential is also symbolised by the opposition between the infertile desert and the sea. As Tamara Bassim reminds us, 'L'eau est un signe de fécondité. Elle est foncièrement germinative'.[13] In 'Lesbos', Sappho's suicide over unrequited love for a man is re-imagined as a self-inflicted punishment for having succumbed to him; as she throws herself into the sea, she sacrifices her life to the symbol of the fertility which she had tried in vain to resist: the *mère-mer* of reproduction. Baudelaire's lesbians, on the other hand, are to be found 'sur le sable couchées' ('Femmes damnées', l.1), embracing the aridity of their environment. The poet also urges Delphine and Hippolyte into the desert, away from fertility:

> Loin des peuples vivants, errantes, condamnées,
> A travers les déserts courez comme les loups.   (ll.101–2)

This desert imagery recalls the prose poem 'Chacun sa chimère', where the men, crushed by the weight of their all-consuming Ideal, are condemned to wander 'dans une grande plaine poudreuse'.[14] These lesbians, then, share Baudelaire's longing for the absolute, and also, in stark contrast to the heterosexual women whom he scorns, have an intimate knowledge of the suffering caused by the *ennui* which inevitably follows all artificial attempts to attain it. In this light, we cannot, as Tamsin Wilton does, simply reduce the Baudelairean lesbian to 'a lost creature, tortured with insatiable lusts, heavy-eyed with lack of sleep and sexual overindulgence'.[15] Far from embodying the male fantasy of a woman possessed by a legendary thirst for debauchery, the lesbian symbolises, rather, the poet's own despair at the ultimate futility of striving towards his unattainable Ideal. Thus the 'Femmes damnées' are seen languishing

---

[13]   *La Femme dans l'œuvre de Baudelaire* (Neuchâtel: À la Baconnière, 1974), 77.

[14]   O.C., I, 282.

[15]   *Lesbian studies: selling an agenda*, 143.

on the sand, staring into the inaccessible distance: 'Elles tournent leurs yeux vers l'horizon des mers' (1.2). In 'Lesbos' the poet himself climbs the rock from which Sappho threw herself and, assuming her position, scrutinises the same unfathomable, infinite expanse:

> Et depuis lors je veille au sommet de Leucate,
> Comme une sentinelle à l'œil perçant et sûr,
> Qui guette nuit et jour brick, tartane ou frégate,
> Dont les formes au loin frissonnent dans l'azur.   (ll.46–49)

Similarly, once young Hippolyte is initiated into the pleasures of the flesh, 'les horizons bleus dépassés le matin' (1.8) are replaced by the vision of 'un horizon sanglant' (1.48). She confronts for the first time the unsettling horror of the *gouffre*, as the bubble of sensual illusion bursts and she is plunged back into reality:

> Mais l'enfant, épanchant une immense douleur,
> Cria soudain: – 'Je sens s'élargir dans mon être
> Un abîme béant; cet abîme est mon cœur!
>
> Brûlant comme un volcan, profond comme le vide!   (ll.74–77)

In 'Lesbos', this yearning is presented as a ritual in which the whole island unites, and 'S'enivre chaque nuit du cri de la tourmente / Que poussent vers les cieux ses rivages déserts' (ll.73–74).

Baudelaire's affinity with these lesbians, therefore, stems from a shared appreciation of the tension between *spleen* and *Idéal*. They understand what the other women of *Les Fleurs du Mal* cannot. In 'Semper eadem', for example, the poet's lover frustrates and disgusts him with her 'âme toujours ravie' (1.9), as she knows nothing of his metaphysical angst. In 'Réversibilité' he asks:

> Ange plein de gaieté, connaissez-vous l'angoisse,
> La honte, les remords, les sanglots, les ennuis,
> Et les vagues terreurs de ces affreuses nuits.   (ll.1–3)

Yet she will never understand, no matter how Baudelaire tries to impart this knowledge. Firstly, in 'À une Madone', it is by piercing her heart with knives representing the seven cardinal sins that he hopes to make her feel his pain:

> Volupté noire! des sept Péchés capitaux,
> Bourreau plein de remords, je ferai sept Couteaux [...]
> Je les planterai tous dans ton Cœur pantelant,
> Dans ton Cœur sanglotant, dans ton Cœur ruisselant!   (ll.39–44)

In the final stanza of 'A Celle qui est trop gaie', which was also banned in 1857, the act of penetration acquires a punitive, instructive force, and requires a new, artificial orifice in order to reduce its reproductive function to nothing:

> Pour châtier ta chair joyeuse,
> Pour meurtrir ton sein pardonné,
> Et faire à ton flanc étonné
> Une blessure large et creuse,
>
> Et, vertigineuse douceur!
> A travers ces lèvres nouvelles,
> Plus éclatantes et plus belles,
> T'infuser mon venin, ma sœur!   (ll.29–36)

The lesbians, however, already have an intimate knowledge of *ennui*, seeking refuge in wine, the 'endormeur des remords anciens' ('Femmes damnées', l.16) and physical pleasure. From a moral standpoint, of course, this is interpreted as a tireless and impenitent devotion to debauchery, and this appears to be the sense of the stanzas added in 1857 to 'Delphine and Hippolyte': 'Descendez le chemin de l'enfer éternel! / Plongez au plus profond du gouffre' (ll.86–87). Yet here the poet encourages the women to continue their vain attempts at sexual transcendence, which represent a gesture of noble defiance in the face of defeat. A similar fearlessness in confronting the gouffre features in 'Lesbos':

> Lesbos, où les baisers sont comme les cascades
> Qui se jettent sans peur dans les gouffres sans fonds.   (ll.6–7)

Baudelaire admires the fruitless debauchery of his lesbian characters in that they refuse to give up the struggle towards absolute experience in the face of overwhelming disappointment.

Thus it seems that these lesbians share none of the spiritual deficiencies which Baudelaire attributes to women in his *carnets*: 'J'ai toujours été étonné qu'on laissât les femmes entrer dans les églises. Quelle conversation peuvent-elles tenir avec Dieu?'[16] Their existential sensitivity and understanding of the poet's plight surely exempt them from the following claim: 'La femme ne sait pas séparer l'âme du corps. Elle est simpliste, comme les animaux. — Un satirique dirait que c'est parce qu'elle n'a que le corps'.[17] If reproductive woman is nothing more than an unreflective animal, Baudelaire at least describes his lesbians as 'un bétail pensif' ('Femmes damnées', l.1), a paradoxical combination, like the poet himself, of *animalité* and *spiritualité*. In 'Femmes damnées', then, the lesbians form a sisterhood both among themselves ('comme des sœurs', l.9) and with the poet ('Pauvres sœurs, je vous aime autant que je vous plains', l.26). This stands in stark contrast to 'À Celle qui est trop gaie', where the poet could only address his lover as 'ma sœur' following the forced injection of venomous *spleen*. Delphine and Hippolyte's communion also transcends the sexual relationship for the sororal, as they call each other in turn 'ma sœur' (l.35), 'ma sœur d'élection' (l.54). In 'Lesbos', the poet declares his allegiance to the women's cause setting both himself and his sisters apart from loathsome bourgeois morality: 'Que nous veulent les lois du juste et de l'injuste?' (l.41). Just as metaphysical concerns bind the poet and the lesbians, erasing any differences of gender or sexual orientation, the poet and Sappho both lose their gender identity in a blurring of gendered terms. Firstly, when the poet follows Sappho's footsteps to the rocky promontory from which she jumped, he appears 'comme une sentinelle' (l.47); in the feminine noun he abandons his male identity and assumes that of the female poet. Similarly, the female poet is then described as 'la mâle Sapho, l'amante et le poète' (l.56), where both genders are reconciled in the attribution of a masculine and a feminine

---

[16] *Mon cœur mis à nu*, XXVII, O.C., I, 693.
[17] Ibid., O.C., I, 694.

definite article to the same person, and in the gender-oxymorons *mâle-Sapho* and *amante-poète*. Far from a facile comparison of Sappho to a man because of her attraction to women, this line highlights the lesbians' intellectual proximity to the Baudelairean poet. This blurring of gender boundaries embodies the poet's desire to reconcile imperfect earthly duality in perfect unity, since 'l'homme de génie veut être un'.[18] Developing this motif, Delphine calls Hippolyte: 'Toi, mon âme et mon cœur, mon tout et ma moitié' (l.36), and in 'Lesbos', as we have seen, the awakening of lesbian desire in the young virgins is stimulated not by the sight of other girls, but rather, by their own reflection, as each individual provides her own other half, perfectly intangible and, therefore, ideal.

In 'Lesbos', the reconciliation of opposites is achieved only by the two poets themselves, Sappho and Baudelaire, and in 'Un Mangeur d'Opium', Baudelaire suggests that this transcendence of gender duality is vital to the artist from an early age: 'les hommes qui ont été élevés par les femmes et parmi les femmes ne ressemblent pas tout à fait aux autres hommes', since they contract 'une délicatesse d'épiderme et une distinction d'accent, une espèce d'androgynéité, sans lesquelles le génie le plus âpre et le plus viril reste, relativement à la perfection dans l'art, un être incomplet'.[19] And so the poet reveals, in 'Lesbos', that he too has enjoyed privileged insight into the lesbians' secrets since his childhood: 'je fus dès l'enfance admis au noir mystère' (l.43). This immersion of the male element in the female, symbolising a quintessentially poetic androgeneity, is perfectly represented by the poem's rhyme scheme which refuses to comply, between stanzas, with traditional prosodic rules of masculine and feminine rhyme alternation. Thanks to the repetition of each stanza's first line at its end, and the insistence on a feminine rhyme at each *a* position in the *ababa* structure, the masculine *b* rhymes are swamped in rich feminine rhymes such as 's'**attir**ent / t'a**dmir**ent / s'**attir**ent' and the *rime pauvre* 'éch**o** / Sapho' (ll.11–15), or '**langoureus**es / amo**ureus**es / **langoureus**es' and the *rime suffisante* 'volup**té** / nubili**té**' (ll.16–20). It is as if the male element were submerged in a richer system of feminine

---

[18]   *Mon cœur mis à nu*, XXXVI, O.C., I, 700; Baudelaire's italics.
[19]   VII, 'Chagrins d'enfance', O.C., I, 499.

correspondences, a process which is completed by *le retour du même* in every fifth line, a prosodic representation of the young virgins admiring their reflections. This verse form is rare in *Les Fleurs du Mal*, featuring in only two other poems, 'Réversibilité' and 'Le Balcon', and the latter proves a particularly useful intertext.

Placed in the cycle devoted to Jeanne Duval, 'Le Balcon' is commonly read as a retrospective evocation of her relationship with the poet. The similarities with 'Lesbos', though, are striking, not least for the identical verse form and the opening lines:

Mère des jeux latins et des voluptés grecques,   ('Lesbos')
Mère des souvenirs, maîtresse des maîtresses,   ('Le Balcon')

In the present context, 'maîtresse des maîtresses' might suggest female homosexuality rather than a superlative evaluation of the poet's lover. Clear echoes of 'Delphine et Hippolyte' also abound in 'Le Balcon', from the 'caresses' (l.3), 'douceur' (l.4), 'sein' (l.8), 'cœur' (l.8) and 'sang' (l.14) to the evening setting, the 'voiles' (l.7), the 'gouffre' (l.27), and the 'mers profondes' (l.29), recalling the sea into which Sappho threw herself. Furthermore, the more mature, less erotic, relationship between the lovers centres on the same hands and feet as the tentative, non-sexual languors of the 'Femmes damnées', with 'fraternelles' echoing the recurrent sororal motif:

Et tes pieds s'endormaient dans mes mains fraternelles.
                              ('Le Balcon', l.19)
Et leurs pieds se cherchant et leurs mains rapprochées.
                              ('Femmes damnées', l.3)

The verb 'endormir' also echoes Delphine's promise to Hippolyte:

Et je t'endormirai dans un rêve sans fin!
                              ('Delphine et Hippolyte', l.40)

The celebration of poetry's evocative power is more central to both 'Le Balcon' and 'Lesbos' than the exploration of sexual mores, but the homosexual references in each text, both explicit and implicit, are crucial to the demonstration. Indeed, given the similarities with the lesbian poems, the speaker of 'Le Balcon' could be read as another woman, making the poem a kind of homosexualised fantasy for the sensual intimacy of the 'Femmes damnées'.

This notion of fantasy is not as far-fetched as it might first appear, for it is clearly expressed in an early poem of homage sent to Sainte-Beuve, 'Tous imberbes alors…', where the poet daringly paints himself as a kind of literary homosexual. The scene is set for Baudelaire's textual outing with a reference to Diderot's infamous tale of 'la Religieuse / Dont chacun sait l'histoire obscène et douloureuse' (ll.29–30); this is confirmed by several of the homosexually charged motifs with which we are now familiar, such as the balcony at night-fall:

> — Quand la sombre Vénus, du haut des balcons noirs,
> Verse des flots de musc de ses frais encensoirs.   (ll.39–40)

and yet another variant on the mirror theme:

> Et puis venaient les soirs malsains, les nuits fiévreuses,
> Qui rendent de leurs corps les filles amoureuses,
> Et les font aux miroirs – stérile volupté –
> Contempler les fruits mûrs de leur nubilité.   (ll.33–36)

Recalling the fruitless horizon-gazing of the 'Femmes damnées', Hippolyte and the poet of 'Lesbos', the young Baudelaire also scrutinises the azur: 'L'œil perdu dans l'azur morne d'un ciel d'été', l.15; moreover, 'la canicule' (l.21) and 'les lourds loisirs d'un jour caniculaire' (l.62) echo the erotic, feverish heat of both 'Lesbos' ('terre des nuits chaudes et langoureuses', l.16) and 'Le Goinfre' ('cette canicule', l.9, 'une nuit chaude', l.28). With the stage set, Baudelaire describes his literary admiration for Sainte-Beuve as an affair between lovers:

> Poète, est-ce une injure ou bien un compliment?
> Car je suis vis-à-vis de vous comme un amant
> En face du fantôme, au geste plein d'amorces,
> Dont la main et dont l'œil ont pour pomper les forces
> Des charmes inconnus.   (ll.72–76)

The formula is even more striking in that the end of line 73 cuts the simile in half; since 'amant' completes a rhyme pair with 'compliment', creating a short pause, a relationship is implied between the 'amant' and 'vous'. Only afterwards does the following line reveal the 'fantôme', the real object of attraction for the 'amant'. Just as Sappho, the original lyric poet, is glorified in 'Lesbos', so Sainte-Beuve's influence on the teenage poet is celebrated here, but the recognition of a literary inheritance in such provocative terms, beyond their initial shock value, is entirely consistent with Baudelaire's early poetics. The poet resembles the homosexual woman or man in his rejection of reproductive nature and his dedication to the pure love of the same rather than the illusory love of the other. Significantly, the poetic awakening of Baudelaire's femininely smooth-cheeked ('imberbes', l.1) adolescent involves the same mirror as the sexual awakening of the 'Lesbos' virgins:

> Et devant le miroir j'ai perfectionné
> L'art cruel qu'un Démon en naissant m'a donné.   (ll.68–69)

With these parallel references to self-discovery in the mirror, Baudelaire explicitly compares himself as a poet to the young girls, cementing the link between lesbian and artist. The mirror is a privileged motif of Baudelaire's early homo-poetic texts, expressing the poetic vocation as the discovery of an ideal other for which the artist yearns. Indeed, in the sonnet 'La Beauté', poets worshipping their unattainable ideal are described as her lovers, as her mirror-eyes reflect an improved image of their own imperfection:

> Car j'ai, pour fasciner ces dociles amants,
> De purs miroirs qui font toutes choses plus belles.   (ll.12–13)

Like the young lesbians, then, the poet also passes through a sort of artistic puberty. Acutely aware of the distance between imperfect earthly forms and their idealised counterpart, he rejects base reality and devotes himself to the asexual pursuit of perfection.

All these themes converge in *La Fanfarlo*, a short story written between 1843 and 1846, and published in 1847 under the pseudonym

Charles Defayis. Most critics see an ironic reflection of Baudelaire himself in the hero, Samuel Cramer, a young romantic poet who is persuaded
by his friend Mme de Cosmelly to steal her husband's lover, a dancer,
away from him. The plan is successful, and yet the young dandy finds
himself tricked, as he falls in love with the dancer and remains with her
even as time erodes her beauty and reality replaces the theatrical artifice
which initially attracted him. The key motifs of Baudelaire's lesbian poems recur throughout the text, such as the mirror, symbolic of sexual /
poetic awakening. Such is the writer's narcissistic satisfaction with his
own poetic sentiments, 'Une larme lui germait-elle dans le coin de l'œil à
quelque souvenir, il allait à sa glace se regarder pleurer'.[20] Indeed, remi-
niscing on their childhood, Mme de Cosmelly remembers specifically: 'je
me regardais moins souvent que vous dans la glace'. Wondering whether
her own beauty is comparable with that of her husband's idol, Mme de
Cosmelly also turns to the mirror, like the poets of 'La Beauté': 'j'ai de-
mandé à Dieu, à ma conscience, à mon miroir, si j'étais aussi belle que
cette misérable Fanfarlo'. In his efforts to explain to her 'le poison de
l'ennui', Samuel echoes the terms of the lesbians' exile by using the feminine noun form: 'on a vu plus d'une voyageuse désolée et perdue dans
les déserts arides du désillusionnement'. The hands and feet, central to the
asexuality of 'Femmes damnées' and 'Le Balcon', are also mentioned.
Mme de Cosmelly gives Samuel her opinion on writers: 'Vous apprenez
au monde que vous raffolez du pied et de la main de madame une telle',
and sure enough, when the poet finally gets his hands on the dancer: 'Notre homme exprimait son admiration par des baisers muets qu'il lui appli-
quait avec ferveur sur les pieds et les mains'. This aversion to reproduction is also echoed in the familiar subversive form of 'un air tiède et
imprégné de bonnes odeurs' which greets Samuel as he opens his window.

   The hero, therefore, shares all those features of Baudelairean poetics
which are figured as lesbian, and both he and the dancer are constantly
described as androgynous, perfectly whole beings. Firstly, this is inscribed in their very names, as Samuel has published poetry under the

---

[20]   All references to *La Fanfarlo* taken from O.C., I, 553–80.

female pseudonym of Manuela de Monteverde, just as the dancer's stage name matches a feminine article *la* to the masculine ending *–o*. This is reinforced as early as the first paragraph, with reference to 'le dieu de l'impuissance [...] dieu moderne et hermaphrodite'.[21] Furthermore, Samuel has a 'double origine', 'le produit contradictoire d'un blême Allemand et d'une brune Chilienne', and does not differentiate between sexual relationships with women, and platonic relationships with men: 'Il raffolait d'un ami comme d'une femme, aimait une femme comme un camarade'. As for the dancer, the narrator is unable to describe the marvellous spectacle of her leg, since it resists comparison to models of either sex: 'une vraie jambe d'homme est trop dure, les jambes de femmes crayonnées par Devéria sont trop molles pour en donner une idée'. Yet despite Samuel's apparently androgynous wholeness, 'il n'a guère eu dans sa vie que des moitiés d'idées'; when he finds his âme sœur, however, his mistress completes him: 'Samuel et la Fanfarlo avaient exactement les mêmes idées sur la cuisine et le système d'alimentation nécessaire aux créatures d'élite [...] ils étaient parfaitement d'accord'. Expressions such as 'accord d'opinions', 'similitude de goûts' and 'confraternité de goûts et de sentiments' leave no doubt as to what Barbara Wright calls 'the androgynous parallels between Samuel and the Dancer', 'a harmony of opposites [...] which lies at the heart of artistic illusion as presented by Baudelaire'.[22]

Yet once they choose to remain together, both figures lose their privileged status and succumb to reproductive life. Samuel initially feels that artists, 'prédestinés que nous sommes à n'enfanter que des morts-nés', forfeit their paternal function: 'il considérait la reproduction comme un vice de l'amour, la grossesse comme une maladie d'araignée. Il a écrit quelque part : les anges sont hermaphrodites et stériles.' The expression 'une larme germait-elle' quoted above also suggests, therefore, that the artist's sole reproductive function is to create some form of expression for his melancholy. Once conjugal life takes over, he becomes a real father; the dancer gives birth (to twins, naturally), and Samuel's creative efforts are henceforth described in suitably prosaic terms: 'elle vient d'accoucher

[21]   My italics.
[22]   Barbara Wright and D.H.T. Scott, *La Fanfarlo and Le Spleen de Paris* (London: Grant & Cutler, 1984), 23.

heureusement de deux jumeaux. — Samuel a mis bas quatre livres de science.'[23] By joining the reproductive cycle of humanity, therefore, the artist is exiled from the mysterious realm of poetry, condemned to simply churning out the physical, down-to-earth stuff of science books.

As Richard D.E. Burton observes, Baudelaire's taste for literary pseudonyms develops in the late summer of 1844, following a bitterly embarrassing episode which sees him deprived of his financial autonomy by his mother and stepfather:

> It was in the immediate aftermath of the imposition of the *conseil judiciaire* that Baudelaire added his mother's maiden name to his surname and so transformed himself into that bicephalous and curiously bisexual being Baudelaire-Dufaÿs (or, alternatively, Baudelaire De Fayis, Charles Dufaÿs, Defayis, or de Feyis and even, using his second given name, Pierre Dufaÿs or de Fayis) who would sign almost all his letters and all his published writings between September 1844 and January 1847.[24]

Although all the texts we have studied belong to this period, it would surely be too gross an abuse of psycho-analysis to suggest that Baudelaire's poetic preference for homosexual, hermaphrodite and androgynous figures had at its root his own sense of financial castration. We might allow ourselves, nevertheless, to see in his various pseudonyms the application of his early lesbian poetics to his own artistic signature, symbolising the idealised trans-gendered wholeness to which the artist must aspire.

In conclusion, Baudelaire is far from the only poet to tackle the theme of lesbianism. Lamartine, in his *Nouvelles méditations poétiques* of 1823, publishes the pedestrian 'Sapho, Elégie antique', in which Sappho, tormented by her unrequited love for a young man, throws herself to the waves. In 1867 both Verlaine and Banville publish lesbian texts clearly influenced by Baudelaire. As Jacques Borel notes, the six sonnets of Verlaine's 'Les Amies' veer towards pastiche or parody.[25] Despite numerous

---

[23] My italics.
[24] *Baudelaire and the Second Republic: writing and revolution* (Oxford: Clarendon Press, 1991), 11–12.
[25] Verlaine, *Œuvres poétiques complètes* (Paris: Gallimard, coll. 'Bibliothèque de la Pléiade', 1962), 1202.

allusions to the Baudelairean intertext, such as the title 'Sur le balcon', the sororal motif or references to 'odeurs' and 'caresses', texts such as 'Pensionnaires' appear designed either to titillate or amuse. As such, the exclusive use of feminine rhymes seems a tacky gimmick with which to labour a crass point:

> L'une avait quinze ans, l'autre en avait seize;
> Toutes deux dormaient dans la même chambre. [...]
> Chacune a quitté, pour se mettre à l'aise,
> La fine chemise au frais parfum d'ambre.   (l.1–6)

Banville's 'Erinna', on the contrary, follows Baudelaire's lead in voicing concerns central to his poetics through the voice of the lesbian poet said, perhaps, to have been a student of Sappho. Like Verlaine, Banville employs purely feminine rhymes, to which he refers rather heavy-handedly, and imports familiar vocabulary and even rhetorical structures from 'Delphine et Hippolyte'. Yet he also proves sensitive to Baudelaire's ironic subversion of the fertility motif, describing Sappho's breast as a fruitless 'pâture des chimères' (l.12).

It is Baudelaire, then, who sets the tone for a serious poetic appropriation of the lesbian as central to a metaphysical poetics. Her importance lies not in the voyeuristic topoi of male fascination to which Verlaine is content to pander, but rather, in shared understanding of the restless spiritual yearning at the heart of *Les Fleurs du Mal*. She embodies Baudelaire's personal definition of absolute Beauty as sketched in his *carnets*: 'un visage de femme [...] qui fait rêver à la fois [...] de volupté et de tristesse; qui comporte une idée de mélancolie, de lassitude, même de satiété [...] quelque chose d'ardent et de triste, – des besoins spirituels'.[26] At the heart of her suffering lies the essentially irreconcilable Baudelairean tension between an all-consuming quest for the infinite and the impossibility of attaining it. As such, these women are 'Chercheuses d'infini' ('Femmes damnées', l.23) whom the poet simultaneously urges: 'fuyez l'infini que vous portez en vous!' ('Delphine et Hippolyte', l.104). All attempts to attain the absolute will be futile, and yet neither the lesbians nor

---

[26]   *Fusées*, X, O.C., I, 657.

Baudelaire can bring themselves to accept the realities of reproductive life. They constantly yearn for the impossible union with the idealised self rather than submit to the heterosexual reconciliation of opposites. As such the lesbian remains a privileged figure in Baudelairean poetics: virgin, demon, monster and martyr ('Femmes damnées', 1.21) like the poet himself, she amply deserves her privileged status as his poetic *âme sœur*. Monique Wittig, who refers obliquely to Baudelaire as 'le poète lesbien', demands: 'il faut détruire politiquement, philosophiquement et symboliquement les catégories d'"homme" et de "femme".'[27] It is an agenda to which Baudelaire would surely subscribe.

Bibliography

Bassim, Tamara, *La Femme dans l'œuvre de Baudelaire* (Neuchâtel: À la Baconnière, 1974).

Baudelaire, *Correspondance*, ed. Claude Pichois, 2 vols (Paris: Gallimard, coll. 'Bibliothèque de la Pléiade', 1973). Vol. 1 repr. 1993 with supplement; vol. 2 repr. 1999.

——, *Œuvres complètes*, ed. Claude Pichois, 2 vols (Paris: Gallimard, coll. 'Bibliothèque de la Pléiade', 1975–1976).

Borel, Jacques, Verlaine, *Œuvres poétiques complètes* (Paris: Gallimard, coll. 'Bibliothèque de la Pléiade', 1962).

Burton, Richard D.E., *Baudelaire and the Second Republic: writing and revolution* (Oxford: Clarendon Press, 1991).

DalMolin, Eliane, *Cutting the Body* (Ann Arbor: University of Michigan Press, 2000).

Marchal, Bertrand, *Lecture de Mallarmé* (Paris: José Corti, 1985).

Wilton, Tamsin, *Lesbian Studies: selling an agenda* (London: Routledge, 1995).

Wittig, Monique, *La Pensée straight* (Paris: Balland, 2001).

Wright, Barbara, and D.H.T. Scott, *La Fanfarlo and Le Spleen de Paris* (London: Grant & Cutler, 1984).

[27]   *La Pensée straight* (Paris: Balland, 2001), 12.

The Lesbian as 'femme-écran'? Balzac's *La Fille aux yeux d'or* and Akerman's *La Captive*

Owen Heathcote
University of Bradford

Although very different in period, medium and style, Honoré de Balzac's *La Fille aux yeux d'or* (1834–1835) and Chantal Akerman's *La Captive* (2000) have a number of characteristics in common. Whilst Balzac is clearly a canonical French male writer and Akerman a Belgian avant-garde / art cinema director,[1] Akerman's *La Captive* is equally literary and indeed canonical in origin, based as it is on two sections of Proust's *À la recherche du temps perdu*: *la risonnière* and *La Fugitive / Albertine disparue*.[2] More importantly, both works feature a sequestered female lover or *captive*: in Akerman, Ariane (Albertine in Proust) who is relent-lessly pursued and spied upon by her would-be and possibly actual lover, Simon (Proust's Marcel) and, in Balzac, the eponymous *fille aux yeux d'or*, Paquita Valdès, pursued by her would-be then actual lover, Henri de Marsay, while virtually imprisoned by her female 'owner', the marquise

---

[1] See *Encyclopaedia of European Cinema*, ed. Ginette Vincendeau (London: Cassell / BFI Publishing, 1995), 3.

[2] For an examination of *La Captive* as a cinematic adaptation of Proust, see Peter Kravanja, *Proust à l'écran* (Brussels: La Lettre Volée, 2003), 107–20. Kravanja is, however, mistaken when he claims Proust uses the expression 'la captive' only once and deduces from this that Akerman 'montre d'emblée qu'[elle] ne se sent pas liée par l'œuvre de Proust' (108) since references to 'la captive' and its cognates in fact occur many times in *La Prisonnière*. See, for example, Marcel Proust, *À la recherche du temps perdu*, eds Thierry Laget *et al.*, 3 vols (Paris: Laffont, 1987), III, 69, 86, 90, 151, 281. A further detailed study of Proust and Akerman, which unfortunately appeared after the writing of this essay, can be found in Martine Beugnet and Marion Schmid, *Proust at the Movies* (Aldershot: Ashgate, 2006), 168–205. According to Beugnet and Schmid, the 'great un-known and aporia of the Proustian text and of the cinema' is lesbian love (204).

de San-Réal. Although literary in origin or style, both works exploit a contrast between colour — whether, in the case of Balzac, the famous colours of Paquita's boudoir, the vivid pictorial reds, pinks, golds and whites associated with the story's dedicatee, Eugène Delacroix, or, in the case of Akerman, the striking blues and golds of the bedrooms in Simon's apartment — and its opposite: both the vacant Simon and the blind-folded Henri pursue their 'captives' through the empty, echoing, unseen streets of Paris, Simon alone in his chauffeured Rolls and Henri pinned down in a swift-moving carriage. A further link between the two works is, therefore, an interplay between visibility and invisibility, with the characters seeing each other — or not seeing each other — through or behind — and, in the case of Akerman, on — a *screen*. Indeed, for Simon, a windscreen. Since both Ariane and Paquita are both *screened*, in the sense that they are both visible, yet invisible, penetrated yet impenetrable, the theme of the *femme-écran*, to which Balzac refers specifically in *La Fille aux yeux d'or*,[3] will, like Ariadne's thread suggested by the name of Akerman's protagonist, be one of the main threads or themes of this paper.

One of the main reasons why both Ariane and Paquita are seemingly behind a screen for Simon and Henri is that they are, at least initially or intermittently, in a prior relationship with a woman. Although living in Simon's apartment, Ariane seems more attached and available to her long-standing friend, Andrée, and Paquita is the slave of a woman who turns out to be Henri's half-sister, the marquise de San-Réal. However obviously lesbian these relationships, few critics have considered the nature or the representation of lesbianism in either *La Fille aux yeux d'or*

---

[3]   In Honoré de Balzac, *La Comédie humaine*, ed. Pierre-Georges Castex, *et al.*, 12 vols (Paris: Gallimard "La Pléiade", 1976–1981), V, 1095. Subsequent references to this text and to Rose Fortassier's introduction will be given as footnotes (*FYO* followed by page number) after the relevant quotation.

or *La Captive*,[4] perhaps because they, too, identified with the puzzled or thwarted male narrator-viewers, or because they, too, felt that the lesbianism was behind a screen: whether lesbianism is a key to a mystery as for Henri de Marsay or an impenetrable, possibly taboo, mystery as for Simon, lesbianism seems to be situated beyond description, beyond comment, beyond analysis: whether a conundrum or the clue to that conundrum, lesbianism and the lesbian defy language. In order to redress this textual and critical silence on the subject of lesbianism, it may be helpful, therefore, to examine precisely this link between the lesbian and the 'femme-écran'. Are lesbianism and 'the lesbian' themselves a screen or are they behind the screen? This question has two implications. First, it asks whether lesbians are themselves the secret or the symptoms of a secret. Are lesbians themselves the closet, or are they *in* the closet? Secondly, if lesbians are *behind* the screen, they may, once uncovered, reveal a welcome, hitherto under-appreciated, essence or identity. Given, for example, Balzac's fondness for typologies, they may be seen as a new social category or species and thus in need of recognition and space other than that of the screen or closet. On the other hand, if part of the screening process, the lesbian herself may be in process, and thus be part of a gendering or even de-gendering *process*. From this perspective, the lesbian may well contribute to an understanding of sexuality and representation and of the relationship between sexuality and representation. It is evident from this that the 'femme-écran' analogy can contribute to the representation of the lesbian as identity or as position — or, indeed, both. Moreover, whether screen or screening process, the lesbian may, like Freud's screen memories,[5] be symptomatic of further secrets or

---

[4]   See however Rose Fortassier's introduction, 771–78 and Michael Lucey, *The Misfit of the Family: Balzac and the social forms of sexuality* (Durham and London: Duke University Press, 2003), 121–23. For an analysis of the visible yet marginal status of lesbian desire in Akerman's earlier films, *Je tu il elle* (1974) and *Portrait d'une jeune fille de la fin des année 60 à Bruxelles* (1993), see Judith Mayne, 'Girl talk: *Portrait of a Young Girl at the End of the 1960s in Brussels*', in *Identity and Memory. the films of Chantal Akerman*, ed. Gwendolyn Audrey Foster (Trowbridge: Flicks Books, 1999), 150–61.

[5]   See Sigmund Freud, *The Psychopathology of Everyday Life*, in *The Penguin Freud Library*, ed. James Strachey; tr. Alan Tyson, 12 vols (Harmondsworth:

further closets: she may disguise, while also gesturing towards, other, potentially even greater taboos, such as female-to-female violence or incest, or, even, the very nature or construction of taboo itself: the lesbian as mystery, as sphinx, may point to the whole problem of (male) questing, curiosity and power.

Alongside Gautier's *Mademoiselle de Maupin* (1835–1836), La-touche's *Fragoletta* (1829) and Baudelaire, whose early title for *Les Fleurs du Mal* was *Les Lesbiennes* (1845–1847), Honoré de Balzac's *La Fille aux yeux d'or* is one of the most frequently referenced French 'lesbian' works of the nineteenth century. It is, moreover, widely seen as one of his most intriguing and provocative novellas. For Camille Paglia it illustrates a Balzac whose 'manipulations of gender are the most complex in literature'[6] and, for Graham Robb, Balzac was, in his representations of male and female homosexuality, 'so far ahead of his time that he is barely recognisable as a pioneer'.[7] Amongst many others, critics as different as Shoshana Felman, Doris Kadish, Dorothy Kelly, Pierre Laforgue and Nicole Mozet have all subjected the story to rigorous scrutiny,[8] and Terry Castle anthologises extracts from the story enthusiastically in her monu-mental *The Literature of Lesbianism*.[9] However provocative and intri-guing it may be, the plot of the story seems straightforward enough. After

Penguin Books, 1991), V, 83–93.

[6] Camille Paglia, *Sexual Personae: art and decadence from Nefertiti to Emily Dickinson* (Harmondsworth: Penguin Books, 1991), 404–5.

[7] Graham Robb, *Strangers: homosexual love in the nineteenth century* (Basingstoke and Oxford: Picador, 2003), 45.

[8] See Shoshana Felman, 'Rereading Femininity', *Yale French Studies*, 62 (1981), 19–44; Doris Kadish, 'Mixing Genders in *Marat assassiné* and *La Fille aux yeux d'or*', in *Politicizing Gender: narrative strategies in the aftermath of the French Revolution* (New Brunswick: Rutgers University Press, 1991), 37–63; Dorothy Kelly, 'The Primal Scene of Castration, Voyeurism, and *La Fille aux yeux d'or*' in *Telling Glances: voyeurism in the French novel* (New Brunswick: Rutgers University Press, 1992), 34–52; Pierre Laforgue, '*La Fille aux yeux d'or*, ou érotique, histoire et politique', in *L'Éros romantique: représentations de l'amour en 1830* (Paris: PUF, 1998), 183–204; Nicole Mozet, 'Une lecture structurale de *La Fille aux yeux d'or*', in *Balzac au pluriel* (Paris: PUF, 1990), 124–42.

[9] Terry Castle, *The Literature of Lesbianism: a historical anthology from Ariosto to Stonewall* (New York: Columbia University Press, 2003), 410–12.

an extended description of a Paris dominated by the search for 'l'or et le plaisir', the reader is introduced to the young *arriviste*, and seeming orphan, Henri de Marsay, sired but then passed on to a succession of substitute fathers by the profligate Lord Dudley, and now in search of 'la fille aux yeux d'or', Paquita Valdès, who is struck by Henri's androgynous beauty. Henri is eventually escorted, blindfolded, into Paquita's red, white and gold boudoir but realises, when she cries out 'Maraquita' during their passionate love-making, why he thought she was virginal but not innocent: she is the sexual slave of the marquise de San-Réal, who, he realises on witnessing her forestall his plan to execute Paquita, is another of Lord Dudley's children and thus his own half-sister and virtual identical twin. In betraying the marquise for himself, Paquita was, therefore, as Henri observes, 'fidèle au sang'.[10] Resisting the sexual overtures of her half-brother, the marquise will retire to a convent and Henri moves on to pastures new, announcing to his friend, Paul de Manerville, that Paquita died '[d]e la poitrine'.[11]

It can be seen from this brief summary that the lesbian and lesbianism are, in a variety of ways, the secret in *La Fille aux yeux d'or*. Although Paquita does emerge, at predictable times and in predictable places, from her unknown site of sequestration, she is invariably escorted by her mulatto, Christemio, and her non French-speaking *duegna*, and, when at home, is sealed in behind a series of coded entrances, locked doors, and male, female and canine guards. Since she is, moreover, even inside, further cloistered within either a dank, dirty salon[12] or in a semi-circular, thickly upholstered, sound-proofed boudoir,[13] there is no doubt that Paquita is firmly closeted in *La Fille aux yeux d'or*. The closeted lesbian does, moreover, hide another, the absent but ever-threatening marquise, in the same way that, as Henri makes clear, one false mistress can hide the real one:

---

[10]   *FYO*, 1108.
[11]   Ibid., 1109.
[12]   Ibid., 1078–79.
[13]   Ibid., 1087–89.

> La meilleure des discrétions est celle dont usent les femmes adroites quand elles veulent donner le change à leurs maris. Elle consiste à compromettre une femme à laquelle nous ne tenons pas [...] pour conserver l'honneur de celle que nous aimons assez pour la respecter. C'est ce que j'appelle *la femme-écran*.[14]

As if this double secret attached to Paquita and the marquise were not enough, Henri himself has to become closeted in order to see his lover: however much the fearless fighter and patriarchal pasha,[15] Henri has to be taken either pinned down or blindfolded to Paquita's house, escorted, moreover, in the mobile closet of a closed coach and preceded by the sealed packet arranging the rendezvous and announcing his arrival.[16] The narrative thus offers a whole *mise en abyme* of human and non-human packages, parcels, containers and closets which combine to ensure that the lesbian and lesbianism are the closely guarded secret of *La Fille aux yeux d'or*. And within that closet is, safely preserved if barely accessible, the essence and the identity of the lesbian. If lesbianism is the secret of the story, then, no sooner is that secret disclosed, than the story itself closes. And it closes in such a way that the secret is triply re-sealed: Paquita is killed, the marquise withdraws into a convent and, for reasons of pride and *arrivisme*, Henri will keep it to himself. At the end of the story, the secret — and with it, lesbianism — is forever secure and intact. There is, therefore, a certain homology between lesbianism, the screen and the narrative: the safety of the lesbian closet is replicated by narrative enclosure, disclosure and then closure or re-closure.

Although, then, the lesbianism of Paquita and the marquise is secured behind screens and within closets, lesbianism is not exclusively screened

---

[14]   Among other 'femmes-écran' in Balzac figures, most notably, Malaga, in the tellingly entitled *La Fausse Maîtresse*.

[15]   *FYO*, 1085.

[16]   See Felman (1981), 35 for further comments on the parcel motif in *La Fille aux yeux d'or*. Mention can hardly be made, even now, of the closet, physical or conceptual, without reference to Eve Kosofsky Sedgwick's celebrated *Epistemology of the Closet* (New York: Harvester Wheatsheaf, 1990), which Diana Knight uses for a reading of Balzac in 'Skeletons in the Closet: homosocial secrets in Balzac's *La Comédie humaine*', *French Studies*, 57: 2 (3003), 167–80.

off in *La Fille aux yeux d'or*. Observant readers will have already noted Balzac's early allusion to one of Lord Dudley's other offspring, 'une jeune fille née d'une dame espagnole, élevée à la Havane, ramenée à Madrid avec une jeune créole des Antilles' and later married to the marquis de San-Réal.[17] They will also have noticed that Henri's friend Paul referred to Paquita's companion, 'une femme qui vaut cent fois mieux qu'elle' and who, moreover, actually resembles Henri.[18] Such readers will add such comments to Henri's readiness to believe Paquita's letters come from the possessive marquis in London even though he sees the marquis in Paris[19] and thus to his self-identification with 'cette éternelle vieille comédie [...] dont les personnages sont un vieillard, une jeune fille et un amoureux'.[20] They will also add references to the marquise not only to Henri's puzzlement at Paquita's mixture of virginity and non-innocence[21] but to at least three of her own remarks: Paquita observes that Henri has the same voice as someone unspecified;[22] she tells him he is forgetting 'le pouvoir féminin';[23] she describes him as 'un de ces anges qu'on [lui] avait appris à haïr'.[24] It can be seen, then, that the supposedly hermetically sealed closet can in fact be opened and that the screen, if not transparent, is at least intermittently holed. By being, despite or because of closets and screens, at least intermittently visible, lesbianism is shown to be itself porous and intermittent. It depends on readings, interpretations and point of view. When Paquita is no longer 'une femme-écran' hiding another woman, but herself, as 'femme-écran', *herself that other woman*, lesbianism is not longer (just) an essence but a position. Indeed, the whole force of the screen is that one can be on either side of the screen — or indeed, on both sides alternately or simultan-

---

[17]   *FYO*, 1058.
[18]   Ibid., 1064. In 'Le Récit euphémique', *Poétique*, 17 (1974), 27–38 (28), Leyla Perrone-Moisés neatly unpicks the early, often unnoticed, references to the marquise.
[19]   *FYO*, 1074.
[20]   Ibid., 1071.
[21]   Ibid., 1091.
[22]   Ibid., 1083.
[23]   Ibid., 1099.
[24]   Ibid.

eously — or simply in-between, like the screen itself. Thus, at the same time as being an identity within the closet or behind the screen, lesbianism and the lesbian in *La Fille aux yeux d'or* are also a process and a performance — in the sense that they depend both on what she does and, perhaps even more importantly, on *how she is viewed*. Small wonder, then, that eyes and seeing — after all, Henri is blindfolded when taken to see Paquita — play such a large part in *La Fille aux yeux d'or*.[25] For in *La Fille aux yeux d'or* lesbianism depends not just on what a woman is, nor even just on who is looking at her, but, as Henri shows, on how much the viewer can, in fact, *see*.

Given that lesbianism is, in *La Fille aux yeux d'or*, not only an identity but a process and a performance, it is hardly surprising that the novel is permeated with references to movement and to theatre. However seemingly artificial the yoking of the opening section on Paris to the later narrative of Paquita and Henri, its emphasis on Parisians' industry, effort and *work* together with its emphasis on the upward movement of 'or et plaisir', is an appropriate introduction not only to a thematics of purportedly perverse passion but to a passion defined by its mobility, by its enactment and by a particular *mise en scène*. When Henri is transported, literally, into Paquita's boudoir, and is asked to cross-dress before they make love, the point is not just to introduce passion and provocation — nor even the rather suspect cliché that he is turned into a woman — but to show sex and sexuality as a process of transformation and performance. Hence, too, the coded entrances and the guarded portals. Lesbianism — *like perhaps all sex and all sexuality* — is a process, a ritual and a play. Henri may have got the play wrong when he refers to 'cette éternelle vieille comédie [...] dont les personnages sont un vieillard, une jeune fille et un amoureux',[26] but he is right to see himself at play,

---

[25]   For important comments on the links between gold, sight and femininity, see Felman (1981). In *Sarrasine*, too, the legibility of sexuality depends on social and cultural contexts: see Owen Heathcote, 'Playing with the *Coup de foudre*: the subversion of drag in *Sarrasine* and *The Crying Game*' in *Peripheries of Nineteenth-Century French Studies. Views from the Edge*, ed. Timothy Raser (Newark: University of Delaware Press, 2002), 268–92 (285–6).

[26]   *FYO*, 1071.

and in a play, in this particular act of Balzac's human comedy. The gender trouble that is announced by his apparent 'femininity',[27] as indeed by his cross-dressing, is only one aspect of a sex and sexuality which, like lesbianism 'itself', is shown to be a process and a performance in *La Fille aux yeux d'or*. As well as being an identity shielded by closets and screens, and as well as being an identity represented by the indomitable marquise,[28] lesbianism is also sufficiently chimerical — Balzac likens Paquita to the portrait of 'la femme caressant sa chimère'[29] — and sufficiently protean to infuse all forms of sex and sexuality.[30] For whether Paquita 'is' a lesbian who makes love to a man, or 'is' a straight woman in an enforced relationship with a woman, matters less than the possibilities of sexual crossings and cross-crossings opened up by 'lesbianism' and less than the voluptuous sexual ecstasies provided by these sexual crossings and criss-crossings. Rather than charting Paquita's 'conversion' from lesbianism to heterosexuality, *La Fille aux yeux d'or* draws the heterosexual, if sexually ambivalent, Henri de Marsay into a kind of lesbian pan-sexuality, from which he emerges with all the force of ill-acknowledged heterosexual melancholia.[31]

In order to show that Balzac is not simply exoticising lesbianism and offering it up for jaded heterosexuals like Henri,[32] it is important to point out that there is a further aspect to the analogy between closets, screens and sexuality in *La Fille aux yeux d'or*. As has been shown, when Paquita is no longer 'une femme-écran' hiding another woman, but *herself becomes that 'other woman'*, lesbianism is no longer (just) an identity but

---

[27]   Ibid., 230.
[28]   For a very different view of the role of violence in *La Fille aux yeux d'or* see Owen Heathcote, 'The Engendering of Violence and the Violation of Gender in Honoré de Balzac's *La Fille aux yeux d'or*', *Romance Studies*, 22 (1993), 99–112.
[29]   *FYO*, 1065.
[30]   See Ibid., 1044.
[31]   According to Judith Butler, *Gender Trouble: feminism and the subversion of identity* (London: Routledge, 1990), 70: 'heterosexual melancholy is culturally instituted and maintained as the price of stable gender identities related through oppositional desires.'
[32]   *FYO*, 1070.

a position, and, moreover, a position marginal or liminal to the text: they are both, with the marquise, outside the closet/screen and, at least partially, but only partially, inside the closet-screen with Paquita. For when Paquita is with Henri, and when the text is with Paquita and Henri, then lesbianism and the lesbian are both inside and outside, or, rather, neither inside nor outside, but in a world beyond both Paquita and the text. Lesbianism and the lesbian not only have their secure identities in closets and behind screens, but are also, always already, otherwise and elsewhere. For lesbianism is not just about to break out of the closet and from behind the screen, but, as the presence-absence of the marquise shows, break into the closet and through the screen — as does the marquise, violently, at the end of the story. *La Fille aux yeux d'or* is not so much a text about *coming out* as about *coming in*. And it can only be about coming in rather than out because it is always already 'out', anywhere and everywhere for those with eyes to see. If lesbianism is in process, it is also in process in the sense of being in the process of becoming, pre-Wittig, a kind of incorporative, universal 'elles'.[33] And, indeed, a universal 'elles' which can attract and absorb the sexual difference rather dubiously embodied by Henri de Marsay in the Venus-Paris of 1814.[34]

It can be seen from the above remarks that the closet / screen motif in *La Fille aux yeux d'or* shows how Balzac's lesbian combines her identity as a typically Balzacian socio-sexual type with sufficient gender mobility to inflect and infect the somewhat feminised masculinity and assumed heterosexuality of Henri de Marsay. This combination of lesbian identity and gendered fluidity is also facilitated by having a pair of lesbians with very different characteristics — the mysterious, even mythical 'fille aux yeux d'or' and the more clearly defined, even monolithic marquise. Before concluding that this combination of lesbian identity and gender trouble places Balzac in the avant-garde of sexual politics, a final question needs to be asked: does a story which claims that '[l']amour vrai

---

[33] See Monique Wittig, 'The Mark of Gender' in *The Straight Mind and Other Essays* (New York: Harvester Wheatsheaf, 1992), 85.
[34] See *FYO*, 1041, 1045.

règne surtout par la mémoire'[35] use lesbianism as a Freudian 'screen memory' for other, more taboo activities such as female-to-female violence or incest, or should the final violence and the incipiently incestuous relationship between Henri and his half-sister be incorporated, like Henri's wavering masculinity and supposedly exclusively heterosexual pleasure, into the above-mentioned pan-lesbianism?

Rather than represent more closeted taboos, the female-to-female violence and the potential incest at the end of *La Fille aux yeux d'or* are in fact so flagrant that they are in danger of sidelining the actual lesbian relationship between Paquita and the marquise. As Michael Lucey writes: 'faithfulness to the bloodline trumps anything we might think of as possessiveness regarding sexual identity.'[36] However, at the same time as apparently sidelining that supposedly taboo sexual identity, the violence also endows lesbian relationships with the same status as any other pairing. As Henri quips on hearing the marquise and Paquita: 'je veux aller voir comment cela se passe là-haut, afin d'apprendre la manière dont se traitent leurs querelles de ménage'.[37] However extreme the violence, it is therefore also banalised and normalised — by no means unusual in a Paris which is, as the extended introduction showed, a kind of earthly Hell: 'Là, tout fume, tout brûle, tout brille, tout bouillonne, tout flambe, s'évapore, s'éteint, se rallume, étincelle, pétille et se consume'.[38] Similarly, the uncanny resemblance between Henri and the marquise explains not only Paquita's *coup de foudre* for Henri — thus again fusing lesbian and heterosexual attractions — but, by anticipating Henri's sexual attraction towards his half-sister, shows the universal appeal of *the same*: Henri follows his sister in desiring Paquita and he also follows Paquita in desiring the marquise and, given his own resemblance to the marquise, is also, in a multiplicity of reflections, desiring not so much the other as himself.[39] Once again, then, lesbianism is not so much the exception as the type, not so much the taboo as the norm. Hence, Henri's lack of

[35]   Ibid., 1093.
[36]   Michael Lucey (2003), 121.
[37]   *FYO*, 1106.
[38]   Ibid., 1039–40.
[39]   See Felman (1981), 24.

surprise at the relationship between Paquita and the marquise. As again Lucey notes: 'Henri is thus *not* a dupe regarding same-sex relations between women. He seems perfectly familiar with them — as would any number of readers in the 1830s.'[40] Indeed, as Diana Knight has shown, open secrets about homosocial / homosexual positions and behaviours abound in Balzac.[41] The lesbian, however, seems to go beyond even the open secret, in that the lesbian combines the seemingly exotic, mysterious and taboo with the normal, the banal and *the same*. While keeping her own securely 'closeted' identity and while remaining as 'femme-écran', the chimera-like lesbian also transmutes, like the alchemist's base metals, into a gold-standard model for the representation of sexuality in the *Comédie humaine*.

Although Monsieur de Charlus, in Proust's *Sodome et Gomorrhe*, is somewhat disparaging about *La Fille aux yeux d'or*, seeing it as illustrating Balzac's familiarity with 'ces passions que tout le monde ignore, ou n'étudie que pour les flétrir',[42] there are clear similarities between the Balzac novella and Proust's *La Prisonnière* and *Albertine disparue / La Fugitive*. Many of these parallels are retained in Chantal Akerman's screen version, the Franco-Belgian *La Captive* (2000). As in Balzac and in Proust, the story centres on the virtual sequestration of a young woman, Albertine in Proust, Ariane in Akerman, within the Paris flat of the narrator, Simon — Proust's Marcel. Like Henri de Marsay, Simon pursues Ariane in a series of journeys through Paris, trying to observe her every movement and every meeting — particularly with other women. For, unlike Henri, Simon suspects, from the start, that Ariane is lesbian. She is particularly familiar not only with Andrée (Proust's Mlle de Vinteuil) whom he invites regularly to the flat, but with a constellation of other 'jeunes filles en fleurs' whom he also watches, at the beginning of *La Captive*, on a black and white holiday film of the girls cavorting in

---

[40]   See Fortassier, *FYO*, and Lucey (2003), 121.
[41]   See Knight (2003).
[42]   See Proust (1987), II, 840–41. By ending her film before Marcel is told that Albertine was in fact 'guilty' of 'vice' (see *La Fugitive*, III, 433) Akerman may well avoid such condemnations of lesbianism, but she also makes it less visible, even, than in Proust.

the sea. Although Albertine-Ariane is, like Paquita, exceedingly difficult to fathom, if only because she, too, is evasive or untruthful when questioned by Simon-Marcel, she remains acquiescent whenever he calls her to his room in the flat. Indeed, one of her favourite lines is: 'Voulez-vous que je vienne?' Eventually, however, — and unlike in Proust where Albertine's departure is a surprise to Marcel — Simon decides they should separate and he drives Ariane to her aunt's house in the country where plans are suddenly reversed: Ariane will after all return to Paris with him. Staying in a hotel on their journey home, Ariane takes a late-night swim and, pursued by a desperate Simon, drowns. Like *La Fille aux yeux d'or* — but unlike Proust where Marcel devotes many pages to reflections on Albertine after her fatal riding accident — *La Captive* closes with the sequestered woman's death. Unlike *La Fille aux yeux d'or*, the cause of death is uncertain: it could be suicide, an accident or even murder.[43] Ariane's death is, like her life, a mystery. Unlike her mythological namesake, she does not lead her hero out of the labyrinth and into the light.

It is apparent from this short summary that closets and screens figure in *La Captive* at least as importantly as in *La Fille aux yeux d'or*. Whilst the precise configuration of Simon's Parisian apartment is almost as unclear as Paquita's house in the rue Saint-Lazare, it, too, combines virtually empty, somewhat inhospitable reception rooms, seemingly in the process of re-decoration, and enclosed, internal and conspicuously draped bedrooms where the ailing Simon passes much of his time. This combination of enclosure and emptiness is repeated in the virtually deserted, echoing halls of the Rodin museum, in the Paris streets, also echoing from Ariane's distant, high-heeled steps,[44] and, perhaps even more importantly, in the huge but entombing private space of the chauffeur-driven Rolls he uses to follow Ariane across Paris, searching

---

[43] On the various possible explanations for Ariane's death, see Tony McKibbin, '*La Captive* and the power of love', *Studies in French Cinema*, 3: 2 (2003), 93–99 (99).

[44] On Akerman's insistence Sylvie Testud (Ariane) wear such uncomfortable footwear, see Olivier Joyard, 'Sylvie Testud ou la certitude du doute', *Cahiers du cinéma*, 550 (octobre 2000), 18–19 (18).

for her through the screen/lens of the windscreens which continually separate him from her and the outside world. If both internal and external spaces of *La Captive* place Ariane within a closet, albeit vast, or behind a screen, however transparent, then this distancing effect is repeated in a variety of other ways, from the film-within-a-film of the young women in the sea — where temporal and technical distance is emphasised by jump-shots and virtually inaudible dialogue — to the blurred vision of Ariane in her bath, indistinctly filmed behind another double 'film' of glass and steam. As in *La Fille aux yeux d'or*, then, the lesbian is both on a screen and, in *mise-en-abyme*, behind a screen and, as a tantalisingly close but mysterious, inexplicable, friend, a kind of literal 'femme-écran'. Being both a screen and screened, both clearly visible, yet often indistinct and inaudible, Ariane combines, like the marquise and Paquita, the distinct identity of sex, of 'le pouvoir féminin', and the more blurred contours of gender. The lesbian has indeed an identity but that identity is, like the Rodin sculpture, like the myth of Ariane — recalling, perhaps the mythical figures of Venus, the chimera and the sphinx evoked in *La Fille aux yeux d'or* — and like the Akerman film, subject to multiple, inter-vening prisms which protect her from the prying male gaze. Resistant but acquiescent, submissive but self-contained, both Paquita and Ariane embody sex, gender and orientational difference while being, reassuringly yet disconcertingly, always already the same.

Notwithstanding the parallel use of closets and screens in both *La Captive* and *La Fille aux yeux d'or* there are important differences between novella and film. A key difference is that, despite her apparent sequestration in Simon's flat, Ariane is much freer than Paquita. If Simon feels the need to pursue her as she circulates, seemingly inexplicably, around Paris, it is a sign that Ariane is indeed free to move, whether to see friends such as Andrée, the lesbian couple Isabelle and Sarah, or the opera singer Léa, or, simply, to go to the Rodin museum or arrange a hotel room for her aunt. This freedom has a number of significant implic-ations. First, it enables Ariane to combine containment and fixity with a nomadic, deterritorialised and thus Deleuzian lack of identity — with what Ivone Margulies has called 'the politics of the singular' and with what Tony McKibbin has termed 'the fluidity of character, the indeterminacy of character' in Akerman.[45] Thus, again the lesbian combines a politics of identity with generic indeterminacy. Secondly, Ariane's relative freedom enables her to be more of a challenge to the often thwarted, frustrated Simon, who never knows how long she is going for, who with, or for what purpose. Thus, however male-controlled Ariane — and *La Captive* might be seen as an example of 'le pouvoir masculin' as much as 'le pouvoir féminin' — it can also be argued that Simon, not Ariane, is, as the jealous obsessive, the true captive of the film: according to Bernard Benoliel, Simon is 'le vrai prisonnier de cette fausse captive'.[46] After all, Simon himself aggravates his own possessiveness by himself arranging Ariane's meetings with Andrée, even though he realises he will suffer from the pleasure they take in each other's company. Thirdly, Ariane's freedom enables her to meet not only Andrée but other women such as Léa, with whom she sings an extraordinary duet, and the lesbian couple, Sarah and Isabelle, whom Simon pathetically questions about what happens between women. Like Marcel who, after Albertine's death, forlornly wishes he had been more understanding of 'ces goûts' in Albertine's relationship with Mlle de Vinteuil,[47] Simon is, even during Ariane's life-time, nonplussed and disempowered by lesbian intimacy. For one of the main differences between *La Captive* and *La Fille aux yeux d'or* is that, unlike *La Fille aux yeux d'or*, *La Captive* repeatedly shows the inviolability not just of lesbian power but of lesbian solidarity. However outwardly submissive to Simon, it is with Andrée that Ariane's barriers come down and it is together vis-à-vis Simon that, however unmaliciously, the lesbian couple Sarah and Isabelle are, like Medusa, laughing.[48] However superficially controlling, Simon is outflanked by a mixture of 'the politics of the singular' and the complicity of the female

[45]   See Ivone Margulies, *Nothing Happens: Chantal Akerman's hyperrealist everyday* (Durham and London: Duke University Press, 1996), 1–20 and McKibbin (2003), 99.

[46]   Bernard Denoliel, '*La Captive*. Le Temps retrouvé de Chantal Akerman', *Cahiers du cinéma*, 550 (octobre 2000), 14–19 (16).

[47]   See Proust, *La Fugitive* III, 412 and above note 42.

[48]   See Hélène Cixous, 'Le Rire de la Méduse', *L'Arc*, 61 (1975), 39–54.

group. Even in death, and even if he kills her, Ariane thwarts him: Simon is, like Henri in *La Fille aux yeux d'or*, outmanœuvred by the woman who seems to obey his every wish. Paquita is killed not by Henri but by an avenging Venus-Aphrodite and Ariane returns, like Aphrodite-Venus, to the sea whence she came.[49]

It can be seen that recourse to the motif of the 'femme-écran' enables both Balzac and Akerman to portray lesbianism and the lesbian as ultimo-ately impervious to male curiosity and unavailable to male power. Despite the flagrant misogyny of some of Balzac's remarks in *La Fille aux yeux d'or* — for example, according to Henri, woman is '[u]ne petite chose, un ensemble de niaiseries'[50] — Paquita's mystery for Henri does not simply repeat the stereotype of woman as a 'dark continent' or the 'monstrous feminine'[51] but her separateness and her unavailability — and Henri's frustration at that separateness and unavailability.[52] Similarly, in *La Captive*, although Ginette Vincendeau, for example, regrets that Akerman shows 'the "mystery" of lesbian desire' from a male perspective,[53] this male perspective is thereby shown to be defective, intrusive and indeed gratuitous. For by self-consciously retaining and re-contextualising the literary and filmic conceit of the 'femme-écran', Balzac and Akerman are hopefully preparing the ground for other, newer and more positively radical representations of the lesbian and lesbianism. This might, at least occasionally, avoid the need to kill off the lesbian lover at the end, which is not yet the case for more sexually explicit and

---

49   On Ariane-Aphrodite, emerging from and returning to the waves, see Denoliel (2000), 17 and on the references to Venus in *La Fille aux yeux d'or*, see above, note 34.

50   *FYO*, 1072

51   That Medusa is not always laughing, especially when she is lesbian, has been shown in such key works as Barbara Creed, *The Monstrous-Feminine: film, feminism and psychoanalysis* (London; Routledge, 1993), and Lynda Hart, *Fatal Women: lesbian sexuality and the mark of aggression* (London: Routledge, 1994). See also Paulina Palmer, *Lesbian Gothic: transgressive fictions* (London: Cassell, 1999).

52   *FYO*, 1082.

53   Ginette Vincendeau, '*The Captive*', *Sight and Sound*, 11: 5 (May 2001), 45.

more supposedly radical productions such as Sande Zeig's *The Girl.*[54] But that, we can hope, will be another story.

Bibliography

Akerman, Chantal, *La Captive* ([London]: Artificial Eye, 2000), video-recording.

Balzac, Honoré de, *La Comédie Humaine*, ed. Pierre-Georges Castex, *et al.*, 12 vols (Paris: Gallimard 'La Pléiade', 1976–1981).

Beugnet, Martine and Marion Schmid, *Proust at the Movies* (Aldershot: Ashgate, 2006).

Butler, Judith, *Gender Trouble* (London: Routledge, 1990).

Castle, Terry, *The Literature of Lesbianism: a historical anthology from Ariosto to Stonewall* (New York: Columbia University Press, 2003).

Creed, Barbara, *The Monstrous-Feminine: film, feminism and psychoanalysis* (London: Routledge, 1993).

Felman, Shoshana, 'Rereading Femininity', *Yale French Studies*, 62 (1981), 19–44.

Foster, Gwendolyn Audrey (ed.), *Identity and Memory: the films of Chantal Akerman* (Trowbridge: Flicks Books, 1999).

Hart, Linda, *Fatal Women: lesbian sexuality and the mark of aggression* (London: Routledge, 1994).

Kravanja, Peter, *Proust à l'écran* (Brussels: La Lettre Volée, 2003).

Lucey, Michael, *The Misfit of the Family: Balzac and social forms of sexuality* (Durham and London: Duke University Press, 2003).

Paglia, Camille, *Sexual Personae: art and decadence from Nefertiti to Emily Dickinson* (Harmondsworth: Penguin Books, 1991).

Palmer, Paulina, *Lesbian Gothic: transgressive fictions* (London: Cassell, 1999).

Proust, Marcel, *À la recherche du temps perdu*, eds Thierry Laget *et al.*, 3 vols (Paris: Laffont, 1987).

---

[54]   Sande Zeig, *The Girl*, a film based on a story by Monique Wittig, Peccadillo Pictures, 2002.

Robb, Graham, *Strangers: homosexual love in the nineteenth century* (Basingstoke and Oxford: Picador, 2003).

Sedgwick, Eve Kosofsky, *Epistemology of the Closet* (New York: Harvester Wheatsheaf, 1990).

Vincendeau, Ginette (ed.), *Encyclopaedia of European Cinema* (London: Cassell / BFI Publishing, 1995).

Wittig, Monique, *The Straight Mind and Other Essays* (New York: Harvester Wheatsheaf, 1992).

Lesbian Desire
in Recent French and Francophone Cinema

Lucille Cairns
Durham University

This study arises from a much broader project on mediations of lesbian desire in French and Francophone film, starting from the earliest exemplars I have been able to locate, viz. Jacques Deval's *Club de femmes* and Jean de Limur's *La Garçonne*, both released in 1936. This wider book project covers a corpus of some ninety films. The present article concentrates more narrowly on films released from 1990 onwards, drawing on a total corpus of thirty-three works, mainly feature-length films but including some shorts. In order to make any kind of meaningful textual analysis, the article will not attempt to cover all thirty-three in detail. Instead, it will begin by providing an overview which notes differences arising from the gender of the directors — female or male — and also from their nationality — metropolitan French, French-speaking Belgian, French Canadian, and French-speaking African. Secondly, it will briefly sketch out the socio-political contexts in which these films were produced, as a first step towards understanding some of these differences. Finally, it will engage in closer textual appraisal of one film from each of the national groupings, chosen partly — but only partly — to exemplify differing permutations on one of the most prominent *topoi* to have emerged in my wider study of the area: that of lesbian desire as a drive towards fusion and in-differentiation.

So, to start with the biggest body of texts, the twenty-four from metropolitan France, do any distinct gendered differences emerge in their mediations of lesbian desire? Of the thirteen female directors, only five appear to have any affinities with lesbian identity or identification, as measured by their participation in *Cineffable*, the international lesbian film festival which has been held annually in Paris since 1988. Not surprisingly, all five — Sylvie Ballyot, Sylvia Calle, Frédérique Joux, Marie Mandy and Keren Yedaya — provide relatively affirmative takes on inter-female desire. However, none of the five texts in question is a full-length feature film (the longest being Sylvie Ballyot's *Alice* at forty-eight minutes), and, to my knowledge, none has achieved a commercial release in France. From a political perspective, these directors are thus unlikely to be making any impact on mainstream perceptions of lesbianism. Of the other eight directors in this French female category, three pathologise lesbian desire, to a greater or lesser extent — Diane Kurys in *À la folie* (1993), Anne-Sophie Birot in *Les Filles ne savent pas nager* (1999), and Catherine Corsini in *La Répétition* (2000); one (Christine Lipinska in *Le Cahier volé*, 1992) presents lesbian desire sympathetically but gives it a stereotypically tragic ending when one of the two young women commits suicide due to maternal censorship of her love; another — certainly the most famous: Josiane Balasko in *Gazon maudit* (1995) — ultimately yokes lesbianism to the straight couple in an implausible threesome; and two adumbrate its potential strength but sideline it by either locating it in a minor character (Tonie Marshall in *Pas très catholique*, 1994) or refusing its narrative development (Virginie Despentes in *Baise-moi*, 2000). Only one of the eight, Claire Simon in *Mimi* (2002), mediates lesbianism as a healthy, unproblematic state of affairs, as one component of a very balanced woman's overall identity.

Turning to the eleven metropolitan French films directed by men, no fewer than four are the work of one single individual, François Ozon (*L'Homme idéal*, 1996; *Regarde la mer*, 1998; *Huit femmes*, 2001; and *Swimming Pool*, 2002). It is not indifferent that of the eight male directors, three (Gabriel Aghion, already director of *Pédale douce* in 1995, François Ozon, and André Téchiné) are openly gay, and another (Stéphane Giusti) has been gay-identified during at least one period in his life (the mainstream, left-of-centre newspaper *Libération* reported his transformation from gay to straight whilst shooting the film!).[1] All four of these men have treated male homosexuality affirmatively in other of their films. Of course, it cannot be inferred from this that their treatment of female homosexuality will be equally affirmative, but that is hardly the point. As it happens, two of the four do provide a politically empowering depiction of lesbianism — Aghion in *Belle maman* (1999), Giusti in *Pourquoi pas moi?* (1999) — and neither Ozon in his four films nor Téchiné (*Les Voleurs*, 1996) fall into the unnuanced, pathologising vein common to the other male-directed films on lesbian desire under consideration here. More relevant is their role in bringing to mainstream film audiences the existence and, as they mediate it, robustness, of a sexual orientation that is, in relative terms, vastly occluded on screen. Of the remaining four male directors — Olivier Assayas in *Irma Vep* (1996), Claude Chabrol in *La Cérémonie* (1995), which presents lesbian desire implicitly rather than explicitly, Jean-Pierre Denis in *Les Blessures assassines* (2000) and Philippe Faucon in *Muriel fait le désespoir de ses parents* (1995) — only one, Faucon, provides a non-pathologising take on lesbianism.

Among the ten *non*-metropolitan French-language films treating lesbian desire, only two were directed by men: Paul Carrière's *Maman et Eve* (1996) from Canada, and Joseph Gaï Ramaka's *Karmen Geï* (2001) from Senegal. Significantly, I have been unable to locate a video or DVD copy of the Carrière text, despite strenuous efforts, so am unable to comment thereon, and was only able to obtain a video copy of the Ramaka film after literally months of internet searching; its reception alone marks a distinct national difference, for it was confiscated by the

---

[1] 'Stéphane Giusti est sûrement un garçon plein de bonnes intentions, et de ressources (homo devenu hétéro en cours de tournage nous annonce le dossier de presse)', Didier Péron, 'Sur les homos ça pionce', *Libération* (6 January 1999).

Dakar government after riots.[2] In terms of style and ideology, it depicts lesboeroticism openly and sensuously, but represents the only 'truly' lesbian character — Angélique, the prison governor who falls for bisexual Karmen — as doomed, and, moreover, uses the old chestnut of her suicide to underwrite this negative fate.

Amongst the eight female-directed non-metropolitan French films in our corpus, four emanate from Belgium, and four from Canada. One of the four Belgian products, Chantal Akerman's *La Captive* (2000), is an extremely loose adaptation of Proust's literary monument *La Prisonnière*. The other three — Dominique Baron's *Tous les papas ne font pas pipi debout* (2001), and Chris Vander Stappen's *La Fête des mères* (1998) and *Que faisaient les femmes pendant que l'homme marchait sur la lune* (1999) — all privilege questions of lesbian kinship / family, be it relations between mother and lesbian daughter (*La Fête des mères*) or lesbian parenting. In contrast, among the twenty-four metropolitan French films, only three deal with lesbian parenting, and only two with parental attitudes towards lesbian children. As for the French Canadian films, the issue of lesbian kinship is quite simply absent. The preoccupations of these four Canadian films, Louise Archambault's *Atomic Saké* (1999),

---

[2] 'When Karmen screened in Senegal there were practically riots, with one group bursting into a theatre with axes threatening to burn the place to the ground. What inflamed people was not the film's depiction of lesbian love, nor its politics, which are provocatively anti-establishment, (Karmen here is the leader of a band of militant brigands who denounce the corruption of the police and ruling class). At issue was a sacred song included in the movie, sung during the funeral of Biddle's character. Because Gaï Ramaka balked at removing the offending piece of music, the movie was subsequently banned in Senegal', Dimitri Katadotis, 'Beat Crazy: Stephanie Biddle gets into the rhythm with *Karmen*, the daring opening film at Vue d'Afrique', *Hour* (2001). But despite Katadotis's denial that the objections were to the film's depiction of lesbian love, this has often been the perception, and objection on religious grounds does not preclude a more latent homophobic objection. Senegal's legal provisions *vis-à-vis* same-sex acts are incontrovertibly homophobic: 'L'article 319 du code pénal prévoit qu'au Sénégal ...sera puni d'un emprisonnement d'un à cinq ans, quiconque aura commis un acte impudique ou contre nature avec un individu de son sexe. Si l'acte a été commis avec un mineur de 21 ans et moins, le maximum de la peine sera toujours prononcé', Plein Sud Sénégal, B.P. 1532, Mbour (Sénégal), http://www.pleinsud.online.fr/conseils.htm.

Manon Briand's *2 Secondes* (1998), Jeanne Crépeau's *Revoir Julie* (1998) and Léa Pool's *Emporte-moi* (1998), are diverse. Only one obvious feature links the three of them (*Revoir Julie*, *Emporte-moi* and *Atomic Saké*): the tensions generated by a lesbian woman's, or in the case of *Emporte-moi*, girl's, attraction to a straight, or seemingly straight, female friend. Briand's *2 Secondes* is refreshingly unconcerned with problems: in it, lesbian attraction is entirely unproblematic, and figures, as in Claire Simon's *Mimi*, as a healthy part of a whole life, reversing the common synecdochal operation by which lesbian-identified subjects are perceived above all in terms of their sexual orientation — an impoverishing and repressive operation.

One important observation to be made in concluding this inevitably limited and broad-brush overview is the generally more upbeat, lesbo-affirmative take of the French Belgian and French Canadian films, all female-directed, as compared to the metropolitan French films. In order to make any sense of this discrepancy, we need to take cognisance of the differing socio-political contexts in France, Belgium and Canada *vis-à-vis* lesbians and gays. First, France lags behind in terms of legal recognition of lesbian and gay partnerships: since 1999 it has had *le Pacs* (*Pacte civil de solidarité*), but this law confers nowhere near the same rights as marriage. Belgium, on the other hand, despite being a monarchy where Catholicism still holds considerable sway, has bettered that by going the whole hog and legalising lesbian and gay marriage (February 2003),[3] as

---

[3] 'Sur le fond, le texte accorde aux couples homosexuels les mêmes droits qu'aux couples hétérosexuels, qu'il s'agisse des droits sociaux, fiscaux ou de ceux liés au patrimoine et à l'héritage. Idem en cas de divorce. Seules exceptions: l'adoption et la filiation. Ainsi dans le cas d'un couple lesbien, la mère biologique sera considérée comme l'unique parent de l'enfant. Le texte prévoit, en outre, qu'un couple homosexuel ne pourra pas adopter d'enfant', 'Infos: Revue de Presse', *Lesbia Magazine* (April 2003), 17.

Quebec has also just done (March 2004).[4] Second, on the issue of lesbian parenthood, France is again less liberal, explicitly limiting artificial insemination to straight couples, whereas the Belgian state provides artificial insemination for lesbians, and Canada's federal government is about to make it illegal to bar lesbians access to artificial insemination.[5]

Finally, it is important to note that, traditionally, there has been no systematic state support for the production of lesbian-themed or lesbian-directed films in France. It was not until 2003 that the Mairie de Paris, headed by the out gay mayor Bertrand Delanoë from March 2001, finally agreed to grant a subsidy to the annual lesbian film festival *Cineffable*, which is now in its fifteenth year.[6] And even this new positive gesture

[4]   'C'est en juin dernier que le gouvernement canadien a approuvé une nouvelle politique nationale permettant aux couples gays de s'unir par les liens du marriage', 'Infos: Revue de Presse', *Lesbia Magazine*, September 2003. See also the following statement: 'La Cour suprême du Canada rejette la demande de groupes opposés au mariage gay qui cherchaient à provoquer l'appel d'un jugement d'un tribunal ontarien qui qualifie la définition traditionnelle du mariage d'inconstitutionnelle. Rappelons qu'il y a quelque temps, le gouvernement libéral a jeté sur papier un projet de législation prévoyant la légalisation du mariage de conjoints de même sexe. Il a ensuite soumis le texte aux magistrats de la Cour suprême afin d'obtenir leur avis, qui devrait être rendu en début d'année prochaine. Dans le cours politique normal prévu par le gouvernement, le Canada deviendrait ensuite le troisième pays du monde à reconnaître le mariage gay', 'Des opposants au mariage gay déboutés en Cour suprême', *Presse Canadienne (PC)* (09 October 2002).

[5]   'Ottawa — Le gouvernement fédéral s'apprête à écrire noir sur blanc dans ses lois qu'il est illégal d'empêcher les lesbiennes d'avoir recours aux nouvelles techniques de reproduction, y compris l'insémination artificielle,' Hélène Buzzetti, 'Feu vert aux lesbiennes pour l'insémination artificielle', *Le Devoir* (24 April 2003).

[6]   'France — Lors de la quatorzième édition de Cineffable, qui se tenait à Paris ce week-end, des associations lesbiennes ont invité Fabienne Leleux, adjointe au Maire du Xème arrondissement, et Nicole Azzaro, conseillère de Paris, pour débattre avec elles de ce qu'elles considèrent comme « une disparité flagrante entre les gays et les lesbiennes pour l'octroi des subventions de la mairie de Paris ». Le mécontentement fait suite au refus de la mairie de subventionner Cineffable (officiellement par manque d'argent, plutôt en raison de la non-mixité de l'événement selon les organisatrices), qui organisait pour la première fois son festival de film lesbien dans Paris intra-muros. Les festivalières ont qualifié les relations avec la Ville « de très décevantes en tant qu'organisatrices

only provides a modest sum to enable the *organisation* of the event, which, symptomatically, has only ever featured a very small number of metropolitan French-produced films on lesbianism, the majority being anglophone productions. By contrast, the 'official' Belgian lesbian and gay film festival held annually in January receives subsidies from the Communauté française de Belgique (as does Pinkscreens, the 'Alternative Gender Festival', albeit on a far smaller scale);[7] and the International Festival of Lesbian & Gay Film in Montreal is also granted a certain amount of financial aid from the city and province.

The remainder of this article will undertake the closer textual analysis signposted earlier. Taking as its *fil conducteur* the (arguably) narcissistic trope of fusion and indifferentiation, but also widening up the hermeneutic to provide a more general working template for the de-encryption of lesbian desire in film, it will compare and contrast the metropolitan French *La Répétition*, the French Canadian *Revoir Julie* and the French-language Belgian *La Captive*. As a French-language African film depicting lesbian desire, *Karmen Geï* is something of a cultural hapax which merits fuller attention than can be afforded it here.

Structured on discontinuity editing, *La Répétition* starts with a sequence showing Louise and Nathalie as pre-pubescent girls dancing joyously together, then flashes forward to them as young women, cycling by the sea together with equal joy and abandon. The happy dyad is soon, however, to be shattered. When the two go to a night-club after an acting début where Nathalie's prowess has put Louise's lesser thespian talents into the shade, Louise obsessively watches Nathalie and almost comes to blows with Nathalie's male dancing partner. The camera then cuts to a

---

du plus grand événement lesbien en France ». Les Archives lesbiennes ont exprimé leur surprise de voir « aussi rapidement » subventionner le prochain Centre d'archives gay et lesbien alors que leur structure qui fonctionne depuis 1984 « continue de vivre grâce aux dons des sympat–hisantes ». Fabienne Leleux, tout en ne niant pas les faits, les a cependant invitées « à bien connaître la logistique des subventions et à interpeller leurs élus de terrain quand un dossier coince »,' Xavier Héraud, Jacques Corre and Anne Vigna, 'Chorale recherche femmes' (4 November 2002), reported in *Les Infos de Têtu* on 27 November 2003.

[7] Marie Vermeiren, in private correspondence with the author, 15 December 2003.

shot of Louise slashing her wrists, a suicide attempt whose failure is elliptically implied by a scene where Louise's mother refuses a hurt and uncomprehending Nathalie access to her daughter.

A second flash-forward stages the chance meeting of the two long-estranged young women ten years later: Louise happens to go with her husband to see a play in which Nathalie (played by Emmanuelle Béart) turns out to be acting. Louise has gone into dentistry, whilst Nathalie has realised her dream of becoming an actress. What follows is an infernal 'répétition' of amorous obsession on Louise's part, destruction and rupture. Many French reviews of *La Répétition* have constructed Louise's obsession with Nathalie as jealousy, a wish to *be* the successful actress Nathalie has become, rather than to *have* Nathalie as a love-object. (In a Lacanian prism, this ascription to the woman of being rather than having reflects ascription of the feminine role of *being* the phallus rather than the masculine role of *having* the phallus... A neat exemplar of how gendered binaries are policed even at the most obscure of connotational levels.) As such, these reviews imply the classical, pathologising model of lesbianism as, ultimately, narcissism: attraction to the same / to indifferentiation and, in a semantic slippage, to the self. I, however, contend that Louise seeks to become Nathalie *only in default of* having her. Put simply, I disagree with the French reviewers who see Louise's obsession with Nathalie as primarily a wish to be like her — a successful actress — and, increasingly, a desire to destroy Nathalie as the living proof of her own relative failure. Rather, I argue that Louise only seeks to *be* like Nathalie, to appropriate Nathalie's identity, when she has failed to *have* her as a desire-object.[8]

The indices to an erotic current between the two accrue steadily. When Nathalie asks Louise to fetch her tights from her hotel room, the camera zooms into a close-up of Louise's hand caressing Nathalie's underwear — a glaring index to her sexual attraction to her so-called 'friend', and nothing to do with the kind of professional thespian envy ascribed to her by the French press — whilst the soundtrack of sinister music augurs ill.

---

[8]   See also *Les Biches* (1968), *À la folie* (1993), *Regarde la mer* (1997), *Les Filles ne savent pas nager* (1999), *La Répétition* (2000).

When the two women share a hotel bed and Nathalie asks her about the scar on her wrist, Louise lies insofar as she refers to a boyfriend, but tells the truth in mentioning 'un chagrin d'amour', and in so doing provides spectatorial confirmation of the lesbian slant to her feelings for Nathalie as a teenager.

When Nathalie phones Louise after splitting up with her boyfriend Sacha and says she misses her, Louise immediately drops husband and job to join her in Paris. One of the scenes in Nathalie's Paris home forms a *locus classicus* of lesbo-eroticism in French cinema: the *scène de la baignoire*.[9] When Nathalie denigrates her own body, Louise tells her she is beautiful, whilst soaping her rhythmically and moving towards her, which appears to disconcert Nathalie somewhat. In fact, Louise's presence increasingly unnerves her, particularly at rehearsals, where she can't concentrate through the knowledge that she is the object of Louise's intent gaze. Consequently, she asks Louise to stop attending them. She also laughs cruelly at Louise's acting when Louise is trying to help her rehearse, prompting Louise to break down in tears. Contrite, Nathalie apologises; Louise then tells her the truth about her suicide attempts ten years ago. Here Nathalie takes the sexual and verbal initiative by stroking Louise, telling her 'Je t'aime', and kissing her on the lips. What follows is an intense sex scene between the two. The camera focuses on their breasts, head, and shoulders, while the soundtrack conveys ecstatic moans plus unmistakable climax. We then cut to the two happily trying on smart dresses in an expensive shop — a 'femme' pursuit, but more important is their joyous complicity, reminiscent of the earlier, post-rupture sequences, with kisses *en plus*.

Director Catherine Corsini betrays extreme (heterosexist symptoms of?) discomfort with this sex scene between the two women: 'cette fameuse scène d'amour où, finalement, Nathalie, euh, j'allais dire, euh, prend le pas, fait le pas et moi [...] je me dis non, c'est inutile [...] moi j'étais tellement gênée à tourner cette scène que j'étais carrément cachée sous la caméra.' Corsini describes the scene which succeeds this, where Nathalie and Louise are trying on dresses in a shop, as 'un moment de

---

9   See also *Gazon maudit*, *Les Voleurs*.

connivence et de bonheur', qualifying the Louise peering through the curtains of the dressing room at Nathalie trying on a dress as 'Louise la voyeuse'. Curiously, Corsini sums up this scene in the dress-shop, rather than the one preceding it, as '*le* moment lesbien du film' (my emphasis); it is significant that the scene consists largely of shots of the two women looking at themselves and at each other in mirrors, thus reinforcing the old chestnut of lesbian as specularity / identification / narcissism.

The lesbian idyll is, predictably for mainstream cinema, very short-lived. Soon we see Nathalie having sex with a man — redeeming herself after her lesbian lapse? — and Louise in a virtual paroxysm of anguish as she listens to them behind the door, gripping her knees manically, rocking back and forth. A point-of-view shot from Louise's jealous perspective shows the man and woman's legs entwined; almost as if she intuits Louise's gaze, Nathalie is unable to reach a climax.

The crisis-point is reached when Nathalie says she is too ill to go on the trip to Rome Louise had arranged without consulting her, and announces 'Faut qu'on se *décolle* un peu, Louise' [my emphasis: note the literal meaning of 'come un-stuck'], explaining 'On s'aime beaucoup mais on s'empêche de vivre', and asking Louise to leave the next day. In these lines, the model of lesbianism as claustrophobic fusion is at its most flagrant in the film. When Louise attempts to caress her neck from behind, Nathalie violently slaps her and yells 'Tu dégages!' Louise is next seen self-harming, in a sense acting out without actualising her previous suicide attempt, but clearly extremely distraught with blood on her fingers (and we may ponder on the lesbo-specificity of this bodily part, along with her mutilation of it). She goes on to tell her husband she no longer loves him. Minatory music accompanies her desperate running through Parisian streets back to Nathalie's house, where she batters on the door and shouts to be let in. When it becomes clear that Nathalie is seriously ill (as it turns out, with peritonitis) and an ambulance ordered by the doctor turns up at the door, Louise refuses to answer, despite Nathalie's terrified pleas. Louise even turns off the light to throw the ambulance crew off the track. Shrouded in darkness, Louise is seen weeping; how is the viewer meant to interpret this? It is clearly not simple desire for revenge that causes her to put Nathalie's life at risk, as some of the French reviewers imply. It is, in fact, more a desire to destroy that which she desires and loves but cannot have, so that nobody else can take her away.

Nathalie obviously survives, though maybe no thanks to Louise: the narrative remains opaque as to whether Louise finally relented and let the ambulance crew in, or whether they broke in. The final cut forward is to a sequence of Paris at night with Louise in a car next to Nathalie's ex-boyfriend Sacha, consecrating at the film's closure the fusional model of lesbian desire which in this particular configuration has involved Louise appropriating Nathalie's past identity as Sacha's lover.

In interesting contrast to the French *La Répétition*, the Belgian *La Captive*, directed by Chantal Akerman, at once conveys a typically masculine take on lesbian desire and yet completely inverts the narcissistically fusional model of lesbianism. Inspired by, rather than a slavish adaptation of, Proust's *La Prisonnière*, *La Captive* is set largely in contemporary Paris. The Marcel character Simon is neurotically possessive of Albertine character Ariane, following her around surreptitiously, nurturing a doomed obsession with knowing her sexual 'truth',[10] and constantly questioning her about her suspected lesbian attractions. He most obviously incarnates the voyeuristic position characterising classic masculine purviews on lesbo-eroticism when he secretly follows Ariane into a museum, gazing at her gazing at a statue of a female bust, then at her being kissed on the cheek by her female 'friend' Andrée.[11] His drive to annex her for himself is visually and spatially conveyed by the preponderance of claustrophobic interiors, narrow corridors and dim lighting which represent the luxurious Parisian apartment in which he confines her.

The film opens with a form of *mise en abyme* as we watch Simon watching a home-video projection of a group of 'jeunes filles en fleur' (who, we learn later from Simon's reference to Ariane's old 'bande' of female friends, share a complicitous history) having fun frolicking on a beach. The haptic harmonises with the visual to suggest a diffuse, sensual

---

[10] 'This kind of truth-seeking is frequently associated with male characters in pursuit of women. Nicholas Roeg's *Bad Timing* is a striking example', Keith Reader, in private correspondence with author, 10 December 2003.

[11] The work of art as mediator of desire is a key Proustian topos.

pleasure between the young women: the camera records their frequent tactility with each other, as well as Ariane's engimatic, aroused smile. Towards the end of the projection we see in the bottom left-hand corner Simon's silhouetted head, emblematising at once his wish to intrude and his spatial marginalisation within this agora of inter-female pleasures. Finally, a long-held shot of Ariane with a young woman who turns out to be Andrée ascribes to the bond between them a particular significance, to be confirmed by the unfolding narrative. The sexual attraction between the two women is implicit rather than explicit, but few viewers would deny its existence, and what is clear is that this is in no sense a fusional or narcissistic relationship: the two women are markedly different from one another in terms of both physical looks and personality.

In a bathroom sequence forming an interesting counterpoint to the lesbian 'scène de la baignoire' mentioned above, the essential mode of the relationship between Simon and Ariane is visually conveyed with striking clarity: whilst physically proximate (living in the same space of the Parisian apartment), they are in every other sense distant — a point effectively conveyed by the glass pane giving the illusion of closeness, since it is transparent and shows them next to one another, but also underlining their actual separation. It also recalls the opening of the film, when Simon had vainly sought intimacy with Ariane through another kind of 'écran', that of the video-film screen.

In his doomed quest to capture the essential 'truth' of Ariane, Simon questions two women in a lesbian relationship, Sarah and Isabelle. The scene curiously resembles a documentary interview, and it is not irrelevant that documentaries generally address social problems. The two women either cannot, or are unwilling, to explain to him what it is like to be a woman making love with another woman, and how this differs from making love with a man. He wants to know about the gestures, but above all about the feelings involved. The women reveal nothing: their stock response is 'Je sais pas'. All they will reveal is that no, it is not just a question of different bodily morphology; and all Isabelle can proffer in terms of specifics is 'J'ai plus de confiance. Nous ne sommes pas des ennemies'. This implies an insuperable, constitutive antagonism between men and women which is to haunt Simon and to prompt an epistemological crisis, as we see from his anguished murmuring to a sleeping Ariane 'Elles ont dit que ce n'est pas la même chose. Qu'est-ce qui n'est pas la même chose?'

It is significant that Simon's ideal of love, says Akerman in interview, is of osmosis — a process of acquisition through absorption — whereas for Ariane it is the opposite, for she actively wants something of him to remain a mystery. Here the fusional model normatively ascribed to lesbianism is incarnated in a straight man (and in Akerman's film there is no suggestion of the sexual ambiguity characterising Proust's Marcel), and its implied opposite to a woman.

In sharp contrast to the pathologising vein of *La Répétition*, and far less coded than *La Captive* in its presentation of lesbian desire, we have *Revoir Julie* (1998), directed by French Canadian Jeanne Crépeau. The Julie of the title is an old 'friend' whom Juliet has not seen for some fifteen years (in this — and only in this — *Revoir* Julie converges with *La Répétition*). The film is based on the consequences of Juliet looking up Julie again, after a painful break-up with a partner whose gender remains unspecified, being referred to only as B. Only once does Crépeau even brush with the narcissistic model of lesbian desire as identificatory fusion when Julie recalls how she had reacted to Juliet's illness fifteen years ago: '*Tu* avais attrapé une de ces grippes montées tellement que *j*'ai failli mourir' [my emphasis].

Interestingly, in contradiction of the gendered stereotypes inherent in gaze theory, we first see Julie through the voyeuristic, furtive gaze of Juliet, who creeps up to the window of her (Julie's) country house and watches her, in medium shot, through the glass pane, dancing in abandonment to (diegetic) music, then jumps and hides when the phone rings inside the house through fear that Julie will spot her.

After comically dramatic *retrouvailles* (Julie mistaking Juliet for an intruder, jumping on her and binding her up under a sack), the two women awkwardly exchange verbal platitudes, but the intensity of the emotions between them is made plain through their alternatively shy, coy, and animated smiles, their frequent eye-contact consisting in gazing, averting the gaze, then tentatively resuming it. Shot-reverse-shots repeat the pattern of smiles, lowered eyes, and renewed smiles. The camera then cuts to an image of the two rocking together on a hammock outside, laughing joyously, sighing in pleasure, their faces shown upside-down to convey their abandoned leaning back in the swinging hammock (the upside-down perspective arguably implying the variance of their pleasure from the [hetero] normative). This image in the diegetic present recalls that of an earlier flashback, collapsing the discrete time-scales to create the illusion of the long hiatus in their intimacy having been abolished.

In conversation as they walk in the countryside, the question of boyfriends arises. Julie says she finds being alone and hoping the right person will come along 'moins pénible' than how she used to feel when with a boyfriend but wanting to be alone. A ludic allusion to lesbians, and to their structural difference from the hetero-environment surrounding them, is made by the interpolation of an old black-and-white documentary sequence about rocks (Julie has just revealed she is a geological researcher), whose commentary refers to sectional lava veins 'appelées "dykes" que l'on reconnaît facilement à la couleur foncée qu'elles opposent au granit environnant [...].' A second interpolation of this type focuses on the production of maple syrup... which prompts very obvious, if crude, lesbian-slanted interpretations.

Shot-reverse-shots of the two drinking wine that evening convey a growing physical arousal. Juliet kneels down close to Julie and, as the conversation evolves, sits back on the sofa with her legs apart, with the camera angle emphasising her jean-clad but otherwise exposed crotch. When Julie challenges Juliet to prove she is not drunk, Juliet kisses her fully and sensuously on the lips. Julie jumps up like a scalded cat, protesting 'Je ne peux pas...'. Both are intensely embarrassed, but when Juliet decides to leave, Julie overrides her decision by giving her a blanket and saying she can sleep in the spare room. The narrative then goes into flashback, again to fifteen years ago, reprising the same abortive kiss instantiated by Juliet and refused by Julie, with the only difference being the setting (before, it had occurred on the hammock).

The viewer is tricked by a dream sequence which we take to be diegetic reality, partly because it is juxtaposed with a diegetically 'real' shot — Julie getting up the next morning, pensive, meditative — but which turns out to be a classic case of wish-fulfilment on Juliet's part. She dreams that next morning Julie brings breakfast to her room, apologises for being rude and having over-reacted, lets her eye stray to Julie's breast, says that she'd actually been flattered by the kiss and wanted to thank her, then lowers Juliet onto the bed and kisses her… At which point Juliet wakens up abruptly.

In diegetic reality, Julie takes much longer to work through her internalised lesbo-phobia. Finally, after an agonised soliloquy and much hesitation, she kisses Juliet on the lips, and their two faces are shown in close-up at this crucial caesura in the narrative. A medium close-up shot shows Julie pulling Juliet closer to her, and the two then rush off into the house where they kiss again, very, very sensuously. Their initial gaucheness is soon overcome by their visually obvious tenderness and rising passion. A close-up shot of their two faces expresses their mutual wonder, diffidence, and desire. A fade-out leads to a curiously fey but well-judged pictorial intercalation of various lesbo-erotic paintings, some of which form part of the Western artistic canon (for example, 'Gabrielle d'Estrée et l'une de ses sœurs', École de Fontainebleau, 1595), and whose computer-manipulated montage — raising of the pictured women's eyebrows — invite a humorous complicity in the creation of a lesbian visual space, complemented by a soundtrack of singing female voices.

The film closes on a 'happy ending' which does not minimise the external obstacles they may have to face, and indeed foregrounds one of them: parental prejudice. Whilst they are in bed together, Julie's mother unexpectedly turns up and, upon finding them semi-clad beneath the sheets, looks appalled, retreats, unpacks the food she has brought for her daughter, and silently departs. Julie, however, has hidden nothing, indeed quite the contrary: she has sat up in bed next to her female lover and said brightly 'Bonjour maman!' Her verbal gesture proudly vindicates the normalcy of lesbian desire set against the social obstacles normatively problematising that desire. In so doing, it cameos a problematic central to the entire corpus of lesbian-themed films which I have attempted to introduce in this article.

Filmography (of films mentioned)

Aghion, Gabriel, *Belle maman* (1999)

Akerman, Chantal, *La Captive* (2000)

Archambault, Louise, *Atomic Saké* (1999)

Assayas, Olivier, *Irma Vep* (1996)

Balasko, Josiane, *Gazon maudit* (1995)

Ballyot, Sylvie, *Alice* (2002)

Baron, Dominique, *Tous les papas ne font pas pipi debout* (2001)

Birot, Anne-Sophie, *Les Filles ne savent pas nager* (1999)

Briand, Manon, *2 Secondes* (1998)

Carrière, Paul, *Maman et Éve* (1996)

Chabrol, Claude, *La Cérémonie* (1995)

Corsini, Catherine, *La Répétition* (2000)

Crépeau, Jeanne, *Revoir Julie* (1998)

Denis, Jean-Pierre, *Les Blessures assassines* (2000)

Despentes, Virginie, *Baise-moi* (2000)

Deval, Jacques, *Club de femmes* (1936)

Faucon, Philippe, *Muriel fait le désespoir de ses parents* (1995)

Giusti, Stéphane, *Pourquoi pas moi?* (1999)

Kurys, Diane, *À la folie* (1993)

Léa Pool, *Emporte-moi* (1998)

Limur, Jean de, *La Garçonne* (1936)

Lipinska, Christine, *Le Cahier volé* (1992)

Marshall, Tonie, *Pas très catholique* (1994)

Ozon, François, *Regarde la mer* (1998)

——, *Huit femmes* (2001)

——, *L'Homme idéal* (1996)

——, *Swimming Pool* (2002)

Ramaka, Joseph Gaï, *Karmen Geï* (2001)

Simon, Claire, *Mimi* (2002)

Vander Stappen, Chris, *La Fête des mères* (1998)

——, *Que faisaient les femmes pendant que l'homme marchait sur la lune* (1999)

Bibliography

Buzzetti, Hélène, 'Feu vert aux lesbiennes pour l'insémination artificielle', *Le Devoir* (24 April 2003).

Héraud, Xavier, Jacques Corre and Anne Vigna, 'Chorale recherche femmes', 4 November 2002, reported in *Les Infos de Têtu* on 27 November 2003.

Katadotis, Dimitri, 'Beat Crazy: Stephanie Biddle gets into the rhythm with *Karmen*, the daring opening film at Vue d'Afrique', *Hour* (2001).

'Infos: Revue de Presse', *Lesbia Magazine* (April 2003), 17.

'Infos: Revue de Presse', *Lesbia Magazine* (September 2003), 17.

Didier Péron, 'Sur les homos ça pionce', *Libération* (6 January 1999).

'Des opposants au mariage gay déboutés en Cour suprême', *Presse Canadienne (PC)* (09 October 2002).

Plein Sud Sénégal, B.P. 1532, Mbour (Sénégal), http://www.pleinsud.online.fr/conseils.htm.

Female Friendships in Contemporary
Popular Films by French Women Directors

Sophie Bélot
University of Sheffield

Critics generally agree that from the 1970s French cinema has witnessed a marked increase in the number of women involved in film-making. Women's presence has constantly evolved, albeit in a different way to how it did in the 1970s. In that decade women mainly made documentaries or avant-garde films, whereas in the 1980s they accessed the mainstream, reaching a larger part of the population. This popularisation of women's film-making prompted Guy Austin[1] to suggest that the days of women's marginalisation as film-makers were over. Although in the 1980s women's presence in popular cinema meant that some of them distanced themselves from militant themes of the 1970s, they still looked at issues related to women, albeit in a less politicised way. In the 1990s, women dealt with themes such as family relationships, relations between the sexes, women's bodies, women's sexuality and female friendship and lesbianism. However it is noticeable that, unlike those of the 1980s, women filmmakers of the 1990s look at these issues in a more radical way, with the aim of shaking up accepted ideas. Carrie Tarr and Brigitte Rollet[2] interpret women directors' position in the mainstream as a 'retour' to a political stance: 'Films of the mid to the late 1990s are informed by the "retour du politique".'[3]

---

[1] Guy Austin, *Contemporary French Cinema* (Manchester: Manchester University Press, 1996).

[2] Carrie Tarr and Brigitte Rollet, *Cinema and the Second Sex: women's filmmaking in France in the 1980s and 1990s* (London: Continuum, 2001).

[3] Ibid., 7.

In this chapter, I have decided to tackle the issue of female friendship and lesbianism in contemporary French film and more specifically in the following productions: *Mina Tannenbaum* (1993) by Martine Dugowson, *Ainsi soient-elles* (1995) by Patrick and Lisa Allessandrin, *Gazon Maudit* (1995) by Josiane Balasko, *La Nouvelle Ève* (1993) by Catherine Corsini, *Pas très Catholique* (1994) by Tonie Marshall and *Baise-Moi* (2000) by Coralie Trinh Thi and Virgine Despentes. With the exception of *Baise-Moi*, released in 2000, all of the aforementioned films were made by women in the 1990s. I aim to examine women's relationships from a feminist point of view to consider the extent to which these films address the issue of female friendship politically. The above list is not exhaustive, but as not all films made by women in the 1990s and the beginning of the new millennium could be included, I have selected those which most explicitly address the issue of female friendship.

Female friendship is hardly new to cultural production: it has inspired novelists and writers through the ages. However, theoretical documentation dealing with it is still scarce. Janice Raymond[4] attributes this scarcity to a male-dominated culture which causes it to be neglected or at best distorted. In France, Simone de Beauvoir[5] tackled this issue in her novels, autobiographies and philosophical essays.[6] In *Le Deuxième Sexe*, although she looks at the relationship between women, the reader may feel disappointed by the conclusions she draws from some of her representations. She concentrates principally on friendship between young female adolescents who always have a 'best friend' in whom they confide. She implies that this behaviour only lasts until they find a man to marry. As they grow up, young girls know that once they are women, they will find their destiny in male companionship. When this happens, the female friend will most likely become a 'rival': 'This concern is often

---

[4]   Janice Raymond, *A Passion for Friends: towards a philosophy of female affection* (Boston: Beacon Press, 1986).
[5]   Simone de Beauvoir, *Le Deuxième Sexe* (Paris: Gallimard, 1949).
[6]   The presence of the theme of female friendship can be felt in Beauvoir's works, such as *Les Belles Images* (1966), *Le Sang des autres* (1945), *L'Invitée* (1943), *Mémoires d'une Jeune Fille rangée* (1958) and *Quand prime le sprirituel* (1979).

destructive of feminine friendships. The "best friend" loses her place of honour. The young girl sees rivals rather than allies in her companions.'[7] The reader is thus warned against the 'dangerous duality' between two women friends. Yet, in a Beauvoirian context, adolescent friendship can sometimes take the form of a lesbian relationship: 'There are lesbian tendencies in almost all young girls, tendencies that are hardly distinguishable from narcissistic enjoyment [...] in her self-adoration is implied the worship of femininity in general.'[8] It appears that lesbianism in *The Second Sex* is considered a logical transition to adulthood for women and is re-appropriated as a societal norm.

Although Beauvoir devotes a few paragraphs to friendship between adult women, alongside those dealing with friendship between adolescent girls, she has no political motive for doing so. When adult women succeed in retaining a female friend, it is usually to speak about 'pregnancies, births, their own and their children's illnesses, household chores'.[9] They exchange recipes, confidences and occasionally help each other. Female friendship is not presented in Beauvoir as an alternative way of life for women — quite the opposite, in fact. It merely reaffirms the lot of the female in a male-dominated society. Beauvoir seems to attribute to women an immutable situation and position. Even when they are together, attempting to take revenge on men, the reader is left thinking that any gesture is doomed to fail. Women together can only create, in Beauvoir's terms, 'a kind of counter universe'.[10] It is only a 'diversion' and not a fundamental transformation. All they are doing is 'waiting for him'.[11] This remark leads Beauvoir to think that only men can experience true friendship. With his male friends, man's position as both subject and object enables him to enjoy a reciprocal relationship: 'each regards himself and the other simultaneously as object and subject in a reciprocal

---

[7] Simone de Beauvoir, *The Second Sex*, tr. H.M. Parshley (London: Pan Books, 1988). 390.
[8] Ibid., 366.
[9] Ibid., 556.
[10] Ibid.
[11] Ibid., 559.

manner.'[12] Only men can experience the equanimity of this situation. Women are not defined as free beings, but rather as 'the other' by men. Women cannot experience a reciprocal relationship for they always 'identify themselves with each other but for the same each is against the others.'[13] Hence, Beauvoir's treatment of the issue of female friendship can be summarised as being limited to a transition in an adolescent girl's life, a transition characterised by feelings of rivalry and antagonism. Her position appears to confirm Raymond's observation that representations of female friendship are often distorted.

It is this distortion that prompted Raymond to undertake a thorough study of female friendship in *A Passion for Friends. Towards a Philosophy of Female Affection*. Sue Limb[14] has undertaken a similar study, and both reach the same conclusion. Like Beauvoir, Raymond and Limb speak of female friendship in terms of companionship and solidarity. For women, a woman friend can share intimacies and is an emotional support. But, in contrast to Beauvoir, Raymond and Limb stress that when together, women can feel complete. Raymond also mentions the erotic dimension that friendship between two women can acquire. Whereas Beauvoir presents a regressive and negative portrayal of female friendship, Raymond has been criticised for idealising it. Her portrayal of female friendship bears no relation to real life and, as such, her representations have no political weight. Pat O'Connor,[15] among others, warns against this mythologising of female friendship by cultural feminists. Raymond's celebration of female friendship is based, according to O'Connor, on 'much essentialist thinking about women's naturally positive characteristics stifled under patriarchy.'[16] Moreover, there is a tendency to reduce female friendship to the sharing of personal intimacies

---

[12]   Ibid., 172.

[13]   Ibid., 558.

[14]   Sue Limb, 'Female Friendship', in *The Dialectics of Friendship*, eds Roy Porter and Sylvana Tomaselli (London: Routledge, 1989), 45–61.

[15]   Pat O'Connor, *Friendship between Women: a critical review* (New York: Guilford, 1992) mentioned in Karen Hollinger, *In the Company of Women: contemporary female friendship films* (Minneapolis: University of Minnesota Press, 1998).

[16]   Hollinger (1998), 24.

which can serve to reinforce women's social disempowerment. Confidences between women can be psychologically positive, but this emphasis on a purely personal relationship also supports women's confinement in the private sphere. Therefore, O'Connor says, a female friendship should be characterised not only by psychological support but, more specifically, by social awareness and engagement. O'Connor's view is thus reminiscent of feminist politics in the 1970s as described, among others, by Françoise Picq[17] in *Libération des Femmes. Les Années Mouvement*. Picq recalls women's rapport with one another as having been characterised by exchanges about both their private lives as well as by issues of concern to every woman. However, whereas Raymond considers that women's personal relationships tie them to the private sphere, in Picq's account women speak about personal matters to raise awareness of their commonalities as women in a patriarchal society. A feeling of belonging to the same social class emerged from these exchanges which resulted in the emergence of a sense of solidarity and unity between them. As women become conscious of their position as objects, they started questioning their existence in a male defined society. For Picq, when women are amongst women, they find the energy and strength to challenge their position as objects and thereby achieve autonomy. Female friendship is therefore a politically potent and constructive dynamic. No longer is there a negative image of gossiping women sitting together talking about themselves: female friendship is seen as creating the power to face down and subvert all forms of male tyranny.

This theoretical backdrop serves to highlight the connection between politics and female friendship. However, there is still debate over its visibility in other general areas of cultural expression such as cinema. No longer considered to be a marginal subject, the topic of female friendship has recently emerged as a popular theme in cinema. As such, an analysis of feminist perspectives in mainstream French films made by women directors would seem to be a logical and timely approach. *Mina Tannenbaum* (1993) by Martine Dugowson looks at female friendship from

---

[17]   Françoise Picq, *Libération des femmes: les années mouvement* (Paris: Seuil, 1993).

childhood through to adulthood. More specifically it centres on a tormented friendship between two Jewish girls, Mina and Ethel. In parallel
scenes, the film first presents Mina as a child and shows her being
rejected by a boy because she wears glasses. For her part, Ethel feels
humiliated at a party when none of the boys invites her to dance and she
has to remain sitting on the bench on her own, because her supposedly
plump figure makes her less attractive than the other girls. The film,
narrated by Mina's cousin, relates their difficult friendship from the time
they meet at dance class at the beginning of the 1960s until Mina's death
in 1991. At the beginning of the film, they are both presented as victims
for not conforming to girls' conventional appearance and behaviour.
Given that the commonality of experience which binds the pair is negative, the viewer construes female friendship as negative. The film implies that their rejection and humiliation by boys of their own age means
that they can only find friendship with girls. Mina emphasises her need
for intimacy with a girlfriend by giving Ethel a reproduction of a painting
of Gainsborough's daughters. Mina has slightly altered the painting by
adding that these two sisters are now whispering in each other's ear.

   In contrast to the similarity between the two girls in the painting, the
film emphasises the differences between Mina and Ethel. Their con-
trasting personalities begin to reveal themselves, as Ethel is shown to be
less rebellious than Mina. Mina is portrayed as being unconventional in
comparison with Ethel's idealised femininity. As they quarrel, Mina
makes Ethel aware of these differences when she declares: 'En fait on dit
toujours qu'on est pareille mais on est pas du tout pareille. (…) en fait on
est différente. Les différences sont plus fortes que les ressemblances.'
Mina's declaration is supported by a shot which shows them sitting next
to each other in a restaurant, as the camera passes from Mina to Ethel to
highlight their differences. These are accentuated still further when Mina
starts having success with her painting. At Mina's exhibition, Ethel reveals her jealousy, when she says to Mina: 'Tout le monde est amoureux
de toi ici. Si, tu as le talent, l'intelligence, la beauté. Tu me parleras encore quand tu seras célèbre? Tu sais c'est une carte de visite de dire que je
suis ta meilleure amie.' This envy of Mina's success comes to a head
when Ethel wonders how she can be famous or leave her mark, which

results in her assuming Mina's identity for an interview with a famous painter.

Mina Tannenbaum can be viewed as a film which looks at female development through the prism of jealousy. In the film, Mina serves as a role model for Ethel but her identification with Mina is tainted by jealousy. From the beginning of the film Ethel is portrayed as a mirror image of Mina. Several times, they are shown sitting next to each other on the bench where their relationship started, with Ethel echoing Mina's words, behaviour and also Mina's experiences with men. Identification with a female friend driven by jealousy corresponds to a Beauvoirian conception of female friendship, conforming as it does to Beauvoir's use of negative cultural stereotypes to characterise women's relationships as rivalry and betrayal. Moreover, just like Beauvoir's description of adult female friendship, the film portrays an actual bond between women involving not only jealousy, but also misunderstanding and conflicts. This discord highlights their differences and thus the impossibility of a true female friendship.

Like *Mina Tannenbaum, Ainsi soient-elles* (1995), a film by Patrick and Lisa Alessandrin, focuses on relationships between young women. The audience follows the adventures of three women in their late twenties and early thirties, Marie and Alice who are single and Jeanne who is married. With its portrayal of a group of women, *Ainsi soient-elles* seems to offer a representation of political female friendship, as defined by O'Connor. For this is a group comprising women, each of whom has a differing outlook on life. They meet weekly in a public space, a swimming pool. It is an opportunity to laugh together, to share their worries and happiness with one another and to seek advice. However, just like Mina and Ethel who confide in one another their feelings about men, the three women in *Ainsi soient-elles* only speak about their sex lives. They rejoice in sharing their sexual feelings and accounts of their encounters with men. Contrary to Beauvoir's theory, their relationship is neither infused with rivalry nor with jealousy about men. Indeed, they do not see one another as rivals or enemies. Rather, they regard one another as allies. They share with each other their feelings about the men they meet or love without any fear of competing with each other. Hence, by contrast to *Mina Tannenbaum, Ainsi soient-elles* does not offer a Beauvoirian image of female friendship, but seems instead to break with earlier stereotypes. However, the fact that those women, like Mina and Ethel, talk to one other about their relationships with men, reduces their relationship to a sharing of intimacies which, if one were to subscribe to O'Connor's view, intensifies women's social disempowerment. Their friendship remains on a personal level, emphasising their belonging to the private sphere and thus reinforcing the separation between private / women and public / men.

Whereas rivalry dominates Mina and Ethel's relationship, an intense intimacy between Marie, Jeanne and Alice is occasionally expressed in the film by physical contact like, for example, the scene at a diner party when they touch each other, implying a feeling of desire. The most intense moment happens at the end of the film, when they are going to the swimming pool together. While walking, they are pictured close together and the camera moves from a close-up of them holding each other's hands to their faces being extremely close. Marie and Jeanne are seen exchanging a desiring look, as though on the point of kissing and Alice is seen kissing Jeanne on the cheek. This moment of celebration of women being together can be read as an expression of female desire. However, the mainstream music as well as the camera work idealises this moment. The film reinforces a portrayal of female friendship as defined by Raymond that is detached from any political aim. This is supported by the fact that this group of women is shown to reveal their own lives not with the intention of evoking commonalities between them to raise political consciousness, but rather to find in each other comfort, advice and justification for their behaviour with men.

Moreover, although the film begins by giving the impression that the narrative will concentrate on a relationship within a group of women, it does not focus so much on them being together as on their individual lives with men. The friendship between these women is undoubtedly ob-fuscated, since it is relegated to providing a background to their relationships with men. At the film's beginning, Marie, Jeanne and Alice are depicted as independent women expressing their own desires and being in control of their lives, but by the end of the film, they have all found fulfilment in a conventional way of living. *Ainsi soient-elles* adopts a regressive position towards women's achievements. It undermines feminist actions and shows instead that fulfilment for women does not lie in challenging women's oppression in a male-dominated society but rather in validating conventional female life choices.

Despite the fact that *Ainsi soient-elles* suggests a certain homoeroticism in the exchange of looks and kisses between the three women, it does not explicitly state this desire. On the other hand, *Gazon Maudit, La Nouvelle Ève* and *Pas très Catholique* refer directly to desire between women. *Gazon Maudit* (1995) by Josiane Balasko revolves around a relationship between two women. More specifically, it looks explicitly at lesbianism as a form of female friendship. As the film starts, it immediately presents its main female character's identity, Marijo, as not conforming to the social construction of the feminine body. Her physical appearance and manner implies an adoption of masculine modes of appearance and behaviour. She smokes little cigars for 'lorry drivers' — according to Loli's husband — she is blunt in her manner and dresses like a man. Moreover, of all the terms used to describe her in the film, none makes reference to her being a woman. The variation and number of concepts used to characterise Marijo reveal the discomfort of a heterosexual society when faced with an unconventional body. Borrowing Diane Griffin Crowder's[18] expression, it highlights 'a profound ambivalence toward the lesbian body as a female body'.[19] *Gazon Maudit* thus shows that gender is not fixed and natural but a concept that can be contested and changed. The division between the categories of man / masculine and woman / feminine reinforced in the two previous films seems to be challenged here, resulting in a questioning of the hegemony of heterosexuality. Indeed, Marijo represents a destabilisation of Loli's normal heterosexual life. Loli is first presented as the epitome of a good housewife; she does not work but looks after her children and her husband. This conventional situation is challenged when she falls in love with Marijo; she starts to appreciate another way of life and changes

[18] Diane Griffin Crowder, 'Lesbians and the (re/de)construction of the female body', in *Looking Queer: body image and identity in lesbian, bisexual, gay, and transgender communities*, ed. Dawn Atkins (London: Harrington Park Press, 1998), 47–68.
[19] Ibid., 51.

accordingly. Loli is then portrayed as a liberated woman who seems to be more in control of her destiny. This change could be seen as lesbianism offering an alternative life to Loli and a liberating alternative to a heterosexual culture.

However, when one looks closely at the changes undergone by Loli, one can see that they are but superficial. Indeed, Loli's change can mainly be read in respect of her sexual behaviour. Whilst at the beginning of the film she wears a plain dress, emphasising her status as a housewife, later she is seen wearing dresses that accentuate her sexuality, thereby inviting male desire. Lesbianism is firmly defined as sexual expression. This can be seen in numerous scenes which show Marijo and Loli's relationship revolving around kissing each other, sleeping in the same bed or having a bath together. Lesbianism is not only defined as purely sexual but also as a volatile sexuality. Marijo speaks about the different women she has met and she is pictured with various women. Marijo's behaviour reflects Loli's husband's unfaithful behaviour and serves as a way to equate lesbianism with heterosexuality. Other examples emphasise the recuperation of heterosexual codes among lesbians. This can be seen in the final scene of the film where Marijo is expecting Loli's husband's child and comes to live with Loli and her husband — Laurent — and by so doing conforms to a heterosexual lifestyle. Marijo has substituted her unconventional behaviour for a well-ordered existence. The narrative is based on a return to a normal order which the film's genre comes to confirm. As a comedy, the film relies on the audience's recognition that any threat to a dominant order lasts while the film is viewed. Typical of comedy, too, is the exaggeration of the main character's outward appearance and behaviour by relying on stereotypes. This is a means to trigger laughter rather than convey any political message. The film sends a reassuring message to the audience by promising a restoration of order by the end of the film. Thus, the audience can relax and enjoy Josiane Balasko as a woman disguised in men's clothes, expressing a temporary subversion of gender roles.

In *La Nouvelle Ève* (1999) by Catherine Corsini, lesbianism, represented by a lesbian couple, is as visible as it is in *Gazon Maudit*. The film centres on Camille's independent life and her interaction with different people. Just like Marijo, Camille defies codes of conventional feminine behaviour. Moreover, like Marijo, Camille has experienced lesbian relationships and is also shown flirting with a woman at her friend's birthday party. On several occasions, desire between two women is mediated through kissing. In Corsini's film lesbianism is not only manifested through a relationship Camille's is implied to have had with her friend and her flirtations with another woman, but is also depicted by way of her female friends, Solvègue and Louise, who are a couple. One might venture that this film provides a political representation of lesbianism as it deals with lesbian characters, lesbian sexuality and lesbian experience. However, a closer analysis of *La Nouvelle Ève* reveals that the representation of lesbianism is limited to Solvègue and Louise rescuing Camille from parties, going to the cinema or spending an evening out with her. It depicts a superficial lesbian lifestyle which does not correspond to reality. Furthermore, the relationship between Camille's two friends is never explicitly shown as lesbian. It is always indirectly revealed to the audience, through Camille who speaks about their relationship. The camera work reinforces the obscurity of this relationship, as the two women are mostly relegated to the background. The audience never knows how long they've been together; no explanation is given about their lesbian relationship. It is offered as a fact and is hence deprived of any political connotation. It is merely an experience, as when Camille experienced a lesbian relationship with Louise during her time at university. Lesbianism is therefore depicted as transitional. Representation of these relationships conforms to Beauvoir's definition of lesbianism as a tendency present in all women. It represents a 'rite of passage' to heterosexuality and hence does not fundamentally threaten heterosexual society. Furthermore, despite appearances, it is a portrayal of lesbianism which, as in *Gazon Maudit*, is a relationship reduced to a sexual attraction between women. When Solvègue and Louise rescue Camille from being drunk, Solvègue suggests 'on se la fait?' This is confirmed in another scene when Camille flirts with a girl at a party and kisses her. The *mise-en-scène* clearly accentuates the erotic spectacle of this scene directed to a heterosexual male audience.

The lesbian representation in *La Nouvelle Eve*, as in *Gazon Maudit*, does not present a challenge to a heterosexist society, but on the contrary serves to reaffirm it. Women, in a lesbian couple, are still defined as being envious; the girl who flirts with Camille at the party succeeds in making her female partner jealous. When Camille's friend reveals to her female partner that she had a relationship with Camille, she becomes jealous too. Jealousy, but also differences, characterise Solvègue and Louise's relationship. Differences in Solvègue and Louise's behaviour are emphasised in the sense that Solvègue is portrayed with masculine attributes while Louise is represented in a more feminine way. Whereas Solvègue is violent, striking a man and and Camille, Louise is the carer. A schoolteacher, she cares for Camille and for people in general. These stereotypical characteristics serve to insert lesbianism into a heterosexual paradigm. This view is reinforced when Solvègue reveals her desire to get married to Louise, as she declares: 'on a des droits comme tous les autres.' Hence, images of lesbian relationships do not represent a threat to a patriarchal *status quo*, but serve on the contrary to reaffirm it.

The same observation applies to Tonie Marshall's *Pas très Catholique* (1994). Although the film relies on a strong female character living a rather unconventional life, it ends by smoothing over any ambiguities. *Pas très Catholique* revolves around a woman, Maxime, who is a private detective and whose investigations take her outside at night. Because of her occupation and her preference for unfeminine clothing, she is characterised as not conforming to dominant codes of femininity, but instead is defined, like Marijo, as unconventional. Moreover, she is not only presented as being independent in her work, but she also leads an autonomous private life. She lives on her own in a small flat and does not want to be attached to anybody. She refuses to show any affection — as the conventional definition of a mother's role implies — to her now eighteen year old son whom she meets again after leaving him and his father seventeen years ago. She is thus presented as escaping the confinement of conventional feminine behaviour and roles. Furthermore, as she refuses to appear feminine, she connotes non-availability to men and is hence presented as challenging heterosexuality. This is confirmed when, in a café, the camera follows Florence who comes to see her lover, Maxime. The relationship between these two women is explicitly shown through look and touch. Florence looks at Maxime and touches her hand in a desiring way. In *Pas très Catholique*, a lesbian relationship is visually depicted when Maxime and Florence are in bed together implying that they have had sex. However, the film has chosen to present this scene in a non-graphic and in a non-voyeuristic way. The film deliberately distances itself from being an erotic spectacle for heterosexual male consumption. Unlike *La Nouvelle Eve*, it seems as though this is a positive representation of lesbianism, as there are no stereotypical images of lesbians. Florence is shown as an epitome of dominant femininity. She wears short skirts with stockings and is represented in a passive way. The audience is deceived because we are made to think that through their appearance, Florence represents the straight woman and Maxime is the lesbian. The film separates gender identity from sexuality and hence challenges assumptions: dressing in a certain way does not indicate a particular sexual identity. A departure from the usual representation of the lesbian as mannish, like Marijo in *Gazon Maudit* or Solvègue in *La Nouvelle Eve*, is thus suggested. It seems that the film concentrates on a representation of lesbianism as an alternative to heterosexuality in order to defy the patriarchal notion that women rely on men economically, socially and sexually.

Seemingly positive in its representation of lesbianism in parts, the film's portrayal of lesbians becomes increasingly problematic as the narrative evolves. Although Maxime's appearance and life could lead the audience to think that she is a lesbian, she unhesitatingly asserts her sexual identity as heterosexual. Maxime's ironic tone during the scene in the café with Florence indicates that the relationship is not going to last. Moreover as Florence looks at Maxime, Maxime does not return Florence's glance, full of desire. This is not an exchange of looks but a refusal by Maxime to assume a lesbian identity. This will be confirmed in the scene when she says to Florence 'J'aime les hommes'. From that moment, any ambiguity suggested by Maxime's behaviour is dissolved. Hence, their relationship is reduced to a sexual attraction. When Florence asks why she made love to her, Maxime answers: 'Parce que tu fais très joliment la cour. C'est très agréable.' Lesbian desire in the love scene is reduced to a passing experience for Maxime and thus confirms Beauvoir's view of lesbianism as merely a tendency present in every woman. Moreover, as in *Mina Tannenbaum* and *La Nouvelle Eve*, where female friendship is based on differences, in *Pas très Catholique* the relationship between Florence and Maxime also reinforces their differences.

This is visually expressed through their appearance, as Florence is dressed in a very feminine way and her behaviour attracts male desire. She symbolises female passivity, as she is usually filmed with her head tilted and speaks in a low and desiring voice. Hence the challenge presented by lesbianism to dominant heterosexual gender structures is here diminished with the re-establishment of the notion of difference.

Although *Baise-Moi* (2000) by Coralie Trinh Thi and Virginie Despentes does not deal explicitly with lesbianism, its narrative is constructed around similarities of life experience and a strong emotional bond between two women. Nadine and Manu both flee from an oppressive environment. Unlike the films discussed thus far, *Baise-Moi* is notable because it explains Manu and Nadine's friendship. Their relationship is not presented as incidental but is portrayed as resulting from a willingness to change their situation in a society where women are dominated by men. Their friendship is thus conferred a political aura.

The beginning of the film works as a precursor to collective activism when parallel scenes present Manu and Nadine's sharing of an oppressed situation in a male society. The film emphasises a sense of closeness and the fact that by being together they will be able to overcome their common situation. To Nadine's remark that it is a surprising coincidence that they met at this specific moment of their lives, Manu replies: 'Non, c'était maintenant ou jamais.' Nadine and Manu's friendship is based on a common understanding of their oppression and their desire to change their status in society. Indeed, as soon as they meet, Nadine and Manu engage in violent action against a male-dominated society. It is through violence and adventure that they can challenge public spaces appropriated by men, as well as stereotypes of women in a patriarchal society. Nadine and Manu are depicted as subverting gender roles, for they challenge gendered binaries by adopting an active subject position.

The notion that active, vital women are associated with same-sex desire can be seen in scenes where Nadine and Manu exchange desiring looks while dancing close together. However, the most prominent scene occurs at the end of the film when Nadine holds Manu dead in her arms, and kisses her before letting her go into the water. Although this is the closing scene, it can be read as progressive, as it challenges the dominant sexual system and establishes a sense of togetherness and reciprocity between the two women. This strong feeling of solidarity between women is furthermore accentuated when Nadine attempts to kill herself in the last scene. Female friendship in *Baise-Moi* is presented as a positive alternative to a dominant culture. Emphasis is put on reciprocity and not difference and it is reciprocity and solidarity that will enable women to change their situation in society.

All the films studied here have in common the fact that they revolve around a main female character, who does not conform to the conventional female type. However, in some of the films, for example *Mina Tannenbaum* and *Ainsi soient-elles*, the political potency of women-women relationships is defused because the films provide a representation of female friendship that is limited to women confiding details of their heterosexual love lives to one another. They confirm Beauvoir's view that a true female friendship cannot exist because women always define themselves in relation to men. The possibility of female solidarity as a threat to patriarchy is thus contained.

The radical position that lesbianism suggests is also diluted in films such as *Gazon Maudit*, *La Nouvelle Ève* and *Pas très Catholique*. Here the lesbian relationship is constructed according to paradigms governing heterosexual behaviours. Indeed, every film discussed in this article reinforces a binary structure on which heterosexual society is based. The only film which stands apart is *Baise-Moi*, in which female friendship is founded on the notion of reciprocity and on finding ways to challenge women's subordinate position in patriarchal society.

Overall, this study of female friendship, including lesbian relationships, has highlighted the fact that female directors do look at hitherto neglected themes. More recent films continue the trend, most notably with Anne Fontaine and Cécile Telerman's *Nathalie* (2003) and *Tout pour plaire* (2004). However, this study has also shown that political comment is rare and that, where it is present, it is too often obscured. Only *Baise-Moi* has explicit political resonance, although the reviews it received upon its release prove that films with political undertones made by women are by no means universally welcomed.

Filmography (of films mentioned)

Allessandrin, Patrick and Lisa, *Ainsi soient-elles* (1995).

Balasko, Josiane, *Gazon Maudit* (1995)

Corsini, Catherine, *La Nouvelle Ève* (1993).

Dugowson, Martine, *Mina Tannenbaum* (1993).

Marshall, Tonie, *Pas très Catholique* (1994).

Trinh Thi, Coralie and Virgine Despentes, *Baise-Moi* (2000).

Bibliography

Atkins, Dawn (ed.), *Looking Queer: body image and identity in lesbian, bisexual, gay, and transgender communities* (London: Harrington Park Press, 1998).

Austin, Guy, *Contemporary French Cinema* (Manchester: Manchester University Press, 1996).

Beauvoir, Simone de, *Le Deuxième Sexe* (Paris: Gallimard, 1949).

——, *The Second Sex*, tr. H.M. Parshley (London: Pan Books, 1988).

Crowder, Diane Griffin, 'Lesbians and the (re/de)construction of the female body', in *Looking Queer: body image and identity in lesbian, bisexual, gay, and transgender communities*, ed. Dawn Atkins (London: Harrington Park Press, 1998), 47–68.

Hollinger, Karen, *In the Company of Women: contemporary female friendship films* (Minneapolis: University of Minnesota Press, 1998).

Limb, Sue, 'Female Friendship' in *The Dialectics of Friendship*, eds Roy Porter and Sylvana Tomaselli (London: Routledge, 1989), 45–61.

O'Connor, Pat, *Friendship between Women: a critical review* (New York: Guilford, 1992) mentioned in Karen Hollinger, *In the Company of Women: contemporary female friendship films* (Minneapolis: University of Minnesota Press, 1998), 23–26, 245.

Picq, Françoise, *Libération des Femmes: les années mouvement* (Paris: Seuil, 1993).

Raymond, Janice, *A Passion for Friends: towards a philosophy of female affection* (Boston: Beacon Press, 1986).

Tarr, Carrie and Brigitte Rollet, *Cinema and the Second Sex: women's filmmaking in France in the 1980s and 1990s* (London: Continuum, 2001).

In the Margins and Off-Centre:
Lesbian Characters on French Television 1995–2005

Brigitte Rollet
University of London Institute of Paris

When the first season of the United States lesbian television series *The L word* was first released on DVD in France in late June 2005, its success was such that it sold out in a week. The *Fnac*, one of the biggest French music, books and film retailers, indicated on its website that it was the fastest selling DVD in the last week of June.[1] Before the DVDs were re-leased, both the mainstream and the specialist French press, devoted articles to the first episode of the series which was broadcast on the pay-to-view channel Canal Plus.[2] Comparisons were made with the British and North American versions of the gay series *Queer as Folk* which the same channel had broadcast a few years previously. The fact that *The L word* was the first ever lesbian series undoubtedly contributed to the media hype which surrounded its broadcasting and the release of the DVDs.

Different explanations can be suggested to explain its success in France: First, there are many more French lesbians than currently thought. Secondly, the series was aimed at a straight (male) audience as well. And thirdly, the scarcity of lesbian characters on French TV is such that all French lesbians and bisexual women bought the series. In this paper, I shall develop the third option, not so much to find the 'real' reason for the success of *The L word*, but in order to present the specific

---

[1] http://www.fnac.com/shelf/articles accessed on 30 June 2005. Most dailies from the communist *L'Humanité* to center right *Le Parisien* offered reviews of the DVD in July 2005.

[2] This episode broadcast on prime-time on 19 June 2005 was presented as the event of the month in dailies such as *Libération*, *Le Parisien,* or the weekly *Le Journal du dimanche.*

situation of lesbian characters on French television, a situation which can contribute to explaining why there was such a craving from French lesbian audiences to see 'themselves', or women with similar sexual preferences, on TV. In the ten years preceding the release of the US series, only eighteen lesbian characters could be seen in French fictions on television, and most of them were not exactly role models or even women that lesbian audiences would conceivably want to identify with.

Before analysing in more detail lesbian characters in French televisual fiction programs broadcast on the French terrestrial channels in the past decade (1995–2005), a short introduction is necessary to understand the peculiarity of French TV as well the society that produces it. After presenting the corpus of fictions that contain lesbian characters, I shall concentrate on those that offer a possible alternative to the general trends.

French Universalism

As recent social upheavals have made tellingly apparent,[3] France does not share its conception of 'difference' and Otherness with its European and non-European neighbours. French universalism, inherited from the French revolution, promotes an ideal of citizenship which transcends particular differences and therefore denies the idea of groups based on gender, age, class, ethnicity, religion or sexual orientation. The first article of the Constitution of the Fifth Republic (1958) states that France is a Republic 'une, laïque et indivisible' (unified, secular[4] and indivisible) which insures the equality of all its citizens regardless of origin, religion or 'race'. Anglo-Saxon acknowledgment and acceptance of various communities, fiercely rejected in France as 'communautarisme à l'américaine', is seen by both sides of the French political spectrum as a major threat to the cohesion and coherence of the French Republic. Becoming or being a French citizen means giving up all individual

---

[3]   See the social riots in November 2005 in the French 'banlieues' and the Bill against signs of religious persuasion in schools (March 2004) which was aimed primarily at female Muslim pupils.

[4]   French 'laïcité' is much more than mere secularism, as it is one of the bases of the French Republic.

specificities within the public sphere and keeping them only within the private sphere. The French myths of integration and equality rely heavily on these notions, which supposedly allow for the emergence and the construction of a unified identity within a unified nation. The importance and the weight of universalism are blatant in every area of French society and culture, including, of course, French television. Since there are officially and constitutionally no 'communities' in France, there is therefore no need for community-specific programming,[5] unlike in other nations such as Great-Britain where various groups are addressed in programmes made by them and designed for them.[6] More importantly, the type of protagonists found on French television is similar to the televisual producers' and managers' perception of an average audience profile: mostly male, of European descent, Judaeo-Christian and heterosexual.

However, despite the influence of universalism, French TV has undergone major changes in the past decade: the development of satellite and cable channels has enabled French audiences to access foreign programmes apart from those broadcast in the PAF.[7] This has led to a radical modification in the types of television fictions seen in France, mostly in terms of narrative and especially characters. French viewers now see many more protagonists from ethnic minorities via these foreign fictions than they do in their national programmes.[8] Similarly, gay

---

[5]   This was clearly expressed by the former director of the private channel TF1 who moved to the public sector before becoming head of the CSA (*Conseil Supérieur de l'Audiovisuel*, the public and national institution in charge of attributing channels among other prerogatives) who declared in 1993 that France did not have communities, these being an 'anomaly' in our country because of republican integration (Hervé Bourges, *La Télévision du public* (Paris: Flammarion, 1993), 82).

[6]   See, for example, *Black on Tuesday* and *Gay time TV* (BBC) or *Out on Tuesday* (Channel 4).

[7]   *Paysage Audiovisuel Français*: French Audiovisual landscape.

[8]   This situation became obvious when a formal complaint for ethnic discrimination on French television was made to the CSA by the *Collectif Égalité* (an association created in 1998 by a group of writers and artists belonging to ethnic minorities). The CSA published a report that showed that although 81 per cent of the fictions broadcast on French mainstream channels included a black character, 74 per cent of these

characters appear more frequently in imported fictions. Furthermore, following the example of French local radio stations growing out of community groups of the 1980s, some French companies have also created their own channels to cater for the assumed needs of specific groups: French viewers can now watch programmes designed for and aimed at religious and ethnic minorities (including the majority religious group of French Roman Catholics for whom a channel exists currently drawing less than 0.01 per cent of the French audience), as well as regional or homosexual groups. After two years of discussion with the CSA, Pink TV, the first ever French gay and lesbian cable channel was allowed to begin broadcasting programmes in October 2004. Pink TV has yet to produce its own home-made programmes and is relying mostly on gay and lesbian 'classics' such as the British and / or American *Queer as Folk* or the British sit-com *Absolutely Fabulous*, to name but a few.

PAF and Domestic and Civil Partnership Laws (PACS)[9]

I have studied gay and lesbian characters in French programmes broadcast in the past ten years (between January 1995 and June 2005), in order to find out whether the situation had changed or not before and after 1998, that is, before and after the PACS (Pacte Civil de Solidarité): the PACS is a bill enabling same-sex couples as well as straight ones, to establish a domestic partnership contract.[10] The end of the last century is

fictions came from the USA. (See CSA, Conseil Supérieur de l'Audiovisuel. *La Lettre du CSA*, 129 (June 2000), http://www.csa.fr.)

[9]   *Pacte Civil de Solidarité*: Domestic and Civil partnership.

[10] This project was initially presented by AIDS associations who fought for years to introduce more equality in the law for surviving partners of AIDS victims who often lost their homes and belongings when their names did not appear on the documents regarding the ownership of property. Despite major opposition from within its own ranks, the Socialist party presented the law to the National Assembly in November 1998. The bill was rejected due to left-wing members of parliament being in the minority. During the month which preceded the second presentation of the project, right-wing groups organised major anti-Pacs demonstrations led by right-wing MPs during which violent homophobic slogans were heard. The bill was eventually passed a year

therefore an important moment in the history of gays and lesbians in France: apart from giving them partnership rights for the first time (although these rights are in no way equal to those enjoyed by married couples and were not labelled nor presented as specifically designed for gays and lesbians), the fiery debates surrounding the PACS have made gays and lesbians visible on French television. After decades when homosexuality was either hidden or the subject of medical and psychiatric television reporting, French gays and lesbians started to appear on various sorts of television programmes after 1999. From 2000 onwards, gay and lesbian couples were regular guests on many TV shows that addressed topics characterised as 'marital issues', such as monogamy, fidelity and weight problems. Both commercial and public channels were affected by this 'homomania' pre and post the passing of the PACS bill, although this representation eventually faded out, once the controversy triggered by PACS had died down.

What impact did the PACS have on changes in gay and lesbian representation on French television? Did they indeed effect change at all? In this paper I focus on the years before and after the PACS bill. By choosing fiction films where the commitment of the channels is greater than in talk shows, I want to assess to what extent it is true that French society and French television have changed their concept of homo-sexuality, which is no longer seen as a 'problem'. Various publications in the specialised or general press echoed the assumption regarding the increase of gays and lesbians on French television and concluded that French audiences were therefore ready to see gays and lesbians on their small screens.[11] Using the data provided by the watchdog group Media.G-

later, in November 1999. Since then, an average 20,000 contracts are signed each year and it is estimated that a large majority are same-sex couples, though this cannot be confirmed due to French Universalist laws that prohibits the collection of data mentioning sexual orientation as well as ethnic origin or religion.

[11] The spreading of this *idée reçue* has been very convincingly investigated and analysed by Isabelle Gavillet, 'Constructions sociales, scientifiques et médiatiques d'un lieu commun. L'acceptation croissante de l'homosexualité à la télévision', *MEI Médiation et Information*, 20 (2004), 83–92.

Net, a volunteer group which compiles lists with all the gays and lesbians seen on TV, mixing together all sorts of programmes regardless of genre and national origin created in 1997, journalists have often reached the conclusion that there is a clear improvement in gay and lesbian repressentation on French television: quantity is therefore seen as synonymous with progress, a simplistic and questionable approach for a much more complex issue, as I shall demonstrate later in this essay.

Although it is now common to find gay or lesbian couples selected to participate in reality television, game shows or talk shows, French televisual fiction programs seem to be more reluctant to introduce gay and lesbian characters, despite an increase in such representation after 1999. It has to be recalled here that fiction is more expensive than other programmes and that the viewing figures for fictional programmes are much higher. Although nowadays there are numerous cable and digital television channels, I have concentrated on the longstanding free to air channels because they draw the majority of French viewers (despite some recent losses to cable and satellite channels). There are currently seven major channels, both private (TF1, Canal Plus and M6) and public (France 2, France 3 and France 5), plus Arte, created in 1993, which is semi-public, bi-national (Franco-German) and specifically devoted to high-brow culture. Since all French channels are submitted to a strict set of regulations (*cahier des charges*) in all areas including fiction, it seems to me that the introduction of gay and lesbian characters into the fictions of these channels is more relevant and significant for this study than an analysis of foreign series with similar characters: home-made fictions with 'different' protagonists represent a financial and ideological investment which says more than programming American series with gay characters such as *Six Feet Under*. It has to be noted here that in order to contribute to the defence of the French language — another issue of national anxiety — against the linguistic and cultural Anglophone hegemony, French TV channels must contribute to the production and / or broadcast of at least 40 per cent of French or French-speaking fiction programmes: those with lesbian and gay characters discussed in this study are part of this quota.

According to figures based on the data available from the Institut National de l'Audiovisuel (INA), the national broadcasting institution, between January 1995 and June 2005,[12] 60 French televisual fiction programs (whatever their narrative genre) included a gay and / or lesbian main character (which represents less than 1 per cent of the overall number of telemovies and scripted series broadcast over the decade). Out of these, only eighteen had a main lesbian character. The discrepancy between men and women is similar in short fictions (in the French context, this means telemovies or scripted series of less than fifty-two minutes). As can be seen in the table given as an appendix to this chapter, most lesbians appear in crime dramas where they are the victim, the suspect or the criminal. Few fictions show other kinds of lesbian characters: a couple show teenagers trying to come to terms with their difference (*Charlotte dite Charlie* and *Muriel fait le désespoir de ses parents*, both in 1995) and a same-sex couple with a son conceived via in-vitro fertilisation (*Tous les papas ne font pas pipi debout*, 1998). The private channel M6, which broadcasts soft-porn erotic fictions on late Sunday nights, has shown two fictions that show women in 'traditional' Sapphic sexual activities before a male character arrives and they start a threesome. A two-part costume drama devoted to the life of the French bisexual writer Colette was also broadcast during April 2004. Before analysing the more interesting of these fictions in detail, some comments have to be made about the global visual construction of the lesbian in French fictions and the popular series in which most of them appear. The only noticeable difference between the trendy lesbian characters in United States' series *The L Word* and the not-so trendy handful of lesbians in French fictions is that the latter are not generally represented as butch. On French television the aesthetic norm for women is that of a young and slim white female who knows her power to seduce (and is prone to playing with the weakness of the male protagonists), and this also applies to the lesbian characters in most French fictional television, to such an extent that they can easily 'pass' for straight women. In crime dramas in

---

[12]   Since the passing of a Bill devoted to 'dépôt legal' in 1992, French channels must transmit all their programmes to the INA which classifies and archives them. The results were obtained by crossing the word 'fiction' and 'homosexuality'. All the programmes (fictions or not) are presented by the INA with a summary and a list of key words.

particular, the characters' sexual preferences, which none of the keen sleuths initially identify, can become the missing element to understanding an enigma: once this is known (and after the recurrent complaint 'what a waste' has been voiced by a male cop), the case is sometimes solved. When couples are involved, they are visually constructed following the traditional opposition of blonde and brunette, noted by Albert[13] and Holmlund,[14] and often are represented with a child.

Lesbians in (French) popular series

Scripted series are currently the most popular fictional format in the PAF. All the channels, private and public, have their regular heroes and heroines who attract a very high percentage of viewers.[15] There are two main types of series on French television: crime dramas and drama dealing with social, sexual or ethnic issues. Both types are broadcast on prime-time, after 20.30 in the evening.

Crime dramas are the most popular genre on French TV.[16] As far as women are concerned, and despite the recent development of series where female police officers are in charge, there is as yet no lesbian as female

---

[13]   Nicole G. Albert, *Saphisme et décadence dans Paris fin-de-siècle* (Paris: La Martinière, 2005), 198.

[14]   Chris Holmlund, 'When is a lesbian not a lesbian?: the lesbian continuum and the mainstream femme film', *Camera Obscura*, 25–26 (1991), 144–79. According to the French researcher Nicole Albert who studied the artistic and literary constructions of lesbians in Paris at the end of the 19th century, there was already what she calls a 'typologie capillaire' (hair typology) between the 'true' lesbian who was recurrently red-haired or brunette and her 'passive victim' usually blond. This construction has also been identified in films by Chris Holmlund (*Desert Heart, Personal Best*). *The L word* also seems to follow the trend.

[15]   The annual report of the CSA regarding the situation of televisual fiction programmes (telemovies and series) is a clear indicator of this trend. (See CSA, Conseil Supérieur de l'Audovisuel. *La lettre du CSA*, 182 (March 2005) http://www.csa.fr.

[16]   See Pierre Beylot and Geneviève Sellier's edited book on crime dramas on French television, *Les Séries policières* (Paris: L'Harmattan, 2004).

protagonist. The culturally inscribed link between homosexuality and criminality is still clearly very vivid, as the presence of gays and lesbians is most prevalent in the crime genre. Both gays' and lesbians' roles in these dramas are generally limited to secondary characters: they have no narrative autonomy and only start to exist when their body is found, when they are heard as a witnesses or arrested for murder. There is no alternative to this distribution of roles. Over the course of the period in question, two lesbian couples appeared on French crime dramas. This included a couple who had signed a PACS in *La Seconde Maman*, which premiered on French TV in 2001. In the other crime drama broadcast (*Intime conviction*, 2004) a married, closeted lesbian kills her secret female lover. It is worth noting that crime drama is the only genre where lesbian characters appear on the French popular (and often populist) channel TF1, which is politically right-wing and caters for the tastes of a conservative audience. Lesbian viewers watching these programmes may well feel themselves to be in the situation of the 'masochist' position Mary Ann Doane identified when writing about female audiences watching classic Hollywood movies where female characters are regularly mistreated: lesbians are clearly not being directly addressed, as these series are specifically designed for the dominant heterosexual group.[17]

Another highly popular type of television programme is the series based on a single hero or heroine whose aim is to solve the problem of a group and to help their neighbours: on the public sector channels, these heroes tend to act within the educational system, while on the private channels, they are more individualistic, solving problems in a very different and sometimes very idiosyncratic fashion and always apart from institutions. Like the crime dramas, most of these series have also introduced a gay character since the beginning of the new century, but unlike them, there is not (yet) a single lesbian in sight.

[17]   Mary Anne Doane, 'Film and the masquerade. Theorizing the female spectator', *Screen*, 23: 3–4 (1982), 74–88.

Lesbians in dramas

Another form of television popular with French primetime viewers are telemovies. These made for television films are often modelled on mainstream French cinema: they last the same average 90 minutes and generally offer similar narrative constructions. Because they were often based on classic literary texts in the early days of French television, telemovies are still (often wrongly) seen as culturally much more prestigious than ongoing series and are hierarchically placed in the highest position in terms of 'added cultural value', which is an important issue in France. Whatever the channel, most of these fictions are fixated upon family issues and generally deal with (straight) couples, marriage, divorce, new and extended families, teenagers' problems and / or intergenerational relationships. Only a tiny minority of these films address social conflict and escape the conventional happy ending of all the channels, which reinforces republican and moral values and offers a sort of 'secular catechism' already found in the series. This is a tradition that contemporary public television inherited from the early days of French television in the 1950s and 1960s, when the motto of the directors and audiovisual managers was to 'morally educate the masses'[18] in a typically French republican and educational fashion.[19]

There are few dramas with lesbian characters in our corpus of fictions and this has not changed greatly after the late 1990s and the PACS. There is, however, a significant difference between the lesbian characters who do appear in these films and those in ongoing series — lesbian characters in these films tend to be the main protagonists. They are therefore given a voice and a gaze and do not rely on a 'straight mediator' to be introduced into the narrative. This does not mean, however, that they escape the dominant ideological views on female homosexuality, as is demonstrated by *Colette* (2004), a telemovie loosely based on the life of the well-known French writer Colette.

---

[18] Capin, in *La Télévision des réalisateurs*, ed. Jacqueline Beaulieu (Paris: INA-La Documentation Française, 1984). 100.

[19] This appears clearly in the series of interviews Jacqueline Beaulieu led in 1984 with directors and managers who worked for French television during these decades (1950–1960). See Beaulieu (1984).

Within this context, however, there were two dramas which tried to avoid the traditional sexual and textual stereotypes and attempted to construct lesbian characters differently. The first of these was made by the male director Philippe Faucon from his own script. Entitled *Muriel fait le désespoir de ses parents*, the film was first broadcast on the Franco-German cultural channel Arte in 1995, before being released in French cinemas in 1997.[20] It tells the story of the eponymous Muriel, a young adult (she is around eighteen years old), who discovers at the beginning of the film that she 'prefers girls', as she soon tells her mother who reacts very badly to the news. The film follows Muriel and Nora, the friend she is in love with (and who does not share her desire despite kissing her 'for fun' at the beginning of the film), and their group of friends. Other scenes show Muriel with her family, building a stark contrast between the open-mindedness of the younger generation compared to the attitude of their parents. Unlike the other fictions where homosexuality is always an issue to be dealt with, *Muriel* follows a different trend: there is no attempt to offer an explanation for her sexual preference and, despite her mother's reaction, Muriel gets on with her life. Recognising that Nora is not a good choice for her, Muriel tries to sleep with a man, before meeting another woman at the end of the film with whom she spends the night. The perspective is always hers and she is the narrative focus of the film. Being different is not the sort of 'curse' it often is in other fictions, and there is a lot of optimism in the way the story is told and ends. Built as a *Bildungsroman*, the film allows Muriel a journey of self-discovery without adding the sort of pathos found in *Charlotte dite Charlie*, a telemovie made in 1995,[21] where the eponymous heroine suffers alone and in silence when she understands her difference. Faucon does not question the sexual orientation of his heroine nor does he

---

[20] Arte's policy is to support fiction on television (more precisely telemovies) and in film for cinema. It is the only channel that aims to break the boundaries between television and cinema. It has greatly contributed to a renewal of fictions on the small screen, from an aesthetic as well as from a narrative and thematic perspective.

[21] The film was directed by female director Elisabeth Rappeneau who also co-wrote the script with Colo Tavernier.

demonise her parents who, significantly, are not given the same importance as in other telemovies dealing with similar issues. Although teenagers coming to terms with their 'difference' are frequent in the overall corpus of French gay and lesbian characters, the depiction of Muriel differs from others, as her discovery is not constructed to allow a consensual speech about the 'right to be different,' nor does it have the implicit moral subtext of other films that implore tolerance. More importantly, in my view, is the fact that the depiction of homosexual sex is not avoided, as is frequently seen on other channels. Last but not least, the film addresses a potential homosexual audience, which is extremely rare elsewhere and especially where lesbians are concerned.

Another interesting movie made for television is the Franco-Belgian[22] drama *Tous les papas ne font pas pipi debout*, made in 1998. It was broadcast on the public channel France 2 during the week preceding the political debates around the PACS at the National Assembly. Directed by Dominique Baron, it is based on a script written by the Belgian lesbian script-writer and director Chris Van Der Stappen.[23] The film is inspired by Van Der Stappen's own experience and tells the story of a lesbian couple who live happily in Belgium where one of them, Zoé, has had a baby using in-vitro fertilisation (which is not allowed for lesbians in France). The film starts with the arrival of Zoé's mother, who comes from France to visit her daughter and grandson. It is clear from the first scenes that she is ill at ease with her daughter's life which she clearly does not understand, and there is palpable tension with Zoé's partner Dan. The two women live in a pleasant neighbourhood where their difference is accept-ed, that is, until new neighbours arrive and change the situation. Unlike

---

[22]   Apart from the telemovies produced by Arte, those providing alternative and positive images and narratives for gays and lesbians tend to be co-productions with either Belgium or Switzerland, as if their bi-cultural origin compensated for the implicit conservative tendency of French television.

[23]   Van Der Stappen wrote the script of the cinema film *Ma vie en rose* (1997) about a young boy who believes he is a girl. She later directed her first film, *Que faisaient les femmes pendant que les hommes marchaient sur la lune?* (2000), an autobiographically-inspired account of her coming out in Belgium, set in the early 1960s.

Muriel, the film *Tous les papas* offers a multiplicity of points of view, all originating from the women's household. Zoé's son is soon bullied by the new neighbours' son who starts a homophobic war against what he sees as an 'abnormal' family. Confronted with the intolerance of the newcomers, Zoé's mother begins to defend her daughter and grandson, therefore implicitly condoning her life-style and sexual orientation. Facing homophobia more virulent and vociferous than her own, Zoé's mother gradually overcomes her own prejudices. Despite using the mother as a mediator and as the person with whom the public is meant to identify, the film gives the same-sex couple some limited intimacy unseen on television before or since. Unlike the films broadcast on Arte where all scenes of same-sex couples kissing or chastely lying in bed are seen by the 'straight mediator' mentioned above, this film allows the lesbian women a degree of narrative autonomy, albeit minimal.

On the negative side, however, it should be said that motherhood is used here, as in other films, as a way of making lesbians less threatening, as it is their status as mothers which is fore-grounded. This is not totally coincidental in a (Catholic) country like France, where gender roles are still extremely traditional and where motherhood is ideologically highly charged. Furthermore, the 'straight mediator' is once again used as the spokesperson for gay and lesbian rights. In *Tous les papas*, Zoé's mother and Dan's father defend their daughters against the 'bad homophobes,' while neither Zoé nor Dan have a public say about their lives. At another level, the film initiates what will become frequent in later telemovies with gay and lesbian parents, where the 'innocent' child is 'punished' for his or her parents' (sinful?) choice, which sometimes implies a debatable conception of 'rights' and 'wrongs' in this matter. However, in the context of French television and society, this fiction was made and broadcast before the PACS and the political hysteria which followed.[24] It also preceded the increase of gays and lesbians on French TV and portrays the only lesbian couple on French television to have conceived with medical assistance and who go on to discuss the matter in the film.

---

[24] See note 9.

Finally, the multiple focalisations within the narrative allow for more than one possible structure of identification for the audience.

The last telemovie with lesbians broadcast on French television before June 2005 was the 'heritage drama' written and directed by Nadine Trintignant, based on the life and writings of the 'scandalous' French writer Colette (2004). I propose to analyse it here as an illustration of the limits of what French television can produce when dealing with lesbians. I will first consider it in the light of the many possible forms of sexual and textual transgressions offered by narratives set in the past which are here missed by the director. As feminist research has shown,[25] costume dramas and historical fictions can allow for the expression of transgressive constructions of the present and can also be read 'against the grain' by the female audience. More recently, some British heritage films of the 1990s have been seen to offer a 'broadly positive view of homosexuality' and to be 'hospitable to homosexual matters'.[26] On British television, the BBC adaptations of Sarah Waters's novels *Tipping the Velvet* (2002) and *Fingersmith* (2005) are interesting examples of alternative constructions of a past which, without being idealised, is nonetheless much more open-minded to female homosexuality than it probably was historically. On the contrary, Trintignant's *Colette* is a reverse illustration of transforming a transgressive figure from the past into a conventional one. Colette's reputation in France is double. There is the 'suitable' writer of texts dealing with nature and animals, studied in schools and colleges all over France. The other Colette is bisexual, an opium-consumer and a music-hall artist who performed mimes and sometimes strip-teases in a typical 'Belle-Époque' fashion, who had many romantic affairs with both men and women, and who led an unacceptable life for the moral and sexual standards of her time. The film

---

[25]   Christine Gledhill (ed.), *Home is where the heart is: studies in melodramas and the woman's film* (London: BFI, 1987); Sue Harper, 'Historical Pleasures: Gainsborough costume dramas', in *Home is where the heart is: studies in melodramas and the woman's film*, ed. Christine Geldhill (London: BFI, 1987), 167–96; and Cook, 1997.

[26]   Richard Dyer, 'Nice young men who sell antiques: Gay men in Heritage films', in *Film / Literature / Heritage*, ed. Ginette Vincendeau (London: BFI, 2001), 43–48.

tries to portray both sides, but only succeeds in offering an 'acceptable' character for prime-time viewers of a French public channel.

Although Colette's attraction to women is not hidden, it is presented in a way which makes it just a phase in an otherwise sexually active hetero-sexual life. The film opens with the 'scandalous' scene at the Moulin Rouge, where Colette does a strip-tease on stage before kissing her female lover Missy, also known as the Countess of Morny, after which a flash-back starts, showing the first meeting between the younger Colette and her future husband Willy. One is entitled to wonder why the director opted for such a narrative construction: from then on, and despite an evocation of Colette's affair with Missy, the lesbian desires of the writer are underplayed. Her joy, pain and sorrow come from her relationships with men, which occupy most of the narrative. Her lesbian affairs are seen and presented as a sort of 'revenge' after Willy's unfaithfulness (this is also how the INA presents it in its summary of the film) and not as the expression of a choice. Like most telemovies discussed here, sexuality between women is never shown, while hints of passionate heterosexual sex are given. Despite the use of Colette's voice-over (based on her writings), Trintignant's Colette is more object than subject of the gaze: while she is almost always in the frame, she is watched more than she watches and her perspective is never clearly shown. Unlike female (cinema) film director Jacqueline Audry who adapted Colette's novels in the 1950s and made 'Belle Époque' films with highly transgressive female characters, half a century later Trintignant fails to construct a woman with whom contemporary female (and lesbian) viewers would want to identify.

Conclusion

Significantly, the only French television film showing a romantic love affair between women on the model of 'girl meets girl' was never screened by the channel which commissioned and funded it. Private channel M6 asked female film director Sylvie Verheyde to contribute to an innovative 'collection' launched by the channel in 2000 entitled *Combats de femmes*. Her film entitled *Un amour de femmes* was made in 2001. No precise details were given to explain their decision, but it is very likely that it did not fit ideologically with the conservatism of the channel, as another cancellation shows[27]. Verheyde's film was subsequently screened in three gay and lesbian film festivals in the United States of America before a DVD was made, in the NTC format, which is unreadable in France. It was not until November 2005 that French viewers could find a European version of this DVD. This anecdote is another illustration of the limits of French television and after watching the film, the reluctance of M6 to broadcast it is 'understandable' in the French ideological context. *Un amour de femmes* tells the story of a married woman with a child who meets another woman,[28] starts her first lesbian affair and eventually leaves husband and child to live with her lover, a choice of narrative which is totally impossible on French television within the current ideological climate.

The common point between the various telefilms and series of the corpus presented here is that, apart from the films shown on Arte, they always use the straight mediator to introduce and to show lesbian characters: in other words these characters have no narrative autonomy and are more often than not voiceless and gazeless. Drawing on Mulvey's theory on the triple male gaze that she identified in Hollywood classical cinema (1975), and after viewing and analysing these fictions, I have come to the conclusion that French scripted television series build a similar 'triple straight gaze' where gays and lesbians are in the comparable position to the women in Mulvey's theory, that is, objects which are

[27]   Another similar event took place on the same channel in 2001, with another director (Christophe Honoré), in another collection, *Carnets d'Ados* (Teen's diaries). His telefilm *Tout contre Léo*, dealing with male homosexuality and AIDS, was not broadcast after the director refused to cut a scene with male homosexual sex (fellatio). M6 objects to such an explanation and declared that the tone and mood of the film did not fit any longer the general trend of their programmes. The telemovie was eventually broadcast on Pink TV in September 2006 (Régis Baillot, 'Divorce consommé entre M6 et Léo', *20 minutes Lille* (21 September 2006). No other case of cancellation has been acknowledged so far regarding the two collections.

[28]   Played by the former porn actress Rafaella Anderson who starred in the controversial film *Baise-moi*, Virginie Despentes and Coralie Trinh Thi (1999).

seen by a straight camera, through a straight character and generally for a straight audience. The main difference from Mulvey's schema is that gays and lesbians are not the objects of desire in French fictions: on the contrary, their narrative plots are aimed at reassuring straight viewers in their sexual preferences. Being regularly victimised, or seen only by others, they are not potential role models for a gay and lesbian audience either.

The main change, however, from the period before the PACS, is the recurrent and almost systematic demonisation of homophobic characters: this is so frequent that it raises many questions for French scripted television, which often aims at giving the audience what I call a 'guide for good behaviour.' As the gays and lesbians are not in charge of the story and have neither voice nor gaze, the point of view is conveyed by the hero or the heroine, a straight character with whom the audience is supposed to identify. This protagonist is generally open-minded and often acts within the narrative as the spokesperson for gays and lesbians. He / she is often confronted with homophobic remarks made by someone who serves mainly as a foil to the hero(ine), and indirectly to the audience, and is therefore quickly rendered harmless. By loading a secondary and insignificant character with homophobia and by symbolically destroying him / her within the narrative, the hero(ine), the channel and the audience are made to feel that they are on the side of good. Apart from *Tous les papas*, there is usually no questioning of where homophobia comes from, and far from denouncing homophobia, the narratives simply single homophobes out without addressing the issue. Apart from this, giving the straight hero-ine the ability to 'defend' gays and lesbians against homophobia tends to deprive the latter of any agency over their own lives.

The increase in the visibility of lesbians on television is therefore not synonymous with a more open-minded view of homosexuality. After analysing all the French fictions with gay and lesbians broadcast over a decade, I have reached a different conclusion from Andrea Weiss's in her study of lesbians in United States of America's cinema, in which she sees positive elements in the increase of films with lesbians in the 1970s and 1980s. For her, 'the cinema has been and continues to be a contested terrain in which people and groups with often opposite interests have staked their claims.'[29] In French television, on the contrary, more lesbian characters do not necessarily mean alternative and more positive opinions about lesbianism. The bi-cultural channel Arte is the only one where these characters are not only more frequent before than after the PACS, but is also the only channel where lesbians are the main protagonists of stories in which their sexual preference is not seen as the problem or 'issue' that it almost always is on other channels. Most popular series in the French public and private sector have followed in the past five years what I would call 'audiovisual opportunism' and started to broadcast programmes with gays and lesbians, more to avoid being seen as old-fashioned narrow-minded bigots than to present homosexuality as an alternative to dominant sexual practices. It is worth noting that most programmes (including films) with gays and lesbians deal with family and couple 'problems' that they share with straight couples. In other words, in order to be visible and seen on French TV, their difference has to be invisible.

In 1989, Epstein and Straub wrote about the United States of America that 'as market-place phenomena such as gay window advertising suggest, capitalism allows marginalised or stigmatised forms of sexual behaviour and identity to filter into consumer society, packaged in the disguised forms which take away the threat posed by those sexualities.'[30] In their introduction, they opposed 'a recuperative [and] conservative cultural mechanism' to 'libratory strategies for breaking with dominant ideologies'.[31] It emerges from what precedes that French television has exploited 'marginalised or stigmatised forms of sexual behaviour and identity' for reasons which have very little to do with offering alternatives to dominant ideological discourse regarding homosexuality in general and lesbians in particular.

---

[29] Andrea Weiss, *Vampires and Violets: lesbians in films* (New York: Penguin Books, 1993), 163.

[30] J. Epstein and K. Straub, *Body Guards: the cultural politics of sexual ambiguities* (London: Routledge, 1989), 10.

[31] Ibid., 5.

Fictions with lesbian characters broadcast on French television between 1 January 1995 and 1 May 2005

Date	Channel	Title	Genre (name of series)	Role/s
03/1995	TF1	*Le secret de Marion*	Crime (*Le Juge est une femme*)	Victim (title role)
05/1995	France 2	*Charlotte dite Charlie*	Psychological drama	Title role
06/1995	Arte	*Muriel fait le désespoir de ses parents*	Psychological drama	Title role
10/1996	M6	*Un amour au féminin*	Erotic	Lover
07/1997	France 3	*Balle perdue*	Crime	-Victim -Former lover
11/1997	Canal +	*Des gens si bien élevés*	Psychological drama	Bisexual (minor role)
11/1998	France 2	*Radiée*	Crime (*Avocats et Associés.*)	-client seeking legal advice after leaving husband for a woman
12/1998	France 2	*Tous les papas ne font pas pipi debout*	Psychological drama	Couple of women
02/99	TF1	*Arrêt de travail*	Crime (*Julie Lescaut*)	Murderess
04/2001	TF1	*La seconde maman*	Crime (*Un homme en colère*)	Couple: suspect partner
05/2001	M6	*Des parents pas comme les autres*	Psychological drama	Mother (+gay father)
04/2002	France 2	*Agressions*	Crime (*PJ*)	Suspect
05/2003	M6	*Marie ou la fascination charnelle*	Erotic	Lover
06/2003	TF1	*Soupçons*	Crime (*Julie Lescaut*)	Suspect
09/2003	France 2	*Délit d'amour*	Crime (*La Crim*)	Victim
10/2004	TF1	*Intime Conviction*	Crime (*Femmes de Loi*)	Victim + her killer
05/2004	France 2	*Colette*	Historical fiction (2 episodes)	Title role

Filmography (of films mentioned)

Despentes, Virginie and Coralie Trinh Thi, dir. Virginie Despentes and Coralie Trinh Thi, *Baise-moi* (1999).

Guyot, Martin and Céline Guyot, dir. Denis Malleval, 'Intime Conviction', *Femmes de Loi,* TF1 (4 October 2004).

Honoré, Christophe, dir. Christophe Honoré, 'Tout contre Léo', *Carnets d'Ados*, commissioned by M6, not broadcast (2001).

Klein, Catherine and Philippe Faucon, dir. Philippe Faucon, *Muriel fait le désespoir de ses parents*, Arte (2 June 1995).

Lecharpy, Véronique, dir. Marc Angelo, 'La Seconde maman', *Un homme en colère*, TF1 (30 April 2001).

Rappeneau, Elisabeth and Colo Tavernier, dir. Elisabeth Rappeneau, *Charlotte dite Charlie*, France 2 (31 May 1995).

Stappen, Chris Van Der, *Ma vie en rose*, script (1997).

——, *Que faisaient les femmes pendant que les hommes marchaient sur la lune?*, script and direction (2000).

——, dir. Baron Dominique, *Tous les papas ne font pas pipi debout*, France 2 (16 December 1998).

Trintignant, Nadine and Marie Trintignant, dir. Nadine Trintignant, *Colette, une femme libre*, France 2 (26 April 2004).

Verheyde, Sylvie, dir. Sylvie Verheyde, 'Un amour de femmes', *Combats de femmes*, commissioned by M6, not broadcast (2001).

Bibliography

Albert, Nicole G., *Saphisme et décadence dans Paris fin-de-siècle* (Paris: La Martinière, 2005).

Baillot, Régis, 'Divorce consommé entre M6 et Léo', *20 minutes Lille* (21 September 2006).

Beaulieu, Jacqueline, *La Télévision des réalisateurs* (Paris: INA-La Documentation Française, 1984).

Belpêche, Stéphanie and Jonathan Bouchet-Petersen, 'Cet été, les chaînes misent sur les séries sulfureuses', *Le Journal du Dimanche* (19 June 2005).

——, 'La télé en DVD', *Le Journal du Dimanche* (7 August 2005).

Beylot, Pierre, and Geneviève Sellier (eds), *Les Séries policières* (Paris: L'Harmattan, 2004).

Bourges, Hervé, *La Télévision du public* (Paris: Flammarion, 1993).

Constant, Caroline, 'Amoureuses amies', *L'Humanité* (30 July 2005).

CSA, Conseil Supérieur de l'Audovisuel, *La Lettre du CSA*, 129 (June 2000), (http://www.csa.fr).

——, *La lettre du CSA*, 182 (March 2005) (http://www.csa.fr).

Doane, Mary Anne, 'Film and the masquerade. Theorizing the female spectator', *Screen*, 23: 3–4 (1982), 74–88.

Dyer, Richard, 'Nice young men who sell antiques: Gay men in Heritage films', in *Film / Literature / Heritage*, ed. Ginette Vincendeau (London: BFI, 2001), 43–48.

Epstein, J. and K. Straub, *Body Guards: the cultural politics of sexual ambiguities* (London: Routledge, 1989).

Gavillet, Isabelle, 'Constructions sociales, scientifiques et médiatiques d'un lieu commun. L'acceptation croissante de l'homosexualité à la télévision', *MEI Médiation et Information*, 20 (2004), 83–92.

Gledhill, Christine (ed.), *Home is where the heart is: studies in melodramas and the woman's film* (London: BFI, 1987).

Harper, Sue, 'Historical Pleasures: Gainsborough costume dramas', in *Home is where the heart is: studies in melodramas and the woman's film*, ed. Christine Geldhill (London: BFI, 1987), 167–96.

Holmlund, Chris, 'When is a lesbian not a lesbian?: the lesbian continuum and the mainstream femme film', *Camera Obscura*, 25–26 (1991), 144–79.

Moreau, Charlotte, 'Les lesbiennes ont leur série', *Le Parisien* (19 June 2005).

——, 'Vu hier soir. *The L Word*: envoûtant', *Le Parisien* (20 June 2005).

Mulvey, Laura, 'Visual pleasure and narrative cinema', *Screen*, 16: 3 (1975), 6–18.

Picard, Jessica, 'Les séries télé s'arrachent en DVD', *Le Parisien* (27 July 2005).

Santucci, Françoise-Marie, 'Série, *The L word* et ses lesbiennes chic débarquent »', *Libération* (19 June 2004).

Vincendeau, Ginette (ed.), *Film / Literature / Heritage* (London: BFI, 2001).

Waters, Sarah, *Tipping the velvet* (London: Virago, 2000).

——, *Fingersmith* (London: Virago, 2002).

Weiss, Andrea, *Vampires and Violets. Lesbians in films* (New York, N.Y.,: Penguin Books, 1993).

Violette Leduc écrivaine et lesbienne : du mythe à la mystification

Mireille Brioude

La notoriété de Violette Leduc auprès des universitaires femmes et des spécialistes de la littérature française féminine n'est plus à faire : par contre elle reste méconnue du grand public et très rarement évoquée dans la presse, même spécialisée. Un numéro récent du *Magazine Littéraire* sur le thème 'littérature et homosexualité' mentionne son nom dans le bandeau-titre parmi une liste d'écrivains homosexuels contemporains.[1] L'ouvrage dirigé par Didier Eribon : *Dictionnaire des cultures gays et lesbiennes* publié en 2003 lui accorde une place de choix : étiquetée comme lesbienne avant d'être reconnue comme une écrivaine hors pair (l'essence précèderait l'existence ? Est-on essentiellement lesbienne ?). Nous étudierons la réception de l'œuvre de Violette Leduc depuis les années 1950 jusqu'à nos jours en insistant sur la polymorphie des censures dont elle fut et dont elle est toujours l'objet : hier la censure et, aujourd'hui l'oubli ou encore, de manière plus pernicieuse, l'annexion abusive dans le champ de la 'culture gay'.

'Amours impossibles' ou : les impasses du scandale

Revenons dans un premier temps sur un point que les spécialistes de Violette Leduc connaissent bien : la censure dont elle fut l'objet au moment de la parution de *Ravages* en 1955, avec la suppression — avant publication — de l'épisode de sa relation avec sa compagne de classe Isabelle.

---

[1] *Le Magazine littéraire*, no. 426 'littérature et homosexualité' (décembre 2003).

Soumis donc aux appréciations de messieurs Raymond Queneau, Jacques Lemarchand et confrères, le début de *Ravages*, qui racontait les amours de Thérèse et d'Isabelle, ne 'passe pas': il fera l'objet d'une publication en 1966, huit ans plus tard, tronquant définitivement le texte original: en attendant on suggère à Violette Leduc de publier ces passages 'sous le manteau' ainsi que le sont tous les ouvrages à caractère pornographique. C'est de cette manière que ces messieurs jugent le récit de la liaison érotique entre les deux collégiennes.[2] De même est jugée inconvenante la scène du 'taxi', qui elle aussi sera publiée — mais en 1971 — ainsi que le récit de l'avortement de Thérèse.

Simone de Beauvoir joue de tout son poids, en vain. On allègue aussi le peu de ventes réalisées par les ouvrages précédents, l'*Asphyxie*, puis l'*Affamée*: le roman *Ravages* doit être lisible par tous, politique éditoriale oblige. Le récit, publié à part en 1955 grâce à Jacques Guérin sera repris partiellement dans *La Bâtarde* (et fera manquer, de peu, le prix Goncourt à cet ouvrage) avant d'être publié in extenso en 2000.[3]

Si le récit d'une relation avec une femme fut l'objet majeur de la censure, celle-ci a sans doute une cause plus profonde. Beauvoir note qu'à la lecture de *Ravages* ce qui avait le plus choqué était que : 'l'objet érotique, c'était l'homme et non la femme : ils se sentirent outragés'.[4]

'Courage, sincérité intrépide' sont les mots de Beauvoir dans sa Préface de *La Bâtarde*. On ne cesse depuis d'user et abuser de l'expression beauvoirienne pour parler de Leduc, créant l'amalgame facile entre être lesbienne et 'avoir le courage de le dire'.

Carlo Jansiti dans sa biographie démontre que l'homosexualité ne fut pas source de culpabilité chez Violette Leduc :

---

[2] *Thérèse et Isabelle*, sera publié par Gallimard en 1966. L'ouvrage est mentionné dans le *Dictionnaire des œuvres érotiques* (Paris : Mercure de France, 1971).

[3] Violette Leduc, *Thérèse et Isabelle*, Texte intégral (Paris : Gallimard, N.R.F., 2000).

[4] *La Force des Choses* (Paris : Gallimard, collection folio, 1963) II, 67.

Si Violette n'a jamais analysé, du moins de façon explicite, la condition et l'identité lesbiennes, elle est demeurée étrangère aux préjugés de son temps. A une époque où l'amour lesbien était considéré comme une tare ou une maladie, son goût pour les femmes ne semble lui avoir posé aucun problème d'acceptation. Dans son œuvre toutefois, à l'exception d'*Isabelle* et des scènes de tendresse entre prostituées en prison décrites dans *la Folie en tête*, Violette Leduc porte un regard assez critique sur les homosexuelles.[5]

Le 'courage' résiderait davantage alors dans le fait de relever un pari littéraire, de dire l'acte amoureux, de le développer jusqu'aux frontières du dicible. Le simple fait que cet acte amoureux soit accompli avec une femme ne constitue pas l'unique intérêt de l'écriture érotique de Leduc. Nous verrons plus loin qu'elle a relevé le même défi avec l'évocation de l'amour hétérosexuel.

Enfin, n'oublions pas que Violette Leduc a eu une vie mouvementée : une vie de femme et même de femme mariée (brièvement certes) mais qui se trouva comme des millions de femmes de sa génération face au problème de la maternité et du refus de celle-ci. *Ravages* fut amputé du récit de son avortement. *Ravages* devint 'son enfant assassiné'. De ce traumatisme, la critique ne parle jamais.[6] Leduc fut donc censurée en tant qu'auteur de récits d'amours lesbiennes ? Certes. Mais on ne peut dire honnêtement que ce fut uniquement à cause de cela.

Examinons maintenant un deuxième aspect du mythe que Violette a elle-même contribué à ériger à travers ses écrits mais dont on a aussi abusé : ses 'amours impossibles' pour reprendre l'expression de Laure Murat.[7] Celles-ci constituent sans doute un leitmotiv de son auto–biographie et concerne les écrivains homosexuels qui la prirent sous leur égide : Sachs, Genet, Cocteau pour les plus célèbres, hommes de lettres

---

[5]   Carlo Jansiti, *Violette Leduc* (Paris : Grasset, 1999), 64.

[6]   À l'instigation de Beauvoir, elle signera le manifeste dit des 343 'salopes' in *Le Nouvel Observateur* (5 avril 1971).

[7]   *Dictionnaire des cultures gaies et lesbiennes* (Paris : Larousse, 2003) : 'Rarement, en effet, écrivaine aura usé d'autant de franchise et de précision dans une œuvre autobiographique marquée d'un double sceau : le récit d'amours impossibles (en général pour des homosexuels) et la description minutieuse de sa passion physique pour les femmes.'

auxquels il faut ajouter l'industriel et collectionneur Jacques Guérin. De Sachs et de Genet, certes, elle fut follement amoureuse. Sachs se cache avec elle à la campagne pendant l'occupation et l'incite à écrire se 'souvenirs' dont elle lui 'rebat les oreilles'. Puis il l'abandonne avant de disparaître dans de sombres circonstances. Genet l'admire et ne lui cache pas à leur première rencontre avoir aimé 'son' *Asphyxie*. Il ne lui pardonnera jamais la critique peu élogieuse d'un de ses livres. Cocteau l'invite à Milly et elle se réjouit de dormir dans la chambre de Jean Marais lorsque celui-ci est absent. Jacques Guérin, enfin, est son mécène et protecteur au même titre que Simone de Beauvoir.

Ces hommes, aimés et admirés, sont avant tout les initiateurs et protecteurs de son œuvre d'écrivaine. En effet, du point de vue d'une approche des conditions de réception des femmes écrivains au milieu du XXe siècle, on s'aperçoit que ces 'amours impossibles' reflètent aussi l'impossible relation égalitaire entre des hommes homosexuels célèbres et une femme écrivain, homosexuelle elle aussi, mais dont la célébrité se forge à l'ombre de ceux-ci. Cocteau et Jean Marais don l'image d'un couple triomphant reste dans les mémoires, lors de la réception de Cocteau à l'Académie française, Sachs sulfureux bénéficiant de publications et d'une biographie sans aucune censure, Genet adulé et joué sans cesse au théâtre... Non, la seule homosexualité ne suffit pas à définir un écrivain ni à mettre un frein à sa carrière : mais être femme...

Violette fut amoureuse de Simone de Beauvoir : il n'est que de lire *L'Affamée* ainsi que sa correspondance. Or, le lien qui s'établit entre elles fut de telle nature que sans le travail de Beauvoir, sa présence, ses critiques et son soutien, Violette Leduc n'eût jamais été un écrivain reconnu et prolifique. Un amour impossible, certes, mais une véritable amitié littéraire.[8]

Leduc, pourtant, est intégrée au milieu littéraire mondain de l'après-guerre et des années 1970. Elle connaît finalement la célébrité, de son vivant et après sa mort quoique de manière relative. On se rappelle le succès de scandale qui s'attache à *La Bâtarde* dès sa publication en 1964

---

[8]   Sur ce thème ainsi que sur tout ce qui concerne Violette Leduc consulter le site http://www.violetteleduc.com.

et on doit noter, malgré le silence de la presse après la mort de l'auteur en 1972, l'émergence d'articles et d'ouvrages universitaires consacrés à Leduc. Quel type de succès rencontra-t-elle alors, quel succès rencontre-t-elle aujourd'hui ?

Revenons donc au moment de la parution de *La Bâtarde* et à son impact dans la presse littéraire. Les deux corpus constitués par les articles français et anglo-saxons débutent, à quelques rares exceptions près, en 1964 et 1965, dates de parution et de traduction de *La Bâtarde*. Bien entendu, les interviews de l'auteur, qui contribuent à la faire connaître, sont plus nombreuses en France, quoique les premiers entretiens radiophoniques ou télévisés ne datent que de 1970, donc de la fin de la vie de Violette Leduc.

Tout d'abord presse anglaise et presse française témoignent toutes deux de ce réflexe que l'on éprouve tous au contact d'une œuvre qui surprend, ou qui dérange : le réflexe comparatiste. Il est rassurant de rapprocher un auteur d'un autre auteur : c'est une opération intellectuelle qui peut s'avérer fructueuse lorsqu'il s'agit de dégager une originalité. Malheureusement, et c'est le cas pour Violette Leduc, de tels rapprochements sont rarement présentés à l'avantage de cette dernière et c'est souvent pour l'amoindrir qu'on la compare à de grands noms. Rares en effet sont les auteurs ayant été à ce point soumis à la comparaison, et avec des personnes si différentes !

C'est la presse anglo-saxonne qui, statistiquement, s'applique le mieux à ce genre d'exercice : de Diderot,[9] à Alain Fournier,[10] en passant par Adamov, Leiris, Blaise Cendrars,[11] Beckett,[12] et même Jules Romains...[13] Le nombre est impressionnant d'auteurs masculins auxquels Leduc est comparée. Entre tous, Jean Genet, son ami, est présenté comme une sorte de 'jumeau en écriture', car, comme l'écrit si bien M. Haynes, notre auteur est 'le Saint-Genet de Simone de Beauvoir.'[14] De tels rap-

---

[9]   'Liaison dangereuse', *Time Literary Supplement* (December 1965).
[10] 'Self inflicted wounds', *The Observer* (2 juin 1968).
[11] N. Bray Booke, 'The cruel time', *Spectator* (février 1967).
[12] T. Bishop, 'A light on loneliness', *Saturday Review* (novembre 1960).
[13] A. Balakian, 'Mad in pursuit', *Saturday Review* (septembre 1971).
[14] M. Haynes, 'The woman with the little fox', *The Nation* (janvier 1967).

prochements véhiculent une image assez méprisante du courant existen-
tialiste et de sa principale instigatrice.

Peu d'auteurs féminins sont cités au palmarès des inspirateurs de
Violette Leduc, sinon Colette, dont elle ferait 'une parodie exagérée'[15] et,
indirectement, Virginia Woolf, lorsque à propos de *La Femme au petit
renard*, on compare l'héroïne de la nouvelle à 'une Mrs Dalloway au
chômage.'[16]

La presse anglo-saxonne semble donc avoir eu fréquemment recours à
la comparaison entre auteurs et ce jusqu'aux dernières publications de
Violette Leduc. Son œuvre a suscité l'attention du public et les
journalistes sans pour autant lui faire obtenir de véritable reconnaissance.
Pourtant il est essentiel de souligner que c'est dans le monde anglo-saxon
que l'œuvre de Violette Leduc connaîtra quelques années plus tard un
succès durable, grâce en particulier à Kate Millet avec *Sita*,
autobiographie dans laquelle l'auteure raconte la façon dont elle
enseignait l'œuvre de Violette Leduc.[17] Cependant, lorsque paraît une
traduction anglaise de *Thérèse et Isabelle*, en 1967, un universitaire
publie aux Etats-Unis un des articles les plus malveillants dont notre
auteure ait été l'objet. Selon ce critique, ce roman occuperait une 'place
de choix dans une anthologie de la littérature lesbienne' et ce 'dans la
tradition du Baudelaire des femmes damnées', elle serait ainsi classée car
elle révèlerait 'une autre facette du nouveau roman et du structuralisme
des années 60'. Pour couronner l'ensemble elle aurait, selon l'éminent
professeur, l'avantage 'd'émerger du troupeau des romancières que la
France a produit depuis 1945.'[18] Notons aussi les titres alléchants autant
que réducteurs tels que 'Passions of a Gallic Sappho' du même auteur à
propos de *La Bâtarde*[19] ou encore 'Autobiography of a lesbian' de E.D
Salem.[20]

---

[15]   Bishop (1960).
[16]   F. Hope, 'A Moveable Feast', *New Statesman* (mars 1967).
[17]   New York : Farrar, Straus, Giroux, 1977, et Paris : Stock, 1978, 361–4.
[18]   H. Peyre, 'Rapture in a little girl's room', *Saturday Review* (juillet
       1967).
[19]   '… the totally uninhibited description of the author's lesbian love has
       contributed not a little to the success of the book.'
[20]   *The Humanist*, 2 (février 1965).

Après 1973, le silence s'installe dans la presse spécialisée. Violette Leduc est morte l'année précédente à Faucon. *La Chasse à l'amour* publié en 1973 est commenté brièvement, et bénéficie d'un avant propos de Simone de Beauvoir. *Le Taxi* est davantage salué, sans doute parce que l'œuvre est plus scandaleuse, s'agissant des amours d'un frère et d'une sœur.

Cependant, dès le milieu des années 1970 elle connaît un succès considérable auprès d'un public féministe et féminin : les premiers travaux universitaires voient le jour.

Étudier Violette Leduc

Les premières thèses sont écrites à la fin des années 1980.[21] Aujourd'hui les chercheuses anglaises et américaines, Locey, Hall, Hughes, Marson sont orientées vers les aspects stylistiques et psychanalytiques de son œuvre. En France, le rapport au temps, à la mère, à la mort, le 'corps morcelé', la 'mise en scène du Je', étaient et demeurent les thèmes de prédilection des chercheuses et chercheurs.[22] L'homosexualité de l'auteur

---

[21] Ghyslaine Charles-Merrien, 'Violette Leduc ou le corps morcelé', Nouveau Doctorat, sous la direction de Jacques Berengues, Université Rennes 2 (1988) ; Marie-Eve Klein, 'Violette Leduc ou la revanche du quotidien', Doctorat 3° cycle, direction Michel Mansuy, Université de Strasbourg 2 (1983) ; V.A Lipton, 'Women in today's world: a study of five French women novelists (Célia Bertin, M. Duras, V. Leduc, F. Mallet-Joris, Chr. Rochefor)', University of Wisconsin (1972). Voir *Dissertation Abstracts International* (juin 1973) ; Marie-Elisabeth Mignoteaud, 'Violette Leduc: récits et subversions', direction Francis Marmande, Paris VII (1989) ; René Pavans de Ceccatty, 'Evidence de Violette Leduc', Doctorat 3° cycle, sous la direction de Yvon Belaval, Paris I UER de Philosophie (1980) ; J.G. Stockinger. 'Violette Leduc, the legitimations of La Bâtarde', University of Wisconsin-Madison (1979). Voir *Dissertation Abstracts International* (décembre 1979).

[22] Elisabeth Locey, *Seducing the Reader: Violette Leduc and the pleasures of the text* (Madison: University of Wisconsin, 1997); Susan Marson, *Le Temps de l'autobiographie: la mort avant la letter* (Vincennes, P.U., 1998); Colette Hall, *Violette Leduc, la mal-aimée* (Amsterdam: Rodopi, 1999); Carlo Jansiti, *Violette Leduc* (Paris : Grasset, 1999); Mireille Brioude, *Violette Leduc, la mise en scène du Je* (Amsterdam: Rodopi,

apparaît comme une composante parmi d'autres de son écriture. A cette époque aucune chercheuse ne se revendiquait des 'gender studies' balbutiantes outre-Atlantique et ignorées en France. Mias il est certain que toutes savaient que s'intéresser à un auteur femme, à cette époque, revenait purement et simplement à s'exclure du monde universitaire français.

Le premier ouvrage entièrement consacré à Violette Leduc est celui d'Isabelle de Courtivron, aujourd'hui professeur au Massachusetts Institute of Technology. Une approche détaillée et systématique de son œuvre y est faite sous un angle thématique et stylistique.[23]

Citons ensuite celui de Martha-Noelle Evans : 'La mythologie de l'écriture dans *La Bâtarde*'.[24] De son côté Jane Rule consacre à Violette Leduc un court essai nuancé et pertinent dans *Lesbian Images*.[25] Loin d'enfermer l'auteure dans une 'image lesbienne' Rule propose une analyse de la personnalité de l'écrivain à travers son œuvre : les titres sont parfois trompeurs et pourtant Rule est une des premières à impliquer Leduc dans un ouvrage du type 'gender studies'.

Les thèses, françaises et étrangères, constituent encore à l'heure actuelle le vivier des recherches sur l'œuvre de Leduc et leur champ d'investigation élargi permet de rendre compte de toute la richesse de son écriture sans la cantonner à une catégorisation forcée dans le camp des écrivaines lesbiennes. Mais encore faut-il que ces thèses soient publiées...[26]

---

[23]   2000).
         Isabelle de Courtivron, *Violette Leduc* (Boston : Twayne, 1976).
[24]   *Littérature*, 46 (mai 1982) voir aussi du même auteur : 'writing as a difference', *The (m)other tongue* (Ithaca and London : Cornell University Press, 1985), 306.
[25]   New York : The Crossing Press, 1982.
[26]   Parmi les thèses, mentionnons l'une d'entre elles, symptomatique de l'état des mentalités en France dans les années 1980, dans le milieu médical : Yvonne Delamare, 'Homosexualité féminine : différents points de vue sociologiques et psychanalytiques centrés sur une œuvre littéraire, Violette Leduc', Sous la direction du Pr Lajeunesse, Hôpital Broussais-Hôte-Dieu, Paris (1983). La doctorante, avec beaucoup de bonnes intentions, visait à démontrer que l'homosexualité féminine n'était pas toujours une maladie : 'Dans quelle mesure V. Leduc est-elle

Plus grave, beaucoup plus grave, me semble-t-il, est la totale absence
du nom de Violette Leduc dans un domaine où on l'attend précisément.
Ce domaine comporte deux champs éditoriaux : le champ des publications destinées à des élèves du second degré, les lycéens préparant le
baccalauréat, et celui des publications destinées aux étudiants spécialistes
de littérature française.

Ravages du silence et nouveaux visages de la censure

Faisons le point sur les ouvrages français destinés à un public d'étudiants
ou de spécialistes de la littérature du XXe siècle. J'ai consulté une
trentaine d'ouvrages: dictionnaires spécialisés, ouvrages d'histoire
littéraire du XXe siècle. Je n'ai trouvé qu'une demi-douzaine d'articles
sur Violette Leduc et son œuvre : ceux de Bernard Valette,[27] Eliane
Lecarme,[28] Guy LeClec'h,[29] Hélène Laprevotte,[30] et Carlo Jansiti.[31] Tous

representative de l'ensemble des homosexuelles et quelle est leur place
dans notre société ?' Et en fin de seconde partie : 'Si Violette Leduc
nous donne un aperçu de ce que peut être la souffrance de certaines
homosexuelles, elle ne nous révèle rien des autres (celles qui ne
souffrent pas). Somme toute il existerait deux sortes d'homosexuelles :
Celles dont la vie affective et sexuelle est perturbée par de graves
conflits : leur homosexualité est peut-être alors une solution mais
souvent empreinte de la même souf–france, leur pathologie plus ou
moins intense est diverse et se distribue dans différentes catégories
nosographiques   sans   systématisation   particulière.   Celles   dont
l'homosexualité   semble   la   solution   la   plus   heureuse   pour
l'épanouissement de leur sexualité et de leur affectivité. Il serait vain de
considérer ces dernières comme malades et de vouloir les guérir à tout
prix.'

[27] *Dictionnaire   des   écrivains   de   langue   française*,   dir.   Couty
      Beaumarchais et Rey (Paris : Larousse, 2001).
[28] *Dictionnaire   de   la   littérature   française*,   collection   Encyclopaedia
      Universalis (Paris : Albin Michel, 2000).
[29] *Dictionnaire encyclopédique*, Laffont-Bompiani, collection Bouquins.
      (Paris : Robert Laffont, collections Bouquins, 2002).
[30] *Dictionnaire des œuvres du XX° siècle,* Le Robert, collection *les usuels*
      paris : Le Robert, 1998).
[31] *Dictionnaire des lettres françaises*, collection (Paris : Le livre de Poche,

articles d'une grande qualité et aucun ou presque ne mettant prin-
cipalement en avant le récit des amours homosexuelles de Violette
Leduc : seuls les aspects stylistiques ou thématiques sont abordés et un
hommage est rendu à l'écrivain. Les œuvres disons 'à caractère
homosexuel' sont citées, mais non en tant que telles, et les amours
(homo)sexuelles de l'auteur sont parfois (pudiquement ?) caractérisées
par des parenthèses. Les notices anglo-saxonnes concernant Violette
Leduc ne sont guère plus rares, mais souvent plus anciennes et plus
détaillées.[32]

Pourtant Isabelle de Courtivron tient des propos décevants et sur-
prenants de la part d'une pionnière des études universitaires consacrées à
Leduc, propos dans lesquels figure justement la référence à l'homosexualité de l'auteur :

> La solitude est le thème majeur, que ce soit celle de la lesbienne vieillissante
> qui se croit « la chienne » de tout le monde, celle de la jeune pensionnaire
> (*Thérèse et Isabelle*) ou de la vieille fille qui ne peut se faire aimer que d'un
> cadavre (*La Vieille fille et le Mort*).[33]

Aucune mention de Violette Leduc ne se trouve dans les manuels de
littérature destinés aux étudiants que j'ai consultés, pas même dans les
rares chapitres consacrés à la littérature féminine... Pour ce qui est des
anthologies on passe allègrement de Le Clézio à Leiris (parfois d'Annie

---

[32]   collection Encyclopédies d'aujourd'hui, La Pochotèque, 1998).
       On trouvera également des articles intéressants dans *French women
       writers*, éd. Sartori and Zimmerman (New York : Greenwood Press,
       1991). Anthony Levi, *Guide to French Literature* (Chicago and London,
       St James Press, 1992) ainsi que dans *The New Oxford Companion to
       Literature in French*, ed. Harvey et Heseltine (Oxford : Oxford
       University Press, 1995). Un récent sondage auprès d'enseignantes
       américaines fait apparaître que Leduc est étudiée dans les universités
       américaines dans les secteurs des 'women' ou des 'gay studies' mais
       aussi dans des cours plus généraux sur l'autobiographie.
[33]   *Dictionnaire littéraire des femmes de langue française*, dir Makward et
       Cottenet-Hage (Paris : éditions Karthala, agence de la francophonie,
       1997).

Leclerc à Leiris) Duras et Colette éclipsent pour longtemps Violette et les autres...

Envisageons le domaine éditorial de l'enseignement secondaire. Lors d'un colloque tenu à Saragosse sur le thème de la littérature féminine j'ai montré les ravages d'une sorte censure inversée dans un manuel scolaire publié en 1985.[34] La double page consacrée à Violette Leduc, les illustrations, le choix des textes, jusqu'aux grossières erreurs sur les titres de ses ouvrages étaient révélateurs de l'ignorance et des préjugés qui entouraient son œuvre dans le domaine scolaire et universitaire. Rassurons-nous, Violette Leduc a aujourd'hui pratiquement totalement disparu des manuels destinés aux élèves qui préparent le baccalauréat en France.[35] Quant aux auteures citées dans ces mêmes manuels, elles sont fort rares.

La censure la plus terrible la plus pernicieuse concernant Violette Leduc est celle qui est le lot commun de nombreuses écrivaines en France : le silence. Silence qui les recouvre parce qu'elles sont des femmes et parce qu'historiquement elles n'eurent jamais la place qui leur revenait au sein de l'institution littéraire. Il faut bien voir que c'est dans ce contexte que ce joue actuellement la notoriété posthume de l'écrivaine Violette Leduc : entre censure silencieuse et surmédiatisation par les adeptes du militantisme gay, quand Violette Leduc finira-t-elle par s'imposer ?

---

[34] M. Brioude, 'Silence, censure et succes de scandale : le cas Violette Leduc', *La Conjura del Olvido* (Zaragoza : Icaria editorial, 1998), 183–95.

[35] Chez Nathan, *Littérature du XXe siècle, textes et documents* (Paris : Nathan, 1997) on consacre tout de même quelques lignes à Leduc dans les rubriques intitulées 'le retour au vécu' et 'la vie est un roman' (sic). À propos de *La Bâtarde*, il est écrit que Violette Leduc dressait en 1964 un 'vibrant réquisitoire contre l'intolérance d'une société misogyne et rétrograde.'

Les gay et lesbian studies : ré-appropriation ou expropriation d'un auteur ?

Revenons un peu en arrière. L'article de Elaine Marks intitulé 'lesbian intertextuality' en 1979 fonde à mes yeux l'inscription de Violette Leduc dans les gender studies.[36] Le critique établit la filiation entre Colette, Leduc et Wittig. En effet, pour Elaine Marks, il existe trois générations d'écrivaines inscrivant le phénomène de l'intertextualité lesbienne : Colette à La Belle Epoque, Leduc à celle de l'existentialisme, Wittig avec le mouvement formaliste et féministe de la fin des années 60. Chaque figure de lesbienne est aussi révélatrice d'une époque : 'la lesbienne maternante de Colette, les collégiennes passionnées de Leduc, les amazones révolutionnaires de Wittig.' Leur mode d'écriture créée un nouveau code à partir de cette figure : nostalgie philosophique de Colette, présent 'parfait' de Leduc, J/e barré dans un présent déjà teinté d'apocalypse chez Wittig.

Du point de vue de la tradition littéraire, Colette et Leduc restent fidèles à la tradition narrative classique tandis que Wittig, elle, fait exploser les repères narratifs et le statut des personnages. Une révolution textuelle et sexuelle s'est progressivement mise en place avec ces trois auteurs. L'image de la lesbienne s'est métamorphosée du couple volup-tueux vers le J/e solitaire et cannibale de Wittig. Seul modèle commun : Sappho. Explicite chez Colette et Wittig il n'est invoqué qu'indirectement par le biais du 'gynécée scolaire' dans Thérèse et Isabelle.

L'héritage de Leduc est en effet revendiqué par Wittig elle-même, dans sa préface pour l'édition américaine de Corps lesbien :

> Le thème [du lesbianisme] n'est pas même tabou puisqu'il n'a pas d'existence dans l'histoire de la littérature. La littérature homosexuelle masculine est dotée d'un passé et d'un présent. Les lesbiennes, elles, sont silencieuses, comme les femmes le sont toutes. Quand on a lu Le Puits de solitude, les poèmes de Sylvia Path et d'Anaïs Nin, La Bâtarde de Violette Leduc, on a tout lu. Seul le mouvement des femmes s'est montré capable de produire des textes lesbiens

---

[36] Homosexualities and French Literature (London : Cornell University Press, 1979).

en totale rupture avec la culture masculine, des textes écrits par des femmes pour des femmes, sans souci de l'assentiment masculin.[37]

Elaine Marks ajoute que Violette Leduc est le seul écrivain reconnu par Wittig comme un prédécesseur. Elle la nomme ainsi car dans *Thérèse et Isabelle* c'est l'expérience de l'auteur qui fournit le sujet de l'écriture. L'acte amoureux occupe la partie centrale de l'œuvre. Elle invente un style, une syntaxe et des métaphores spécifiques... Violette Leduc dit-elle, est reellement le premier écrivain français à nous entraîner au-delà du modèle de Sappho, en restant un auteur lesbien. Cependant ce style reste soumis aux exigences de l'autobiographie et dès que l'épisode du gynécée, lieu clos et féminin prend fin, le corps féminin n'occupe plus une place centrale. Ce que ne fait pas Wittig qui poursuit l'expérience du corps écrit dans toute son œuvre.

Il paraît important de souligner que la revendication de l'appartenance de Violette Leduc à la lignée des écrivains lesbiens n'est pas le fait de l'écrivaine elle-même. C'est une relecture de la part de Monique Wittig, une sorte d'annexion sincère de la critique, soucieuse de donner à une certaine époque au discours lesbien une existence dans le discours critique et historique.

L'annexion de Leduc par Wittig est donc hautement revendiquée par celle-ci au nom de son souci de fonder le discours lesbien en tant que tel. C'est un geste politique que l'analyse de Wittig, s'autorisant dans le champ critique des années 1970 : linguistique, lacanien et féministe.

Ce geste a pourtant été perçu comme la porte ouverte à une classification ultérieure qui annexera Violette Leduc dans un champ plus large et aux contours plus flous, que des hommes et femmes, au nom de leur appartenance à la communauté homosexuelle, s'autoriseront à leur tour.

Est-ce un tel souci qui anime Laure Murat, figurant parmi les auteurs du *Dictionnaire des Cultures gays et lesbiennes,* lorsqu'elle affirme dans l'article 'littérature lesbienne' que Leduc est la 'représentante de l'écrit lesbien assumé' avec le *Puits de solitude* et les *Guérillières* ? Or c'est au

---

[37] *The Lesbian Body*, tr. from the French by David Le Vay (1975; Boston : Beacon Press, 1986).

nom de la volonté de mettre en perspective une histoire de la littérature lesbienne qu'on néglige le fait que l'histoire appartienne aussi à ceux qui ont le souci de la construire : Leduc n'a jamais revendiqué ses écrits érotiques lesbiens en tant que tels mais en tant qu'émanant de sa volonté de jouir en se rappelant ces amours : elle se situe non dans l'autorité verbale mais dans le plaisir du texte. Wittig elle, est écrivaine et c'est cela même qui fait autorité dans son geste de fonder une tradition littéraire lesbienne coupée du discours phallocentrique.

Laure Murat[38] présente Violette Leduc dans l'article qu'elle lui consacre, comme une femme 'de tempérament excentrique' dont l'œuvre censurée, Thérèse et Isabelle' est remarquable par son 'style baroque' et son 'audace' : un bon tiers de l'article est consacré à cet ouvrage, aux dépens des milliers de pages de son autobiographie. Pis, le troisième tome de celle-ci *La Chasse à l'amour* n'est tout simplement pas mentionné ! Oserait-on ne parler que du *Deuxième sexe* dans un article présentant Simone de Beauvoir sans mentionner *Les Mémoires d'une jeune fille rangée* ?[39]

Pour mieux comprendre l'esprit qui préside à l'entreprise du *Dictionnaire*, relevons dans le même ouvrage il faut relever la remarque de Didier Eribon sur Gide : le début de *Corydon* est consacré à une réflexion sur Walt Whitman que Gide entend présenter à son interlocuteur comme un véritable chant d'amour entre hommes. Eribon commente alors :

> Gide procède ici à une véritable ré appropriation gay d'un écrivain, mais surtout il décrit la bataille que les gays doivent mener pour que la dimension homosexuelle d'une œuvre ne soit pas purement et simplement gommée par le commentaire hétérosexuel.

---

[38] 'Violette Leduc', *Dictionnaire des cultures gays et lesbiennes* (Paris : Larousse, 2003)

[39] Mauvais exemple car Sylvie Chaperon consacre l'article Simone de Beauvoir dans le même ouvrage à ses prises de position concernant l'homosexualité. Cependant l'on sait que l'on peut trouver Beauvoir ailleurs, ce qui n'est pas le cas pour Violette Leduc…

Le terme de 'réappropriation gay' (comme si Gide devait être affublé du qualificatif 'gay' !) et le comminatoire emploi du verbe 'devoir' laissent à penser. Un écrivain, parce qu'il est ou fut (ou pourrait être ?) homosexuel, doit-il être exproprié de son texte et devenir par là-même la propriété exclusive du commentaire homosexuel ? Un écrivain, doit-il être la propriété d'une communauté littéraire ? Encore faut-il qu'il le veuille...

Voici l'exemple d'une autre 'réappropriation gay' : il s'agit d'une étrange étude qu'on pourrait appeler 'monographie narcissique' consacrée à Leduc mais surtout au rapport personnel que l'auteur, René de Ceccatty, entretient affectivement avec l'écrivaine.

Tout en regrettant — mais sans s'en expliquer davantage — que Violette Leduc soit catégorisée dans le domaine des 'écrivains homosexuels' et tout en consacrant les deux-tiers de son ouvrage à l'analyse de l'œuvre de Violette Leduc, René de Ceccatty éprouve le besoin de se livrer en une centaine de pages (!) à une confession exposant les raisons profondes de son intérêt pour Violette Leduc :

> Qu'est-ce qui me menait vers Violette Leduc ? Un processus d'identification. Sa conception de la sexualité et de l'amour, c'est certain. Et pourtant, ce que j'avais écrit ne ressemblait à rien de ce qu'elle écrivait elle-même.. J'ai un caractère impulsif et qui déconcerte...[40]

L'identification d'un écrivain pour un autre écrivain semble être aussi la justification du discours légèrement narcissique de Nina Bouraoui, jeune écrivaine, qui dans un numéro du *Magazine Littéraire*, cède aussi à la tentation de s'approprier l'auteure :[41] 'J'achète tous ses livres, sur les quais, Place Clichy, des éditions originales. Je deviens sa collectionneuse. Elle devient mon fantôme. Je sais, sa solitude, son visage, sa voix.' Un peu plus loin, dans ce court article, elle proclame : 'ici il n'y a pas d'homosexualité. Il s'agit de liens, d'histoires, de sexualité, c'est tout.'

---

[40] René de Ceccatty, *Violette Leduc, éloge de La Bâtarde* (Paris : Stock, 1994).

[41] *Le Magazine littéraire*, no. 426 "littérature et homosexualité" (décembre 2003).

Dernière remarque révélatrice : Nina Bouraoui souhaiterait enfin aller au-delà du mythe et considérer le discours amoureux en lui-même... Car qu'y a-t-il derrière ces écrivains dont on fait en dépit d'eux-mêmes un mythe, un porte-drapeau ou un miroir narcissique ? Il y a le piège que tend le texte autobiographique qui par sa nature même me fait céder à la tentation de m'approprier l'histoire de l'Autre, d'en faire, que sais-je, un double caché, un autre moi-même.

La Chasse à l'amour : un livre qui gêne

Le texte est la seule chose qui compte lorsqu'il s'agit d'approcher un écrivain. Bien évidemment, lorsque ce texte est autobiographique on peut éprouver le besoin de se référer à la biographie, qui jouera le rôle d'alibi au sens 'd'être ailleurs': mais l'être est-il ailleurs que dans son texte ? Bref, lisant la biographie écrite par Carlo Jansiti on sera rassuré : Violette n'a pas (trop) menti : elle a eu des liaisons avec des femmes, on apprendra qu'elle en a eu (beaucoup !) avec des hommes.

Supposons maintenant une étudiante, amenée à connaître Violette Leduc et lisant, comme on le fait souvent d'abord, *la Bâtarde*. Séduite par la force audacieuse des premières pages proches de Thérèse et Isabelle, elle a envie de connaître l'auteur : elle ouvre *La Folie en Tête*, se prend dans le récit de la folie, fascinée et en même temps distante. Enfin, elle lit le troisième tome de l'autobiographie, *La Chasse à l'amour* :

> René s'est soulevé. Mon bras autour de sa taille. C'est mince, c'est flexible, c'est fort. C'est de l'homme, il était temps.
> Je dessinais des ronds autour de son téton. Un homme qui a des seins me répugne. Je veux que la nature ne se trompe pas. Pas d'équivoque avec René. Son buste bronzé était chaud à deux heures du matin, chaleur d'abricot.[42]

Le mythe de l'écrivaine lesbienne s'effondre : lui aurait-on menti ou la vérité d'un style est-elle ailleurs que dans des catégorisations ridicules ?

---

[42]   Violette Leduc, *La Chasse à l'amour* (Paris : Gallimard, collection N.R.F, 1973), 183.

Loin de s'affirmer comme écrivaine lesbienne, Leduc s'écrit femme, a aimé des femmes puis a aimé des hommes. Voilà tout.

Le complexe du plexiglass

Finalement la question qui se pose est encore et toujours celle de la catégorisation : écrivaine-lesbienne ou écrivaine et lesbienne : dissociation ou assimilation ? La meilleure analyse en la matière est celle de *Gabriele Griffin*.[43] Au début de son ouvrage consacré aux représentations lesbiennes dans la littérature féminine du vingtième siècle, elle pose la question de la définition à donner à ce que l'on appelle l'écriture lesbienne :

> The answer to the question 'what is lesbian writing ?' depends, in part, on where the locus of the establishment of meaning in relation to a text is sited. One may consider this meaning, in this instance, the lesbian identity of a text, to be determined primarily by the author, by the text itself, or by the reader.[44]

L'enjeu idéologique de la lecture 'lesbienne' et du classement d'un texte dans la catégorie 'écritutre lesbienne' est ici parfaitement posé, à travers la question du lieu de l'énonciation critique. Mais l'enjeu théorique et littéraire est, dans le cas de Violette Leduc comme dans tous les autres cas où l'auteur est 'classé', dépassé par un enjeu idéologique sérieux. Cette idéologie ne réactive pas seulement la coupure entre l'étude textuelle et la lecture contextualisée, historicisée d'un texte. La contextualisation, issue du courant de lecture marxiste est, à mon avis, parfaitement justifiée. Ce qui l'est beaucoup moins c'est justement l'appropriation idéologique d'un auteur complètement décontextualisée : ne voir un auteur non plus en fonction d'un contexte social et littéraire mais le considérer comme intrinsèquement lié à une catégorie socio-

---

[43] Gabriele Griffin, *Heavenly Love, lesbian images in twentieth-century women's writing* (Manchester : Manchester University Press, 1994), 3.

[44] Nous traduisons: 'la réponse,' écrit-elle, 'dépend en partie du lieu d'où l'on établit cette définition : l'identité lesbienne du texte peut être déterminée d'abord par l'auteur, ou par le texte lui-même ou encore par le lecteur.'

sexuée sans aucun recul historique. Griffin cite un article de Judith Butler dans lequel cette dernière souligne avec virulence que le mot 'lesbienne' implique une totalisation provisoire du moi en partie fondée sur l'exclusion de tout autre constituant de ce moi.' et que de tous temps' les catégories identitaires ont été l'apanage des régimes autoritaires'[45]

Mary Meigs, toujours citée par G. Griffin,[46] a cette amusante comparaison : 'toute écrivaine qui s'avère être lesbienne quelque soient ses écrits ou le pourcentage de textes lesbiens dans son œuvre demeure à tout jamais prisonnier de son identité lesbienne comme un insecte dans du plexiglass'.

Le 'complexe du plexiglass' pourrait être celui de toutes les écrivaines aux prises avec le mythe de la lesbienne et de tous les écrivains dit 'gays'. Il ne s'agit bien évidemment pas de nier que Violette Leduc écrivit, avant les autres, de l'amour lesbien, mais il s'agit de voir que ceci ne doit pas occulter le reste : l'œuvre achevé qui épouse une vie entière, avec ses mouvements, ses sautes, ses changements, et surtout un refus persistant de se laisser réduire, de son vivant, à cette identité lesbienne.

Que nous offre aujourd'hui le paysage critique français sur Violette Leduc ? Un désert, avec quelques rares et austères publications. A côté de cela, une vitrine (en plexiglass) appelée 'culture lesbienne' dans laquelle figure Violette, photographiée en pleine page. Entre les deux, une écrivaine méconnue, prisonnière d'un mythe qui tourne à la mystification.

Bibliography

Beauvoir, Simone de, *La Force des choses* (Paris : Gallimard, Folio, 1963), II.

Brioude, Mireille, *Violette Leduc : la mise en scène du Je* (Amsterdam : Rodopi, 2000).

---

[45]   Gabriele Griffin, 'Imitation and gender insubordination', in *Inside / Out: lesbian theories, gay theories*, ed. D. Fuss (New York: New York University Press, 1991) 13, nous traduisons.

[46]   Mary Meigs, 'Falling between the cracks', in *Lesbian Texts and Contexts : radical revisions*, éd. K. Jay and J. Glasgow (New York : New York University Press, 1990).

Ceccatty, René de, *Violette Leduc : éloge de La Bâtarde* (Paris : Stock, 1994).

Courtivron, Isabelle de, *Violette Leduc* (Boston : Twayne Publishers, 1976).

Eribon, Didier, *Dictionnaire des cultures gaies et lesbiennes* (Paris : Larousse, 2003).

Fuss, Diana (éd.), *Inside/ Out : lesbian theories, gay theories* (New York : New York University Press, 1991).

Griffin, Gabriele, *Heavenly Love : lesbian images in twentieth-century women's writing* (Manchester : Manchester University Press, 1994).

Hall, Colette, *Violette Leduc, la mal-aimée* (Amsterdam : Rodopi, 1999).

Jansiti, Carlo, *Violette Leduc* (Paris : Grasset, 1999).

Jay, Karla and Joanne Glasgow, *Lesbian Texts and Contexts* (New York : New York University Press, 1990).

Leduc, Violette, *La Chasse à l'amour* (Paris : Gallimard, N.R.F., 1973).

——, *Thérèse et Isabelle* (Paris : Gallimard, N.R.F., 2000).

Locey, Elizabeth, *Seducing the Reader : Violette Leduc and the pleasures of the text* (Madison : University of Wisconsin, 1997).

Marks, Elaine, *Homosexualities and French Literature* (London : Cornell University Press, 1979).

Marson, Susan, *Le Temps de l'autobiographie : la mort avant la lettre* (Paris : Presses Universitaires Vincennes, 1998).

Sartori, Eva and Dorothy Zimmerman, *French Women Writers* (New York : Greenwood Press, 1991).

Wittig, Monique, *The Lesbian Body*, tr. David Le Vay (Boston : Beacon Press, 1986).

The Lesbian Body in Motion:
Representations of Corporeality and Sexuality in the Novels of Mireille Best

Stephanie Schechner
Widener University

I. Introduction: Figuring the Lesbian Body

How can one represent lesbian bodies without confining them, mutilating them, or distorting them? How can one convey a sense of motion, of vitality and of diversity with respect to the lesbian body? At the heart, so to speak, of contemporary French writing by and about lesbians, these questions remain open ones demanding consideration by both fiction writers and critics alike. Scholars such as Jennifer Waelti-Walters have thoroughly documented the long tradition of both misrepresentation and ambiguous representation of lesbian bodies in French literature. Historically, to portray lesbian bodies has meant to distort, to mythologise, even to fantasise about them. Until the second half of the twentieth century, lesbian bodies, along with all other aspects of lesbian characters, were rarely, if ever, examined with the intent of portraying them in a positive light. In her study titled *Damned Women: lesbians in French novels*, Jennifer Waelti-Walters traces 'the literary construction of lesbian characters and the social and psychological context in which they are set within the larger frame of the history of the modern novel in France' (5) from 1796 to 1996.[1] She reveals an extensive tradition of misrepresentation in which lesbians have most often been figured as, at best, repressed and confused or, at worst, monstrous and evil. Well-known feminist writers such as de Beauvoir, Cixous, and Wittig marked a transition from

[1] Jennifer Waelti-Walters, *Damned Women: lesbians in French novels* (Montreal: McGill-Queens University Press, 2000).

123

earlier predominantly negative portrayals of lesbians to more affirming contemporary ones. All three of these authors were committed to exploring lesbian existence from new points of view. Much of their work remained theoretical however, leaving the fictional landscape relatively speaking under-developed. Unfortunately, following the impressive work of these forerunners, much of the first significant wave of lesbian fiction writing, dating from the 1970s to the 1990s, suffered from the imposition of a political agenda on to relatively weak literary forms. The result was a number of unsatisfactory texts whose ideological stance took precedence over literary concerns. Examining writings from the period 1968 until 1996, several scholars have issued a call for more lesbian writing such as the one expressed here by Lillian Faderman: 'The canon is in desperate need of expansion, which will come in time as more writers who escape from orthodoxy [...] emerge' (58). Even so, scholars such as Waelti-Walters and Lucille Cairns have noted the emergence of a small number of lesser known writers, such as Jocelyne François, Jeanne Galzy and Mireille Best, whose images of lesbians challenge both the dominant heterosexist ideology and the limiting idea of the lesbian novel as manifesto in order to offer new visions of sexual identity. Authors have only in the last several decades embarked upon more positive reflections related to lesbian corporeality and sexuality. In the field of contemporary French lesbian writing, Mireille Best (1943–) has distinguished herself as one of a small group writers who has successfully crafted a complex literary approach to lesbian existence.[2]

   A native of Roquebrune in Normandy and the author of three novels as well as several collections of short stories, Best has anchored her narratives both literally and figuratively in the coastal communities

---

[2]   Mireille Best's work, though impressive, has recieved little scholarly attention to date. At the time I wrote this essay, I was aware of only the publications listed in my bibliography. Only after presenting this essay, did I become aware of Lucille Cairns's book titled *Lesbian Desire in Post-1968 French Literature* (Lewiston: Edwin Mellen Press, 2002) which devotes part of several chapters to Best's work. I have done my best to retrospectively consider Cairns's argument as it intersects with my own.

typical of her *région natale*.[3] Her novels to date each recount in the first person the coming of age of young lesbians living in seaside towns. As Janine Ricouart puts it in her article, the first full-length one to my knowledge to be published on Best: 'le choix de personnages enfants ou adolescents permet à Best d'explorer les remous et les émois de jeunes lesbiennes en devenir.'[4] In all three texts, intimate lesbian relationships are only one part of the dramas which unfold as the young protagonists seek their way in the world. While lesbianism is occasionally contested, attacked, or at issue, it is not always so. Instead, the development of sexuality parallels other aspects of the protagonists' growth. For instance, in each story we see how the heroine's relationship with her mother evolves and changes shape in such a way as to free her from her past so that she can pursue adult connections with other women. As the young women explore love and sexuality, we are offered glimpses of intimacy which emphasise the physical and emotional movements of those characters involved. Ultimately, Best crafts rich narratives in order to explore a variety of relationships and psycho-social life transitions. All the while, she experiments with figurative language and punctuation creating multidimensional texts that demand the close attention of the reader. Best's representations of lesbian bodies are particularly interesting since it is in the course of figuring the body that Best deploys some of her most complex discursive strategies.

Mireille Best's fragmented descriptions of bodies and her association of both corporeality and sexuality with images of water illuminate the particular developmental and cultural situations of her adolescent lesbian protagonists. This paper will discuss in detail how Best conveys the

---

[3]   Mireille Best is the author of the following three novels: *Hymne aux murènes* (Paris: Gallimard, 1986), *Camille en octobre* (Paris: Gallimard, 1988), and *Il n'y a pas d'hommes au Paradis* (Paris: Gallimard, 1995). From this point on I will refer to these novels by the following abbreviations in footnotes: *HM*, *CO*, and *IH*. Best makes frequent use of ellipses in her writing. The ellipses found in quotations in this essay reflect the original texts.

[4]   Janine Ricouart, 'Enfance magique ou infernale? Un regard socio-critique sur l'œuvre de Mireille Best', *Women in French Studies*, Special Issue (2003), 150–65 (152).

motion of lesbian bodies through the use of fragmentation and water images. My argument will suggest that these stylistic choices allow Best to capture both the specific experience of young lesbians in coastal regions and the general mobility which might be desired by readers of all ages who seek freedom from static images. Furthermore, these narrative strategies reflect Best's attitude toward writing which emphasises the notion of the writer as a conduit for her material, thereby highlighting the movement of language and writing. In my conclusion, I will demonstrate that water is central to Best's understanding not only of lesbian sexuality but also of writing.

II. Fragmentation: Our Bodies, Ourselves

The bodies in Mireille Best's novels are most often presented in bits and pieces. Rarely do we find conventionally realist descriptions which seek to paint a visual picture for the reader. Instead, we catch sight of bodies in motion, usually a hand, shoulders, eyes, or hair. Rather than focusing on the usual erogenous zones of the body (breasts and genitals), Best more often demonstrates an awareness of body parts visible to all in everyday life. The attention given to hands and eyes is extensive and reflects a concern with those bodily features which people use most often to make contact with others. In this way, Best opens her narrative to a wide readership, noting the kinds of connection that anyone might find familiar. Best herself has stated that she does not write for a specifically lesbian readership and the fact that her descriptions of bodies often retain a certain neutrality, not to say asexuality, supports this claim. Additionally, Best does not reduce her lesbian protagonists to their sexuality. Their bodies, like those of heterosexual characters, are composed of many parts, not merely those related to the stereotypical expression of sexuality. Best, by shifting her gaze, and ours, from shoulder to eyes to hands, recognises both the full expression of her protagonist's personalities (they are not simply sexual beings) and an expanded notion of sexuality (all aspects of the body might be sexual at any given moment). As we will see, Best thus frees her characters from stultifying definitions of both lesbianism and of conventional sexuality in any form.

If we examine her first novel, *Hymne aux murènes* (Hymn to the Murena / Moray Eels), we will find a number of examples of fragmented descriptions. This text tells the story of Mila, a young woman living in a sanatorium of sorts in preparation for a medical procedure to cut off the 'wings' (as she calls them) protruding from her shoulder blades. At the sanatorium, Mila discovers her attraction for several young women but is rebuffed by them for a variety of reasons.[5] The novel ends with her escape from the sanatorium and her plan to return home to her family.

Additionally, I would like to briefly address the positioning of this text in a sanatorium before examining the fragmented descriptions of bodies. While one might suggest that the story metaphorically dramatises an attempt to control Mila's sexuality as represented by the impending surgery to remove her wings (such is the hypothesis put forth by both Ricouart and, to a lesser extent, Cairns), this argument is undercut by the diversity of the young women found at the sanatorium who are all preparing for a similar surgery.[6] Instead of reading the novel as a commentary on society's attempt to regulate lesbian sexuality, I would suggest that Best might have chosen the somewhat artificial setting for the novel since it allows the reader to focus more closely on how Mila's sexual and psychological development parallels that of the other young women (both heterosexual and homosexual) with whom she lives. If she were living at home, she would most likely have less contact with her peers than in this dormitory setting. I would thus resist seeing the choice of the sanatorium as a simple and direct commentary on how society tries to control lesbian sexuality.

---

[5] Mila's first crush, Paule, falls in love with another young woman, Odile, and subsequently loses interest in Mila. Other objects of Mila's affection include Lili and Josette. Although there are brief encounters between Mila and each of these young women, neither seem inclined to pursue an on-going intimate relationship with Mila. In Lili's case this may be because she leaves the sanatorium before Mila. As Mila herself leaves the institution, Josette refuses to promise to write to her. While Mila's bond with these two women is strong, neither engages with her in a consistently romantic way.

[6] Ricouart (2003), 153.

In the following citation from this first novel describing interaction between Mila, the main character and Paule, her first major crush,we get a preliminary sense of how the bodily fragments are presented in Best's texts: 'Entrebâillement de porte. Œil noir sous la huppe noire. Froncement de sourcil. Oui, je viens. Porte refermée. Je refrappe, ah mais!'[7] Seen from Mila's perspective, only Paule's eye, hair and eyebrow figure in this brief description. These particular details make sense here since Paule opens her door very briefly allowing Mila only a quick viewing. But, a later scene creates a similar effect:

> Et tandis que je réenfonce les mains dans mes poches son regard se réfugie derrière une pellicule de clarté, venue de la fenêtre ou de la lampe et à l'abri de laquelle ses yeux ne sont plus que surface d'infinie réfraction.[8]

This sentence is rather long and lyrical, like many in the novel, and illustrates well the stream of consciousness monologues typical of the narrator. Here, we see again a focus on a few body parts, hands and eyes. The intimacy between the two characters 's'exprime surtout par le regard ou les gestes', as Ricouart notes.[9] The rest of the body is limited to a general presence conveyed by the relation between the two women as they face each other. A little later in the text, we find this third example which gives a more complete description of Paule's face even as it jumps from one feature to another:

> Alors je regarde son visage où ce qui s'est défait se reconstruit plus lentement Ce flou inhabituel dans les traits de la bouche Ce qui dans son regard se ramasse comme je viens de me ramasser moi-même et qui ne retrouve plus sa place exacte Infime désordre de cils, de petits plis autour de l'œil, où l'arrogance en voie de se réinstaller soudain dérape et se disperse... Le regard de Paule brusquement me manque, comme on manquerait une marche, tandis que tous ses traits s'immobilisent dans ce sourire indéfiniment soutenu, devenu fixe, qu'on voit aux gens sur le quai des gares.[10]

---

[7]   Best, *HM*, 68.
[8]   Ibid., 141.
[9]   Ricouart (2003), 155.
[10] Best, *HM*, 158.

This citation is the most interesting of the three since here we get a sense of the barely perceptible motion that Best is trying to capture. The movement is less physical than psychological and here the small facial movements are evidence of internal reactions. As Cairns puts it:

> Best's distinctive skill is, again, in verbally evoking the diegetically ineffable, the elusive currents of desire and revelation that pass between subjects of the same sex who never explicitly acknowledge to one another the erotic basis of their intimacy.[11]

At the conclusion of this passage, contact between the two characters is ruptured as Paule's face becomes immobile. Thus, we can see how Best begins to valorise motion as a key component in emotional contact. We can find similar examples of fragmentation and motion in Best's second novel.

Camille en octobre again foregrounds a young lesbian protagonist, this time living at home with her family in a coastal community. Camille experiences her first love affair with her dentist's wife. Although their romance ends (the dentist's wife becomes pregnant and decides to stay with her husband), it is clear that Camille's love for women was not a phase that she will pass through. We find this, the first of several passages which portray fragmented bodies, relatively early in *Camille en octobre* when Camille encounters her future lover Clara: 'Sourire reçu en plein visage. Fossettes. Bouillie sous mon crâne. Et devant moi le bras de Clara, gainé de bleu jusqu'au-dessous du coude, qui me sert le thé.'[12] This time, short, telegraphic sentences convey Camille's anxiety resultant from being in such close proximity to Clara. Again, the body is caught in pieces: a smile, dimples, an arm, each one separate from the rest. Later in the novel, as their relationship progresses, Camille reflects:

> Je ne l'ai encore jamais touchée, sauf sur le scooter à travers sa veste. Le modelé de ses épaules sous le tissu mince de la robe, leur chaleur, leur proximité me bouleversent encore un peu plus. Puis je perçois leur imperceptible rétraction, comme si elles fondaient sur place, glissant elles

---

[11]   Cairns (2002), 277.
[12]   Best, *CO*, 77.

aussi dans un réflexe d'évasion ou au moins de prudente soustraction au contact imposé, qu'on aurait envie ni de repousser ni de supporter.[13]

Camille's full attention is focused here on Clara's shoulders: their shape, their warmth, their closeness to her and ultimately their movement away from her. The shoulders are not so much sexually objectified as carefully examined for signs of attraction or repulsion. The body begins to serve as a means of communication between two lovers well before any explicitly sexual contact is made. As we saw in *Hymne aux murènes*, motion and the perception of motion assist characters as they negotiate their relationships. Motion provides the characters with a sense not only of physical proximity to one another but also of emotional closeness or distance. This emphasis on physical movement which demonstrates the psychological complexity of a relationship is found in Best's third novel as well.

Il n'y a pas d'hommes au Paradis again takes up the story of a young lesbian. The most complex and 'markedly upbeat'[14] of the three novels, this text treats a complicated family drama intertwined with significant socio-political events (specifically World War II and the Spanish Civil War). The love affair in this novel is short lived and instead at the centre of the novel we find the story of how Josèphe, the protagonist, relates to her own abusive, alcoholic mother and to the loving Rosa, the mother of her ex-lover Rachel. The novel ends on a hopeful note which suggests that Josèphe and Rachel may reunite in the future. A passage from *Il n'y a pas d'hommes au Paradis* reinforces the effect produced by the series of quotations presented thus far: 'Car, tout en évitant de nous toucher ne serait-ce que le bout des doigts, nous mettions peu à peu nos âmes à nu.'[15] In this brief sentence, Best reveals how the most minimal of contact between two women (all we see here are the tips of their fingers) can render their souls naked to one another. The physical is once again subordinated to the more profound emotional contact that Best aims to demonstrate.

---

[13] Ibid., 125.
[14] Cairns (2002), 297.
[15] Best, *IH*, 83.

Fragments are also used to describe other characters in the novel. The following citation recalls how Josèphe's mother reacts to the suggestion of a visit from Rachel, 'Et à ma plus grande stupeur, ma mère a acquiescé d'un sec petit coup de menton sur le col de sa blouse. Elle n'avait toujours pas desserré les dents.'[16] Throughout the novel, Josèphe's mother is portrayed as rigid, literally and figuratively frozen by hatred and depression. In this text, movement, specifically the kind associated with melting water, is especially valued as a necessary component of positive intimate relationships. Josèphe spends much of the novel trying to warm up in order to facilitate her connection with Rachel. As the following citation shows, this is an on-going process: 'D'ailleurs en me rejoignant Rachel cherchait toujours son châle ou sa veste ou ses gants, en reserrant imperceptiblement les épaules. C'est ainsi que je ressentais ma mère: avant tout comme une insidieuse percée du froid qui peu à peu raidissait l'atmosphère.'[17] Once more, the highlighted element seems to be the movement of the body part, rather than the part in and of itself.

In all of these citations, the look that passes between two characters, the exchange of a glance and an almost imperceptible vibration seem more important than any physical contact. As a result, Best describes not a unified body, but instead fragments which emphasise the way in which bodies come together. Throughout, it is the sense of connection (or lack thereof) which is significant. Bodies here are not static, but constantly in motion experiencing almost indiscernible movements toward and away from others.[18]

The fragmentation found in all three novels is closely linked to the disjointed sense of self that Best's protagonists display. These are young women slowly coming to understand themselves and others. The splintering effect conveyed by these partial descriptions portrays not only

---

[16] Ibid., 118.

[17] Ibid., 191.

[18] One is strongly reminded here of Nathalie Sarraute's tropisms which seem an important intertexual point of reference. Sarraute defined the tropism as 'des mouvements indéfinissables, qui glissent très rapidement aux limites de notre conscience; ils sont à l'origine de nos gestes, de nos paroles, des sentiments que nous manifestons, que nous croyons éprouver et qu'il est possible de définir.' (*L'Ère du soupçon* 8)

the way in which they see the world around them, and thus represents an effort at a general sort of psychological realism, but also seems to comment on the particular stage that these young women are passing through at the moment of the novels. Adolescence and early adulthood are times of confusion, of attempting to assimilate new forms of knowledge about oneself and others. In this way, the motion represented in Best's use of fractured images reflects the developmental movement of the young women.

In addition, I would suggest that this refusal to fix bodies in time and space long enough to provide photographic descriptions of them is ultimately a choice to liberate bodies from the limitations of physical description, which can have the unintended effect of rendering otherwise mobile beings as fixed entities, at least apparently, incapable of future mutation. This discursive strategy was shared by other lesbian writers in the 1970s and 1980s who 'found anti-essentialist concepts, emphasising fragmentation, difference and mutability, useful in undermining the monolithic notion of the Lesbian Self (with all its rules and boundaries) that often resulted from earlier theorizing.'[19] To be sure, the most famous example of this type of experimentation with form is Monique Wittig's *Le Corps lesbien*, a text which, despite its singular title ('le corps' as opposed to 'les corps'), embraces the multiplicity of lesbian experience.[20] For Wittig, an almost surgical dissection of the body frees it from the restrictive notions of singular identity. Wittig provides an important intertextual reference for Best who cites a passage from Wittig and Zeig's *Brouillon pour un dictionnaire des amantes* at the beginning of one of the chapters in her first novel.[21] This connection might be worth exploring in more detail than the scope of my current argument permits.

[19]   Bonnie Zimmerman, 'Lesbians Like This and That: some notes on lesbian criticism for the nineties', *New Lesbian Criticism*, ed. Sally Munt (New York: Columbia University Press, 1992), 9.

[20]   Janine Ricouart compares Best's style to Wittig's in *L'Opoponax* writing: 'Elle utilise notamment un style elliptique avec l'omission d'un ou de plusieurs mots, ce qui n'est pas sans rappeler le style de l'*Opoponax*.' (2003), 152.

[21]   Monique Wittig and Sande Zeig, *Brouillon pour un dictionnaire des amantes* (Paris: Grasset, 1976) and Monique Wittig, *Le Corps lesbien*

III. Young Women and the Sea: Water Images

The second main strategy that Best employs to explore corporeality and sexuality is the deployment of a set of images related to water. As we can begin to see from some of the quotations I have discussed thus far, water and liquids are recurrent metaphors.[22] For example, we have seen in the citations from *Camille en octobre* references to a 'bouillie sous mon crâne' (her brain has turned to mush) and Clara whose shoulders 'fondaient sur place'. These images of liquidity are intimately linked to the idea of fragmentation. Best's characters' bodies are not static, fixed entities, but instead are in motion and hence are only perceived as fragments. In order to fully convey their vibrations and movement Best turns to water, a useful image, one that other women writers have explored. In the introduction to an edited volume devoted to water in the writings of women, Yolande Helm reminds us that 'l'élément aquatique et les fluides en général constituent l'un des espaces de prédilection de l'imaginaire féminin'.[23] Water ignites the feminine imagination, according to Helm, on many levels and in many forms:

> La substance aquatique alimente le texte par ses masques multiples: le corps féminin, les sources de l'enfance, les phénomènes météorologiques, le pays natal, le gouffre, la vie et la mort. Ambivalente, elle est à la fois génitrice et 'bonne mère', amante sensuelle ou monstre qui tue et engloutit: elle manifeste une nature bienveillante et paradoxalement une force maléfique.[24]

---

[22] (Paris: Éditions de Minuit, 1973). In addition to images of water, bodies are regularly compared to mythical beings and to animals in order to convey corporeality. Angels and sirens figure prominently in the first novel whose title evokes the moray eels. The god Hermès is referred to in *Il n'y a pas d'hommes au Paradis*. Dogs are recurrent figures throughout all three of the novels. The scope of our current argument does not permit a full discussion of these other images, but they might serve as a productive avenue of inquiry for future scholars.

[23] Yolande Helm (ed.), *L'Eau: sources d'une écriture dans les littératures féminines francophones* (New York: Peter Lang, 1995), 1.

[24] Ibid., 2.

Best's texts employ water in all of these forms.[25] We find torrential downpours which serve to remind us of the weather typical of the coastal region from which Best originates. We find the mothers' bodies at the centre of all of the texts, recalling the fluid state of the womb. Our interest here will focus on how water images are used to illustrate bodies and sexuality, often serving to illuminate moments of intimacy be they physical or emotional.

Most significantly for my argument, water is invoked to express the reaction of the protagonist to interactions with the woman she likes or loves. In such scenes the narrator describes the sensation of melting or liquifying. We find an example of this early in *Hymne aux murènes*:

> Son sourire, qui sépare les séquences avec une lenteur hésitante, lui blanchit le visage. Clarté indépendante de toute source de lumière, dissolvant comme de l'intérieur tout angle brusque toute arrête toute architecture de repli, abolissant toute distance. Quelque chose en moi glisse et se dénoue.[26]

Best relates the coming together of two women to a meltdown which will ultimately unite the two. Here, we witness the initial stages of contact during which the distance between the two is progressively being destroyed. While other images are evoked, namely those of architectural space and of knots untying, the reference to water by means of the participle 'dissolvant' will resonate with other examples found throughout Best's novels.

Similarly, in the following passage from *Camille en octobre*, the young Camille has an experience which parallels Mila's, 'je me sentie soudain mollir et me liquéfier mentalement et couler à l'état de flaque aux pieds d'une femme belle et douce et rieuse comme on n'en voit jamais ici.'[27] Here, the protagonist finds herself soft, liquid and without distinct boundaries in the face of her future lover. This moment is all the more

[25] I have explored the images of water in the novels at length in a previous article titled 'The Young Woman and the Sea: lesbians coming of age in coastal communities in the novels of Mireille Best', *Women in French Studies*, 11 (2003), 50–63.

[26] Best, *HM*, 45.

[27] Best, *CO*, 61.

striking since it occurs in Clara's absence and only shortly after Camille has encountered her for the first time. Even the older protagonist in *Il n'y a pas d'hommes au Paradis*, who is much more cynical and emotionally distant from those around her, undergoes this type of transformation when encountering her love, 'Et je sens mon cœur chanceler dans le courant d'air comme une flamme de bougie au bord de se noyer.'[28] Although the image here is one of fire, it seems worth noting due to the use of the verb 'se noyer' which is associated with liquid. Later, we again find water suggested when Josèphe describes her reactions as she watches Rachel play violin for her:

> Je sentais vibrer les ondes brûlantes et impalpables qui nous reliaient l'une à l'autre, et j'étais consciente qu'un autre faisceau d'ondes reliait entre eux les danseurs Nous étions dans le même remous, que l'inexorable accélération du boléro portait par paliers à incandescence...'[29]

In this scene, waves are the connection points between the two women. While these waves might be ones of vibration, rather than liquid, when considered in light of all the other references to water, the connection seems more than plausible. Here, I would highlight that this image of waves allows Best to convey a connection between two characters who are not in physical contact with one another. In fact, the connection is compared to a physical one experienced by dancers in the room. This psychological contact is portrayed then through the use of a physical image.

Best often employs water images, not only when describing her protagonists emotional reactions to other women, but also in scenes which represent physical intimacy. The most striking use of this is found in *Camille en octobre* where the protagonist's first sexual experiences take place in the beach house belonging to Clara. The water in this scene is everywhere: the ocean beside the house, the rain beating on the roof, the drinks imbibed by the lovers. 'It is as if, congruent with her fantasy of corporeal fusion, Camille is incorporated into Clara's body, and her own

---

28 Best, *IH*, 21.
29 Ibid., 84.

isolated subjectivity dissolved into continuity at one with her partner.'[30] And finally, this is the lingering memory after the event:

> Je n'ai presque rien gardé de cette nuit-là, sauf une énorme vague intérieure éternellement soulevée, avec l'envie de déferler encore et encore et encore, balayant tout ce qui se présente et qui se coince et qui obstrue et qui empêche mon absolu et vertigineux besoin du corps nu, éblouisssant, grand ouvert, de Clara.[31]

Sexual intimacy here is condensed into the figure of a wave which returns over and over, leaving nothing in its wake except desire, nay need, for the body of Camille's lover. The body is described in terms of relatively abstract qualities, not concrete attributes. This scene like so many others contains a 'fade-out' like the ones described by Gabriele Griffin in her study of the representation of lesbian sex.[32] Rather than reveal the actual experience of sexuality, Best focuses her attention on the residue of sex, memories and impressions that remain after the act itself has ended.

Best's first novel, *L'Hymne aux murènes* did not contain any fully realised sexual scenes, but the interactions which approached intimacy were described like this one with Lili:

> Pendant qu'elle chuchote, il y a eu comme un glissement de lune. Les yeux de Lili sont comme deux flaques claires, immobiles, et sans fond [...] Et si je te caressais les cheveux les épaules et tes petits seins si légers qu'on les devine à peine Si je promenais mes mains sur toi, sur ce que tu as de plus chaud, de plus vivant Si je les refermais autour de ta taille tellement flexible qu'elle donne brusquement l'envie de serrer plus fort [...] Si je faisais vraiment Comme Si [...][33]

Once again, water is suggested by the 'deux flaques, immobiles, et sans fond' of Lili's eyes. One gets the impression that Mila might fall into

---

30   Cairns (2002), 288.
31   Best, *CO*, 165.
32   Gabriele Griffin, 'Lines on Lesbian Sex: the politics of representing lesbian sex in the age of AIDS', *Canadian Woman Studies / Les Cahiers de la Femme*, 16: 2 (Spring 1996), 103–09.
33   Best, *HM*, 74.

these 'flaques' and drown somewhere deep within Lili. The scene ultimately remains hypothetical, like most of the sexual scenes in this novel. Mila is on the verge of realising her sexuality in terms of actual action, but she is not yet prepared for extensive contact. Best thus captures perfectly the supreme adolescent moment of hesitation on the cusp between childhood and the adult world.

Ironically, the third novel which has the oldest protagonist is the least sexual of the three. Even here though when sexuality is discussed explicitly, images which recall water or the ocean prevail as in this scene in which the narrator describes how she wanted to visually examine her genitals with a mirror in order to form an opinion of them. In the end, she concludes 'Bref, ça ressemblait à une moule et je n'ai jamais pus croquer dans une moule même cuite'.[34]

Water images are the currency Best uses to illustrate not only moments of contact, but also moments of emotional disconnection. In the first novel, the young Mila's world has been marked repeatedly by chaos and confusion. A series of father figures passed through her household, leaving two half-brothers for Mila in their wake. Mila's reaction to this chaos has been to withdraw emotionally from those around her and to explore an interior psychological space. This self-examination is likened to a deep sea adventure in which a submarine dives under water. In the third novel, in place of discussion of physical intimacy we find instead long meditations on what blocks such intimacy between Josèphe and Rachel. Josèphe comes to realise that she has become frozen like her mother, incapable of making contact with others. Throughout the novel, we find images of crystals and ice such as this one: "Ma mère est dans une grotte rougeâtre hérissée de stalagtites et de stalagmites Je la vois Elle est adossée à une paroi Immobile Comme emmurée dans un cristal en formation Un cristal rouge De plus en plus rouge'.[35] In this citation we get a sense of the family legacy that Josèphe will ultimately have to reject if she is to emerge as an adult capable of forming healthy relationships.

---

[34]   Best, *IH*, 23.
[35]   Ibid., 15.

When Rachel finally leaves a note saying that she wishes to end their relationship, Josèphe reacts strongly:

> Et je déchirais le papier en morceaux de plus en plus petits avec le sentiment de déchiqueter mes propres entrailles Eclaboussant de mon sang les parois hérissées du gouffre Et courant courant pour me déchirer encore plus fort, encore plus vite, jusqu'à ce que tout autour de moi ne soit plus que pics de glace et sang figé [...][36]

As Josèphe shreds the letter, she figuratively rips herself apart. Her blood initially splashes around, but in the end, all around her is ice and frozen blood. At this stage, Josèphe's attempts to make sense of this situation are only partially successful. She can express her emotions, but, once articulated, her feelings remain fixed or frozen for the moment. Near the end of the story, we get the sense that Josèphe has begun to thaw. Although Josèphe does not fully transform herself in time to save her relationship with Rachel, we do see a glimmer of hope in the way Josèphe relates to a dog named Cornélia. The first time she encounters the dog, she returns it to its abusive owner. When the dog reappears, Josèphe is ready to accept its unconditional love. The novel ends with woman and dog at home together during a rain storm: 'Mais ici et maintenant, sur les barres d'appui des fenêtres où Cornélia s'en vient humer les gouttes de pluie, c'est bel et bien la fin de la nuit'.[37] Ironically, rain here represents progress. Josèphe's heart has melted and has allowed her to love another, though for the moment her affection is directed not toward humans but toward animals.

IV. Conclusion: Mouvance

If we are to fully appreciate the complexity of Best's work, we need to develop an integrated understanding of the two narrative strategies which she employs to construct a vision of lesbian bodies. On the most basic level, one might note that Best seeks to achieve a certain kind of psycho-

---

social realism. Both fragmentation and images of water thus serve to positively convey a very particular experience: that of young lesbians coming of age in coastal communities. The fragmentation allows us to grasp the uncertainties and fleeting sensations of adolescents trying to make sense of their sexuality and of increasingly complicated relationships with others. The water offers a connection to the geographic situation of the novels and at the same time conveys the fluidity of the slowly developing sense of self explored by each protagonist. To this extent, Best's novels might provide what Lucille Cairns has called a 'site of identification for lesbian readers and thereby provide more solid grounds for the formation of a (non-monolithic) lesbian subjecthood.'[38] One could argue that Best accurately and lovingly portrays a specific subject position which will expand the range of options possible for identification by lesbian readers.

At the same time, Best resists the notion that she writes for a lesbian readership thereby refusing that identificatory purpose. In her response to Anne Garréta who asked Best 'Do you believe there exists a specifically lesbian readership on the lookout for works and authors not alien to its own experience and identity?', she wrote she did not believe in such a readership and that such a thing would be a 'sad kind of mutilation'.[39] This comment leads me to believe that my first proposal, that we see Best's work as a source of identification for lesbian readers, is a limiting one. Instead, her intense work on literary form, specifically her development of narrative techniques such a fragmentation and imagery, forces the reader to see her texts as something more than simply 'lesbian novels'. In order to preserve what Wittig calls the 'polysemy' of minority texts, I would suggest that we try to avoid reducing these novels to their themes. Wittig asserts that, 'A text by a minority writer is effective only if it succeeds in making the minority point of view universal, only if it is an

---

[38] Lucille Cairns, 'Le Phallus Lesbien (Bis): Lesbo-Erotic French Writing of the Late 1990s', *Nottingham French Studies*, 41: 1 (Spring 2002), 89–101.

[39] Anne Garréta, 'A Questionnaire: French lesbian writers? Answers from Monique Wittig, Jocelyne François and Mireille Best', *Yale French Studies*, 90 (1996), 235–41.

important literary text.'[40] Since it is clear that Best has read Wittig and is influenced by her work, we might conclude that Best attempts to achieve this goal of 'making the minority point of view universal'. If she succeeds, it is by de-centring the question of lesbianism and allowing compelling emotional and psychological dramas to unfold in texts which experiment with literary forms such as fragmentation, metaphors, and images. It is my belief that this is Best's literary quest.

Furthermore, I believe that Best's interest in writing, in the process of writing, is an intense one. This is evidenced by the following quotation. When asked about her aims as a writer, she answered that her work 'only goes through me, coming from somewhere else, but where? [...] I like being in this somewhat magical locus, a passageway, like a harbor or a river estuary, where waters from different sources or horizons flow together.'[41] Best uses water images here not as a commentary on lesbian sexuality and love but as a meta-commentary on her writing project. Rather than seeing her writing as simply an expression of her self, of her identity as a lesbian, she instead remarks upon the variety of sources which inform her writing. As she writes, diverse waters come through her (presumably not only her experiences but her readings as well). Best has signaled the impact that different authors have had on her by including quotations from them at the beginning of chapters. Among the authors she cites are Wittig, Samuel Beckett, Villon, Victor Hugo, and Andrée Chédid. Additional citations are found in the form of a quotation from the Bible and the songs, many of which evoke marine life, that are sung by various characters in the novels. All of these references serve to remind the reader that Best has been shaped as a novelist by various influences. Her writing ought to be appreciated, then, not for its presentation of lesbian bodies, but precisely for its re-presentation of them from a perspective informed and shaped by incredibly diverse set of intertextual references. Best, like her characters, then is perhaps most appropriately understood as a lesbian in motion. In the end, we might say that it is only on the surface of texts such as those Best has written that we will catch

---

[40] Monique Wittig, 'The Point of View: Universal or Particular?', *The Straight Mind and Other Essays* (Boston: Beacon Press, 1992).
[41] Anne Garréta (1996), 241.

glimpses of this new literary figure which will most often elude our attempts to fix her in time and space.

Bibliography

Best, Mireille, *Les Mots de hasard* (Paris: Gallimard, 1980).

——, *Le Méchant Petit Jeune Homme* (Paris: Gallimard, 1983).

——, *Une Extrême Attention* (Paris: Gallimard, 1985).

——, *Hymne aux murènes* (Paris: Gallimard, 1986).

——, *Camille en octobre* (Paris: Gallimard, 1988).

——, *Orphéa trois* (Paris: Gallimard, 1991).

——, *Il n'y a pas d'hommes au Paradis* (Paris: Gallimard, 1995).

——, 'Le Livre de Stéphanie', tr. Janine Ricouart, *The Vintage Book of International Lesbian Fiction*, eds Naomi Holoch and Joan Nestle (New York: Vintage Books, 1999), 21–34.

Cairns, Lucille, 'Mireille Best', *Who's Who in Contemporary Gay and Lesbian History from World War II to the Present Day*, eds Robert Aldrich and Garry Wotherspoon (New York: Routledge, 2001), 36–37.

——, 'Le Phallus Lesbien (Bis): lesbo-erotic French writing of the late 1990s," *Nottingham French Studies*, 41:1 (Spring 2002), 89–101.

——, *Lesbian Desire in Post-1968 French Literature* (Lewiston: The Edwin Mellen Press, 2002).

de Ceccatty, René, 'Les traine-soleil de Mireille Best: des tragédies dans un monde gris et timore', *Le Monde* (15 March 1991).

——, 'Ça s'appelle l'amour', *Le Monde* (7 April 1995).

Faderman, Lillian, 'What is Lesbian Literature? Forming a Historical Canon', *Professions of Desire: lesbian and gay studies in literature*, eds George E. Haggerty and Bonnie Zimmerman (New York: The Modern Language Association of America, 1995).

Garréta, Anne F., 'A Questionnaire: French Lesbian Writers? Answers from Monique Wittig, Jocelyne François and Mireille Best', *Yale French Studies*, 90 (1996), 235–41.

Griffin, Gabriele, 'Lines on Lesbian Sex: the politics of representing lesbian sex in the age of AIDS', *Canadian Woman Studies Les Cahiers de la Femme*, 16: 2 (Spring 1996), 103–09.

——, 'Mireille Best', *Who's Who in Lesbian and Gay Writing* (New York: Routledge, 2002), 18.

Helm, Yolande (ed.), *L'Eau: sources d'une écriture dans les littératures féminines Francophones* (New York: Peter Lang, 1995).

Ricouart, Janine, 'Enfance magique ou infernale? Un regard socio-critique sur l'œuvre de Mireille Best', *Women in French Studies* (Special Issue 2003), 150–65.

Sarraute, Nathalie, *L'Ère du soupçon* (Paris: Gallimard, 1956).

Schechner, Stephanie, 'The Young Woman and the Sea: lesbians coming of age in coastal communities in the novels of Mireille Best', *Women in French Studies*, 11 (2003), 50–63.

Slawy-Sutton, Catherine, Review of *Orphéa trois*, *The French Review* 66: 6 (1993), 1037–8.

Waelti-Walters, Jennifer, *Damned Women: lesbians in French novels* (Montreal: McGill-Queen's University Press, 2000).

Wittig, Monique, *Le Corps lesbien* (Paris: Éditions de Minuit, 1973).

——, 'The Point of View: Universal or Particular?', *The Straight Mind and Other Essays* (Boston: Beacon Press, 1992).

Wittig, Monique and Sande Zeig, *Brouillon pour un dictionnaire des amantes* (Paris: Grasset, 1976).

Zimmerman, Bonnie, 'Lesbians Like This and That: some notes on lesbian criticism for the nineties', *New Lesbian Criticism*, ed. Sally Munt (New York: Columbia University, 1992).

Female Masculinities and Simone de Beauvoir

Ursula Tidd
University of Manchester

In a recent issue of the British lesbian magazine, *Diva*, an article entitled 'Phallus through the looking glass' describes a first visit to a women's erotic emporium by two women who have just embarked together on their first lesbian relationship. They experience the sex shop as a scary utopia of sexual experimentation in which any recourse to the theories of Simone de Beauvoir or Freud on lesbianism seems rather beside the point. The writer describes how she felt like Electra in Wonderland wandering around a Freudian Early Learning Centre with toys for all varieties of sexually curious children. Yet she exclaims 'you can read all the De Beauvoir and Freud you want, but [...] despite decades of feminist voices applauding the philosophical completing nature of the lesbian relationship, and voices of psychologists identifying where it was in my childhood I became a sexual deviant, there's actually no voices to give you practical advice'.[1] Simone de Beauvoir's theory of lesbianism in *Le Deuxième Sexe* does not, admittedly, help resolve this particular conundrum, even though when the English translation of the text was published in 1953, it *was* initially marketed in the United States of America as a sex manual. But the writer of this article does raise the issue of how lesbian identity and sexuality might be performed in the everyday. In the present discussion, I intend to address whether Beauvoir's analysis of lesbianism and of transgender issues in *Le Deuxième Sexe* is still helpful to us in a Butlerian climate in which we are productively engaged in endless 'gender trouble'. As Foucauldian 'reverse discourses' are generated which enable formerly pathologised categories of gender and sex-

---

[1] Sarah Morning, 'Phallus through the Looking-Glass', *Diva* (January 2004), 98.

uality to gain empowerment in certain contexts, do Beauvoir's analyses of lesbianism and transgender issues still offer us any useful points of theoretical reflection? I intend to address these questions by looking at the discussion of female masculinity in the chapters on 'la jeune fille' and 'la lesbienne' in *Le Deuxième Sexe* and at broader transgender issues in Beauvoir's first published novel, *L'Invitée*, which pre-dates the publication of her study of gender by six years. Female masculinity is a completely neglected area in its non-pathological sense in Beauvoir studies, and yet, by examining how female masculinity and transgender issues are explored in *Le Deuxième Sexe* and *L'Invitée*, it will be argued that Beauvoir's radical analyses remain relevant to contemporary debates on gender and sexuality.

The theorisation of female masculinity has been mainly associated with Judith Halberstam's eponymous 1998 study. Her work can be viewed as a developmental offshoot of Judith Butler's groundbreaking work on the performativity of gender which first came to prominence in her text, *Gender Trouble*, published in 1990. In Halberstam's study, she argues that masculinity cannot and should not be conflated with the male body and its effects, that masculinity has been historically produced and performed by girls and women just as femininity has been produced and performed by boys and men. However, not all masculinities are equal in a traditionally patriarchal society. Performances of alternative masculinities such as the tomboy, the invert, the lesbian butch, the drag king are deemed inauthentic and melancholic, as 'the rejected scraps of a dominant masculinity in order that male masculinity may appear to be the real thing.'[2] Such a configuration of masculinity equates heterosexual male masculinity with authenticity and what is 'natural', stable and non-performative, and female masculinity with inauthenticity, artifice and role-playing. In this way, the sex-gender binary remains intact and notions of 'true sex' and 'true gender' prevail. But Halberstam questions why it might be so difficult to imagine masculinity as produced through a range of different subject positions? Why is heterosexual male mascul-

---

[2]   Judith Halberstam, *Female Masculinity* (Durham and London: Duke University Press, 1998), 1.

inity so protected and over-determined? Why are female masculinities, sometimes produced by lesbians, so neglected, so abjected? Why is female masculinity figured as the wrong sort of masculinity? Halberstam's project, then, is to invite us to consider female masculinities as specific gender expressions which sometimes, but not always, mobilise lesbian desiring identities. Thus, female masculinities can be understood not as melancholic renditions of a failed heterosexual male masculinity, but as 'real' as any other artifice of sex and gender, and as a challenge to the hegemony of the sex-gender binary.

Indeed it is Halberstam's contention that modern masculinities are most convincingly and ethically performed in the contemporary context as female masculinities. For masculinity need not be aligned with an ethic of carelessness with regard to self and others, with sexism and misogyny, with biological maleness. It can exist in plural forms, which reinterpret the historical vocabulary of masculinity with a perpetual twist. In short, to use Butler's term, masculinity can become performative, reveal its true fictionality.

Turning to Beauvoir's *Le Deuxième Sexe*, specifically to the chapters in volume two on 'la jeune fille' and 'la lesbienne', it will now be now argued that her analyses help us think productively about female masculinities and their effects on male masculinities. As Halberstam notes, whenever female masculinities are conjoined with the queering of identity, it becomes much more troubling to the gender status quo.[3] Although *Le Deuxième Sexe* might be viewed as advancing a hetero-normative position in certain respects, it also poses a significant challenge to hegemonic models of gender and sexuality, not least in Beauvoir's non-pathologising focus on female masculinity.

Volume two of *Le Deuxième Sexe* is entitled 'l'expérience vécue de la femme' and it is this *phenomenological* understanding of gender and sexuality, the emphasis on everyday lived experience that enables Beauvoir, in my view, to conceptualise gender and sexuality in a more radical way. Seeking to expose the relationship between the lived experience of gender and sexuality and the essentialising patriarchal myths which dis-

---

[3]   Ibid., 9.

cursively shape them, Beauvoir's focus on gender as a becoming, as a constructionist process, alerts us to think about how all gender identities as constructed, not just feminine identities. As Halberstam argues in her discussion of female masculininity, thinking about the plurality of gender and sexuality does not entail inventing a vast taxonomy of speculative identities. Rather, it is to recognise and understand *existing* configurations of gender and sexuality and thereby challenge governing binaries which relegate certain identities, such as female masculinity, to the abject margins.

Alongside Beauvoir's phenomenological understanding of gender and sexuality, it is also crucial to note her critique of classical psychoanalysis in *Le Deuxième Sexe* for it enables her to think about female masculinity and lesbianism in a much less pathologising way. In the 'psychoanalysis' chapter of *Le Deuxième Sexe*, one of Beauvoir's main criticisms of Freud's account of psycho-sexual development is that his account of female sexuality is grafted onto a model of biological maleness, so that the girl can only consider herself as a mutilated boy. Heterosexual biological maleness is connoted as authentic, the real thing. Beauvoir rejects this 'universalist' view of female sexuality and that girls might envy the penis in the way that Freud describes. She argues instead that the girl's entire situation in patriarchal society contributes to her sense of inferiority, not simply the fact that she does not have a penis. It is rather the privileges associated with biological maleness which are envied by the girl. As a result, classical psychoanalysis cannot account for the non-pathological existence of female masculinity or lesbianism because it conceptualises female sexual and gender behaviour as already derivative of heterosexual male masculinity, as a paler and inauthentic imitation. Beauvoir's critique of classical psychoanalysis signals her recognition of its investment in a true sex-gender binary, premised on a supposed naturalisation and authenticity of heterosexual male masculinity. She argues that classical psychoanalysis condemns women to experience a conflict between her masculine and feminine tendencies — so that in asserting her independence within this binary she can only become virilised *and* inauthentic. But this virilisation of women is not presented as pathological in *Le Deuxième Sexe* but merely a part of girls and women's lived experience of identity, as evident in Beauvoir's recourse to sexological and sociological theory and her discussions of 'la jeune fille' and 'la lesbienne', which will now be considered.

Sexological theory is not, in my view, especially valuable as a means to theorise the plurality of gender and sexuality for, as Foucault has argued in *La Volonté de savoir*, sexology among other discourses, acting as a *scientia sexualis*, served to produce the notion of true sex and of sexuality as the truth of the self.[4] Both sexology and psychoanalysis have contributed to the pathologisation of various forms of gender and sexuality, as a result of their investment in the 'true' sex-gender binary. Nevertheless, both Beauvoir and Halberstam have greater theoretical recourse to sexology than to classical psychoanalysis. Halberstam explains that sexology is more useful for her study of female masculinity because there existed — at least on the part of Havelock Ellis — some attempt to catalogue a range of sexual expressions and female masculinities as social constructions in a vague bid for sexual tolerance, although the larger cultural imperative was to 'reduce sexuality to binary systems of sexual difference'.[5] It is this sexological taxonomisation and calibration of sexual identities which is helpful to both Beauvoir and Halberstam. In addition to sexology, Beauvoir also draws on the 1948 Kinsey report on male sexuality, *Sexual Behaviour in the Human Male*, but was unable to consult the equivalent for women as that was not published until 1953. Kinsey's notion of a continuum of sexuality was radical in the 1940s. It prefigures Adrienne Rich's notion of a continuum of lesbian experience from her groundbreaking article of 1980 'Compulsory Heterosexuality and Lesbian Existence' and more recent work, such as Halberstam's, on transsexual and transgender identities.[6] Beauvoir's references to sexology and to sociological accounts of sexual behaviour, such as Kinsey's, are consonant with her focus on the lived experience of gender and sexuality in *Le Deuxième Sexe* and her recognition of the plurality of their expression.

---

[4] Michel Foucault, *L'Histoire de la sexualité I, La Volonté de savoir* (Paris: Gallimard, 1976), 85–91.

[5] Halberstam (1998), 76.

[6] Adrienne Rich, 'Compulsory Heterosexuality and Lesbian Existence', *Signs*, 5 (1980), 631–60.

In the chapters on 'la jeune fille' and 'la lesbienne' she productively challenges the pathologisation of female masculinity and of the sexological category of the 'invert'. In the former chapter, Beauvoir argues that girls experience their growing up as a mutilation of the expression of their full subjectivity: 'pour la jeune fille il y a divorce entre sa condition proprement humaine et sa vocation féminine'.[7] The young girl recognises that she must renounce her subjectivity to fulfil her destiny as absolute Other in patriarchal society.[8] Beauvoir argues that most girls are 'tomboys' at around ten or twelve years of age, and she defines 'tomboys' or 'garçons manqués' as 'des enfants à qui manque la licence d'être des garçons', so all they are lacking is the ontological freedom of boyhood![9] So, feasibly, certain boys might experience their masculinity as 'garçons manqués', that is to say that they might not experience and produce their male masculinity as authentic or as a free expression of their subjectivity. This is a form of alienated male masculinity, in certain cases staged as a male femininity, to which Beauvoir gestures in the scarcely concealed episode from Sartre's childhood in which he had his 'girlish' curls shorn off.[10]

In a traditionally patriarchal society, Beauvoir argues that girls are prevented from expressing their exuberance and energy to possess the world. The young girl reacts to her alienated situation in various ways: if a 'tomboy', she may experience a burning disappointment which may lead her directly to lesbianism or it may not if she consents to the patriarchal femininity proposed to her and its dubious advantages of passivity, coquettishness and vanity. Halberstam echoes this point when she argues that conventional female femininity is not only unhealthy for girls because it promotes inactivity, passivity and helplessness but also because it entails their precociously early heterosexualisation.[11] She

---

[7]   Simone de Beauvoir, *Le Deuxième Sexe II* [1949] (Paris: Gallimard Folio, 1987), 99, hereafter *Le DSII*.

[8]   Ibid., 100.

[9]   Ibid., 51.

[10]   Ibid., 17; incident cited in Jean-Paul Sartre, *Les Mots* (Paris: Gallimard, 1964), 83–85.

[11]   Halberstam (1998), 268–9.

proposes instead the cultivation of female masculinity as a more fulfilling option for girls and women. This troubles the traditional gender status quo because it dislodges masculinity from heterosexual biological maleness and challenges what Beauvoir depicts as an implicit and naturalised sado-masochism in the heterosexual erotic relation and the patriarchal mythological construction of wives and mothers. In other words, it questions the power relations which conflate biological maleness and masculinity, biological femaleness and femininity and which stage the heterosexual coupling of naturalised dominance and passivity as an authentic erotic experience.

Female masculinity, then, might be seen as a powerful discursive strategy, and one which is not necessarily deployed by lesbians nor does it necessarily increase lesbianism. However, as noted earlier, the conjoining of female masculinity and queer identities have a greater subversive potential. Beauvoir's chapter on 'la lesbienne' is attentive to these issues but it has come in for some criticism, partly, I think, because of its references to the sexological debates on inversion which have had a rather pathologising legacy. Halberstam argues that when lesbian feminism rejected inversion as a same-sex sexual category, it also rejected female masculinity as an overriding category of lesbian identification, replacing it with the woman-identified woman who is most often gender-androgynous and sometimes seemingly desexualised.[12] As Halberstam explains, while androgyny entails some gender mixing, it does not entail total ambiguity or gender confusion.[13] Beauvoir's discussion of female inversion in her chapter on lesbianism may be construed as out-of-step with a second wave feminist configuring of lesbian identity as gender-androgynous, however I contend that it remains valuable for its non-pathologising engagement with female masculinities.

Nevertheless, the chapter on 'la lesbienne' has its pathologising blindspots. Positioned between 'L'Initiation sexuelle' and 'La Femme mariée', it closes the 'Formation' section, suggesting that, as Marie-Jo Bonnet has also noted, that Beauvoir rules out lesbianism as a potentially

---

[12]   Ibid., 82.
[13]   Ibid., 57.

long-term or lifelong option for women.[14] This marginalisation of lesbianism prevents her arguments about lesbianism having any major impact on her central thesis concerning the social construction of femininity in patriarchal society. It also fosters the heterosexist notion that lesbianism is a 'phase' of women's sexual development which prepares a more authentic adult heterosexuality. Further, it disregards the experience of those women who might choose to pursue lesbian relationships later in their lives, as an alternative choice concerning the mode of their sexual self-expression.

Beauvoir argues that the lesbian is neither a 'femme manquée' nor a 'femme supérieure'. Lesbianism is a choice or an attitude adopted by certain women as an attempt to reconcile their autonomy and their alienated experience of their body. She argues that a lesbian relationship is at least as valid as any heterosexual relationship: 'l'homosexualité peut être pour la femme une manière de fuir sa condition ou une manière de l'assumer'.[15] One is neither irrevocably heterosexual nor homosexual; one chooses one's sexuality perpetually and what is more pertinent is the authenticity of the choice. Beauvoir challenges here the notion of 'the lesbian' as a discrete pathologised identity as figured by sexology and psychoanalysis and says that all women are predisposed to have a physical affinity with women: 'Et si l'on invoque la nature, on peut dire que naturellement toute femme est homosexuelle. La lesbienne se caractérise en effet par son refus du mâle et son goût pour la chair féminine; mais toute adolescente redoute la pénétration, la domination masculine, elle éprouve à l'égard du corps de l'homme une certaine répulsion; en revanche le corps féminin est pour elle comme pour l'homme un objet de désir'.[16]

This is an excellent example of Beauvoirian irony: she turns the rhetorical strategy of naturalistic essentialism on its head and argues that there is a fundamental physical affinity between girls and women, an erotic *mitsein* or 'being-with the female Other'. The male body, she

[14]   Marie-Jo Bonnet, 'De l'émancipation amoureuse des femmes dans la cité', *Les Temps Modernes*, 598 (1998) 91.
[15]   *Le DSII*, 195.
[16]   Ibid., 195.

argues, for the adolescent girl, is connoted with the threat of penetration and male domination and hence it is repulsive to the girl. However, she soon internalises the male objectifying gaze, and the degree to which this is internalised and other psycho-social factors (for example, her relationship with her primary carers and other women and men) will result in the specification of her erotic choice.

Beauvoir argues that women do not necessarily choose lesbianism as an alternative to being objectified by heterosexual men; it is not a choice necessarily made in response to a dysfunctional and oppressive operation of heterosexuality. In *Le Deuxième Sexe*, heterosexual sex is represented as an act in which each participant is torn from him or herself and becomes temporarily the Other for that Other, but one in which women have little chance of expressing their autonomous subjectivity. More often, patriarchal ideology encourages them to adopt the roles of 'the woman in love' or 'the narcissist' in which they become fascinated and authenticated by the passivity of their bodies being reflected in male heterosexual desire. Lesbian sex is not, however, necessarily experienced in a more authentic manner, even if it is, according to Beauvoir, a more reciprocal and plural experience.

Overall, as Toril Moi has argued, Beauvoir presents an ambiguous picture of lesbianism: arguing for the greater authenticity of lesbianism as an erotic choice but also indicating its potentially narcissistic ability to mirror the Other — a mirroring process which, in terms of Beauvoir's existentialism, seems to lack the necessary difference between self and Other which makes for true reciprocity.[17] Elsewhere in *Le Deuxième Sexe*, narcissism is exposed as an inauthentic justificatory response to woman's alienated situation in patriarchal society. Importantly, though, Beauvoir characterises the entire human condition (including lesbianism) as existentially ambiguous; ambiguity is a fundamental characteristic associated with freedom and choice and what counts is the authenticity of the lived experience as a reciprocal encounter between self and Other. So, it is worth considering what 'same' and 'different' might mean here. Does

[17] Toril Moi, *Simone de Beauvoir, The Making of an Intellectual Woman* (Oxford, UK and Cambridge, USA: Blackwell, 1994), 199–203.

Beauvoir mean that lesbians have the same corporeal morphology and
therefore the same erotic experiences? Can those same experiences, if
they exist, dictate a similar social positioning? Or does she mean that
lesbians have a psychic or behavioural sameness, despite the diversity of
lesbian experience that she has elsewhere indicated? Beauvoir is probably
referring to an experience of sameness rooted in a similar situated subject
position relating to gender and sexuality. Even if individual experiences
and responses might be different in their detail, heterosexual women and
lesbians are — to use Althusser's notion — discursively interpellated
according to their respective situations in broadly similar ways. Subjected
to a certain sameness of historically, politically and socially contingent
discourses of gender and sexuality, they interface individually with those
discourses in differently detailed ways.

Beauvoir's account of lesbian sex also contrasts to what she presents as
the rather sadomasochistic 'sound and fury' of the heterosexual encounter. In this, she appears to extract the urgency of desire from lesbian
erotic exchange, yet depicting it with an almost Irigarayan multiplicity of
desire and erotic reciprocity. Consider, for example, 'entre femmes,
l'amour est contemplation; les caresses sont destinées moins à s'approprier l'autre qu'à se recréer lentement à travers elle; la séparation est
abolie, il n'y a ni lutte, ni victoire, ni défaite; dans une exacte réciprocité
chacune est à la fois le sujet et l'objet, la souveraine et l'esclave; la
dualité est complicité'.[18] So libidinal multiplicity and reciprocity seem
unable to co-exist here alongside a passionate urgency of desire between
women — becoming instead, an endless exchange of similar, yet muted,
pleasures.

At an ideological level, the chapter on 'la lesbienne' is also not quite a
rallying call for political change. Specifically, there is no analysis of
heterosexuality as a political institution and its attendant oppression of
lesbians, as subsequently analysed by Adrienne Rich and Monique
Wittig.[19] Beauvoir does not argue that the combination of misogyny and
homophobia experienced by women identifying as lesbians has its roots

---

[18] *Le DSII*, 208.
[19] See Monique Wittig, *The Straight Mind and Other Essays* (Hemel
     Hempstead: Harvester Wheatsheaf, 1992).

in the political institution of heterosexual patriarchy. Similarly, she does not argue that homophobia is a heterosexual 'problem'. In this failure to identify the ideological operation of heterosexuality and its role in the construction of lesbian identity, Beauvoir does not posit the oppression of lesbians as an oppression which co-exists and operates in conjunction with sexual and racial oppressions, elsewhere analysed in *Le Deuxième Sexe*.

Overall, Beauvoir appears to assume that most women *are* irrevocably heterosexual. This implied stasis of sexual orientation which does not posit stasis as the result of an emancipatory strategy or as the consequence of oppression is inconsistent in the context of Beauvoir's general arguments elsewhere concerning gendered and black identities where 'être, c'est être devenu'. The crucial point of interpreting mythologised, oppressive identities relating to gender, race and sexuality as processes of being, as becomings, is that they can then be considered to be mutable and plastic — which is why Judith Butler partly bases her notion of gender performativity on Beauvoir's notion of 'devenir femme'. But in terms of sexual orientation, Beauvoir seems to say that it is both simultaneously a choice and not a choice, that at some level, it is experienced as fundamentally *ambiguous* in patriarchal society. As a sometimes situated erotic choice, the implications of that choice are not fully explored by Beauvoir in her largely individualistic and ahistorical approach to lesbianism.[20] However, as explored below, her discussion of female masculinity and female inversion in the chapter on 'la lesbienne' is historically attentive and does posit the existence of lesbian communities, albethey comprised of bourgeois women writers and artists.

Beauvoir's research into lesbianism in the 1940s was hampered by the paucity of non-pathological, theoretical accounts of lesbianism available to consult. Hence, she read psychoanalytical, sociological and sexological theories of sexuality and one can only speculate that Kinsey's 1953 report on female sexuality might have enabled her to present a more positive,

---

[20] Ann Ferguson, 'Lesbian, Identity, Beauvoir and History' in *Hypatia Reborn, Essays in Feminist Philosophy*, eds Azizah Y. al-Hibri and Margaret A. Simons (Bloomington and Indianapolis: Indiana University Press, 1990), 280–9.

thorough analysis of lesbianism, rooted in 'le vécu', as she had formulated with regard to heterosexuality in *Le Deuxième Sexe*.

Beauvoir's portrayal of lesbianism is also rooted in her own particular experience, which was not always empowering or very positive. Her sexual experiences with women, often taking place within a teacher-student scenario, perhaps did not allow her to conceptualise the power and range of erotic difference in lesbian relationships, rooted in equality. Much of Beauvoir's sexual experience with women can be categorised according to Claudia Card's notion of a 'Sapphic' pattern of lesbian relationship, in which one partner is significantly older or younger.[21] Such teacher-student relationships are more likely to be rooted in inequality of status and a desire for sameness or emulation on the part of the student, which tends to preclude the exploration and experience of erotic difference between two reciprocal subjectivities.

A final issue concerning Beauvoir's presentation of lesbianism is significant. As she demonstrates in *Le Deuxième Sexe*, the oppression of women takes place through institutional, mythological and individual practices and is enacted through a specular economy. The male, heterosexualised 'gaze' positions woman as 'Other' in a patriarchal society. Yet this does not apply in the same way to lesbians because they cannot always be visually identified in society as lesbians. Sometimes they can easily 'pass' as heterosexual women or heterosexual men in a heterospecular economy in a way that black heterosexual women and men and white heterosexual women cannot pass as white men, unless lesbians assume an overt identity manifest in dress and body codes and social practices which identify them as lesbian to the heterosexual and homosexual gaze. Moreover, the heterosexual male gaze — perhaps ignorant that its specular object is a lesbian — is subverted by the lesbian's knowledge that she can elude the oppressive implications of that heterosexualised objectifying gaze, although only insofar as she is not a heterosexual woman. As women, lesbians are still subject to the male gaze as an instance of patriarchal power in practice. There is, then, a

---

[21]   Claudia Card, 'Lesbian Attitudes and *The Second Sex*' in *Hypatia Reborn*, 298.

limited fluidity of identity for lesbians in a heterosexual, specular economy (even if they do not exploit it) that is unavailable to some other traditionally oppressed groups and which perhaps encouraged Beauvoir to view (literally) lesbians as a separate case in her study. In this way, reminiscent of Wittig's formulation of lesbians as runaway slaves from the heterosexual contract, the lesbian might evade the heterosexual specular economy as it pervades *Le Deuxième Sexe*.[22]

The heterospecular economy figures in the chapter on 'la lesbienne'. One of the fallacies that Beauvoir exposes is that female masculinity equates to lesbianism. In a point echoed almost fifty years later in Halberstam's *Female Masculinity*, Beauvoir argues that 'définir la lesbienne "virile" par sa volonté "d'imiter l'homme", c'est la vouer à l'inauthenticité.'[23] Beauvoir advocates lesbianism as a positive choice, not as a melancholic, inauthentic failure to imitate male heterosexuality. In fact, she argues that 'la femme dite "virile" est souvent une franche hétérosexuelle'.[24] The performative dimensions of lesbian identities are highlighted as Beauvoir argues that lesbians sometimes stage butch and femme roles but these are parodic and pleasurable in purpose and do not indicate anything necessarily about the expression of lesbian sexuality:

> À plus forte raison est-il vain de prétendre ranger les lesbiennes en deux catégories tranchées. Du fait qu'une comédie sociale se superpose souvent à leurs véritables rapports, se plaisant à imiter un couple bisexué, elles suggèrent elles-mêmes la division en 'viriles' et 'féminines'. Mais que l'une porte un tailleur sévère et l'autre une robe floue ne doit pas faire illusion. A y regarder de plus près on s'aperçoit que — sauf dans des cas limites — leur sexualité est ambiguë.[25]

Beauvoir then argues that, in any case, nothing is more unnatural than conventional feminine dress, just as masculine dress is unnatural although at least the latter has the merit of being practical.[26]

---

22 Wittig, 'One is not born a woman' in *The Straight Mind*, 20.
23 *Le DSII*, 197.
24 Ibid., 200.
25 Ibid., 211.
26 Ibid., 215.

Beauvoir distinguishes, however, between heterosexual women who adopt male dress and traditionally masculine styles of behaviour to acquire greater freedom — that is, heterosexual female masculinity which is very widespread — and lesbian masculinity. As Halberstam argues, heterosexual female masculinity may challenge gender conformity, but compared to lesbian masculinity, it is much more acceptable.[27] Drawing on a case study cited by Krafft Ebbing of a Hungarian lesbian named Sandor, Beauvoir examines a lived experience of lesbian masculinity. Sandor was raised as a boy, and as she grew up she had relationships with feminine women, who often mistook her for a man to the point where she married. Physically she had feminine anatomical characteristics, although she had begun her menstruation very late and her genital development was partial. Arrested temporarily for impersonating a man and marrying a woman, she was subsequently acquitted. Sandor expressed her sexuality by making love to women but never allowing them to make love to her — what we would term these days a 'stone butch'. Sandor despised men and was especially attracted to older feminine women. This suggests, argues Beauvoir in a further critique of classical psychoanalysis, that Sandor had a masculine Oedipus complex in relation to her mother. She formed a couple identity with her mother and sought to protect and possibly to dominate her. In this way, Sandor performs, according to Beauvoir, a fragile masculine identity which is psychically 'completed' by an older feminine partner.

So it seems that Beauvoir uses the chapter on 'la lesbienne' to explore gender variance as well as lesbian sexual preference — this is probably the legacy of her use of sexological sources. However, unlike sexological approaches to gender variance and sexual orientation, Beauvoir's discussion does not, on the whole, pathologise the gender-variant women and lesbians whom she studies. In Sandor's case, for example, she argues that it was society's intervention which destroyed her equilibrium in its attempt to fit her into the sex-gender binary. Like Halberstam, Beauvoir seems to be challenging why we construct certain sex roles as authentic and unaccountable (such as heterosexual male masculinity) and others

---

[27]   Halberstam (1998), 28.

such as transgender lesbianism as inauthentic and accountable to the point of their annihilation. As Butler argues in *Gender Trouble*, exclusive homosexuality and exclusive heterosexuality are equally melancholic in their exclusion of each other.[28] All sexualities are both closed and open to certain erotic practices but only some are pathologised and deemed inauthentic according to specific ideological agendas and within part-icular historical circumstances.

Finally, I want now to consider briefly Beauvoir's first published novel, *L'Invitée*, for its representation of female masculinity, on the grounds that it is, in my view, the most gender troubling fictional work in her corpus. Much work has been done on *L'Invitée* and readings draw on a range of perspectives from existentialism, feminism, psychoanalysis and narratology. The text stands apart from Beauvoir's later fictional production in that it lacks any significant historical context, despite its setting on the threshold of the Second World War. It focuses intensely on interpersonal relationships, specifically a triadic relationship between one man, Pierre, and two women, Françoise and Xavière, among the theatrical milieu in Paris. The text's epigraph 'chaque conscience poursuit la mort de l'autre', taken from Hegel's *Phenomenology of Spirit*, encourages us to read the text as an existentialist drama. However, I want to suggest a queer dimension to the epigraph in that the otherness at issue here is not only the Other as other consciousness, but also the Other within the self, a melancholic otherness which is figured in the performativity of genders and sexualities in the text. Specifically, I want to look at the perform-ativity of masculinities in the text and the queering of sexualities. This is an area which has been largely neglected in the text's reception because there has been little discussion of masculinities in Beauvoir studies and because the lesbian desire between Françoise and Xavière has tended to be read through the chapter on 'la jeune fille' in *Le Deuxième Sexe*, there-by containing it as an inauthentic phase in the relationship between the older Françoise and the younger Xavière.[29] Moreover, issues concerning

---

[28] Judith Butler, *Gender Trouble* (London and New York: Routledge, 1990), 57–72.

[29] For an exception, see Sarah Fishwick's *The Body in the Work of Simone de Beauvoir* (Oxford and Bern: Peter Lang, 2002).

male homoerotic desiring positions, for example, in the relationship between Gerbert and Françoise or Gerbert and Pierre have not been considered, perhaps because the sex-gender and heterosexual-homosexual binaries still govern the reading positions from which the text is usually approached, despite a wealth of textual evidence relating to the queer identities in play.

A powerful queer motif occurs early in the text which signals that gender trouble is at work. Xavière reproaches Françoise and Pierre for always making people more complicated than they are. Françoise replies that people are only simple if one considers them superficially. Xavière then tells her that an Austrian hermaphrodite lives in their hotel, having taken refuge in France following her / his expulsion from Austria.[30] Françoise replies sardonically that it must have been a lucky break to have been an hermaphrodite in Austria in the heyday of psychoanalysis and sexology. Xavière relates how her hermaphroditic neighbour cries all the time because she/he lives in poverty and is attracted to men but this attraction is not reciprocated. Incidentally, this same example of Austrian intersexuality also features at the start of the chapter on 'la lesbienne' in *Le Deuxième Sexe*. In *L'Invitée*, this brief vignette troubles normativity relating to gender and sexuality and encourages a queer reading of the text.

This is further facilitated by the precarious female masculinity of Françoise which is allied both to a lesbian desiring position in her relationship with Xavière and becomes a male homoerotic desiring position in her relationship with Gerbert. Beauvoir anticipates her sub-sequent argument in *Le Deuxième Sexe* that female masculinity is not necessarily allied to lesbianism but is also produced through female heterosexuality and, as I will argue, through Françoise performing a gay male identity with Gerbert.

Françoise's masculinity is also measured against the masculinity of Pierre, her long-term partner. Fallaize has described Pierre's masculinity in *L'Invitée* as 'caricatural' and as being closely linked to his gift for

---

[30]   Beauvoir, *L'Invitée*, 171–2.

words.[31] A melancholic Don Juan, Pierre exploits language and his role in the phallogocentric order to seduce women. Yet his symbolising power is contained by his absence as focaliser, the focalisers being Françoise, Elisabeth and Gerbert. He appears to exist as a fantasy projection, idealised by all three focalisers as the incarnation of traditional masculinity, but one which, with the advent of Xavière – who does not idealise him – becomes a traditional masculinity in crisis.

In his relationship with Françoise, Pierre is represented in her focalised narrative as a dominating force. Yet assuming focalising control to represent Pierre as melancholic seducer, Françoise appropriates key attributes of his masculinity, namely, his gaze and phallogocentric power which he uses to seduce women. This appropriation of the gaze to represent Pierre, among other things, is crucial for Françoise because a central aspect of the novel is concerned with her quest for autonomous subjectivity. But her quest largely fails, I would argue, because she fails to reinterpet the traditional model of masculinity represented by Pierre. Equipped temporarily with the signifying phallus, she appears not to know how to queer it. In Butlerian terms, she fails to deploy the lesbian phallus, that is to say, to challenge the Lacanian binary of the feminine being the phallus and the masculine having the phallus.[32] Hence the competition between Pierre and Françoise to seduce Xavière becomes a multiple Hegelian struggle that takes place between Pierre and Xavière to restore Pierre's traditional masculinity, between Françoise and Xavière for Pierre, between Françoise and Pierre for Xavière, and between Françoise and Gerbert for both Pierre and Xavière. At the heart of these struggles is the performativity of gender and sexuality, and a constant play of sexual substitutions in a theatre of transgressive queer possibilities. In this, Françoise fails to reinterpret traditional masculinity, enacting her masculinity as a lack of care towards self and Other (exemplified in her illness and her final assassination of Xavière) and as a

---

[31]   Fallaize, *The Novels of Simone de Beauvoir* (London and New York: Routledge, 1988), 37.

[32]   Judith Butler, 'The Lesbian Phallus and the Morphological Imaginary' in *Bodies that Matter, On the Discursive Limits of 'Sex'* (London: Routledge, 1993), 57–92, especially 85–91.

need to maintain a relationship of dominance and submission. This leads her to conceptualise her lesbian desire for Xavière phallically, as an attempt to control Xavière, to objectify her physically and ultimately to annihilate her. Despite her eroticised attention to Xavière's physicality, and as Sarah Fishwick has convincingly argued, the plurality of the female desiring body as represented in the eroticised encounters between Xavière and Françoise, Françoise feels paralysed by 'ce beau corps qu'elle ne savait même pas désirer'.[33] Dancing with Xavière in a Parisian club, Françoise is at a loss to identify her feelings for Xavière as authentic sexual desire. This can be explained by the phallocentric model of desire with which Françoise is inculcated. As Fishwick argues, recourse to alternative feminist models of desire, such as that proposed by Irigaray in *Ce Sexe qui n'en est pas un* allows this phallocentric model of desire, premissed on the possession and objectification of each partner, to be challenged.[34] An alternative gynocentric model of rather muted desire is sketched, as argued earlier, in the chapter on 'la lesbienne' in *Le Deuxième Sexe*. But Françoise's inability to challenge this phallocentric model of desire is related, I contend, to her overall lack of autonomy and to her inability to value her own female masculinity as an authentic ethical and desiring subjectivity. She is left, in effect, with the discarded scraps of Pierre's phallic masculinity and unable, hence, to conceptualise an alternative desiring position. She functions therefore largely as a surrogate for traditional masculinity, as is also evident in her relationship with Gerbert.

Initially, at the start of the novel, this relationship is staged as a mother-son scenario: Françoise casts an affectionate but concerned gaze over Gerbert's weary face as they work together on a script for Pierre. She cherishes their intimacy together and the routine of their working patterns. Yet they also appear to have a blokish camaraderie together for they drink whisky and barely communicate. A further dimension to their relationship is Françoise playing a heterosexual male role to Gerbert's role as 'jeune fille', with his beautiful green eyes, his curling eyelashes

---

33   Beauvoir, *L'Invitée*, 316.
34   Sarah Fishwick, *The Body in the Work of Simone de Beauvoir* (Oxford: Peter Lang, 2002), 203.

and expectant mouth.[35] Yet in all of these roles in which Françoise desires Gerbert, she is shown as not knowing what she 'could want'.[36] The performativity of gender and sexuality in the text casts Françoise into a stasis of desiring confusion. In Gerbert's own narration, Françoise is depicted as disdainful of the conventional trappings of femininity: wearing down-at-heel shoes, laddered stockings, not prone to sudden changes of mood or to a predilection for feminine ornamentation.[37] Gerbert has a traumatised relationship to women, feeling ill at ease and bored with them. Indeed, he reflects that if he had the luck to be homosexual he would not frequent women at all.[38] But with Ramblin, a gay actor at the theatre, he appears ill at ease and grateful that Ramblin had never made a pass at him. He seems, in fact, most at ease with Pierre of whom he says he is fonder than of anyone else, which suggests that Françoise's masculinity acts as surrogate masculinity for Pierre's in her relationship with Gerbert. Unable to desire Pierre's masculinity safely because it is attached to a biologically male body, Gerbert can safely desire Françoise's masculinity instead, attached as it is to a biologically female body. Indeed, towards the end of the novel, just before Françoise and Gerbert finally do sleep together, he tells her that she is 'comme un type!' This suggests that in Françoise's relationship with Gerbert, as with Xavière and Pierre, there is a complex web of sexual identifications in play, one of which entails Françoise's performance of masculinity for Gerbert's gratified reassurance so that they, in effect, perform a gay male couple identity.

Female masculinity is therefore performed in *L'Invitée* both as the remnants of traditional heterosexual masculinity in Françoise's relationship with Pierre and Xavière and as gay male surrogate masculinity with Gerbert. Unable to conceptualise an ethical lesbian female masculinity in her relationship with Xavière, Françoise stages her annihilation. Too threatened by the autonomy that Xavière represents and desperate to retain Pierre as the original referent for her own masculinity, Françoise

---

[35] Beauvoir, *L'Invitée*, 18.
[36] Ibid., 18.
[37] Ibid., 317.
[38] Ibid., 337.

murders the Messianic Xavière in a queer rewriting of the Christian narrative. Although this is framed at the end of the text as an act of self-affirmation for Françoise and as a choice, 'elle s'était choisie', it is, as Beauvoir recognised, a wholly unethical choice and hence a moral failure. A choice which shrinks Françoise's world into a melancholic iteration of a dysfunctional surrogate heterosexual masculinity, so that she remains just like Pierre, the performative possibilities of identity shut down.

In conclusion, the radicalism of Beauvoir's analyses of gender and sexuality in *Le Deuxième Sexe* is particularly evident in her analyses of female masculinity. As *L'Invitée* illustrates and *Le Deuxième Sexe* develops further, the cultivation of authentic, ethical female masculinities, especially when conjoined with the queering of identities, deeply troubles the prevailing binaries of sex and gender and heterosexuality and homo-sexuality. Hence, Beauvoir's theorisations of gender and sexuality may not provide assistance with the practicalities of one's sex life, but they help refine how we think about the trouble it might cause us.[39]

Bibliography

Beauvoir, Simone de, *L'Invitée* (Paris: Gallimard, 1943).

——, *Le Deuxième Sexe* (Paris: Gallimard, 1949).

Bonnet, Marie-Jo, 'De l'émancipation amoureuse des femmes dans la cité', *Les Temps Modernes*, 598 (1998), 85–112.

Butler, Judith, *Gender Trouble* (New York and London: Routledge, 1990).

——, *Bodies That Matter, On the Discursive Limits of 'Sex'* (New York and London: Routledge, 1993).

Card, Claudia, 'Lesbian attitudes and *The Second Sex*' in *Hypatia Reborn, Essays in Feminist Philosophy*, eds Azizah Y. al-Hibri and Margaret A. Simons (Bloomington and Indianapolis: Indiana University Press, 1990), 290–99.

---

[39] I would like to thank Laura Doan for her comments on an earlier draft of this article. All errors and misjudgements that remain are, of course, my own responsibility.

Ferguson, Ann, 'Lesbian Identity, Beauvoir and History', in *Hypatia Reborn, Essays in Feminist Philosophy*, eds Azizah Y. al-Hibri and Margaret A. Simons (Bloomington and Indianapolis: Indiana University Press, 1990), 280–9.

Fishwick, Sarah, *The Body in the Work of Simone de Beauvoir* (Bern and Oxford: Peter Lang, 2002).

Halberstam, Judith, *Female Masculinity* (Durham and London: Duke University, 1998).

Moi, Toril, *Simone de Beauvoir, the making of an intellectual woman* (Oxford, UK and Cambridge, USA: Blackwell, 1994).

Robinson, Christopher, *Scandal in the Ink, Male and Female Homosexuality in Twentieth-Century French Literature* (London: Cassell, 1995).

Simons, Margaret A., *Beauvoir and the Second Sex, Feminism, Race and the Origins of Existentialism* (Lanham, Maryland, USA: Rowman and Littlefield, 1999).

Spelman, Elizabeth V., *Inessential Woman, Problems of exclusion in feminist thought* (London: The Women's Press, 1988).

Tidd, Ursula, *Simone de Beauvoir, Gender and Testimony* (Cambridge: Cambridge University Press, 1999).

Wittig, Monique, *The Straight Mind and Other Essays* (Hemel Hempstead: Harvester Wheatsheaf, 1992).

Outings on the Inside:
Lesbian Spaces in the Prison Narratives of
Albertine Sarrazin and Elisabeth Cons

Amanda Crawley Jackson
University of Sheffield

It's fascinating to spot the immediate differences in a women's prison to Belmarsh. Not least the searching procedure, the fact that lesbianism is far more prevalent in female prisons than homosexuality is in male establishments, and, if you can believe it, the level of violence is higher. They don't bother waiting in the shower before they throw the first punch. Anywhere, at any time, will do.[1]

L'imagerie populaire qui transforme les prisons de femmes en répliques de la Lesbos antique, c'est du crayonnage naïf. Du naïf violent, lorsque vous écopez d'un rapport de mœurs pour avoir fait la bise à une camarade qui avait le bourdon, ou pour vous être fait épiler avec la tête sur les genoux de l'opératrice; mais de là à prétendre que nous sommes de purs esprits...[2]

Jeffrey Archer's statement — based on his reading of a screenplay written by a fellow (male) inmate — reveals, at three levels, a preoccupation — or, more accurately, a fascination — with a perceived *openness* in women's prisons. First, there is the intrusion of the specular examination (of the body, of the site of inhabitation); second, the prevalence and openness of lesbian practices and behaviours; third, he describes an anarchic deconstruction of previously bounded spaces and the opening up (or

---

[1] Jeffrey Archer, *A Prison Diary* (Basingstoke and Oxford: Macmillan, 2002), I: *Belmarsh: Hell*, 129–30.

[2] Albertine Sarrazin, *La Cavale*, in *Romans, lettres et poèmes: L'Astragale, La Cavale, La Traversière* (Paris: Jean-Jacques Pauvert, 1967), 205.

spilling over) of intimate (closed) *loci*. Albertine Sarrazin and Elisabeth Cons, both of whom have written narratives describing their time spent in prison, describe lesbian spaces in remarkably similar terms. In Sarrazin's trilogy of autobiographical works, the narrator, Anick, is seen to engage in various relationships — intimate and sensual, if not sexual — with other women. However, throughout the corpus, her husband — Julien — is established and apostrophised as a privileged and loving interlocutor, the very symbol of her life and identity *extra muros*, which thus leads her to disavow this 'other', 'pragmatic' aspect of her 'walled' sexuality. Cons, for her part, is engaged in a continual dialogue of desired identification with penal and social authority and as such descries what she perceives as the deviant sexual relations enjoyed by certain of her co-detainees.

In this paper, I will argue that the existence — and disavowal — of lesbianism in the carceral space must be understood within the historical parameters of the 'new' prison. I will show how the rigid geometric economy of the old model (grounded in panopticism and manifest in binaries of open / closed, visible / invisible, powerful / powerless) has given way to a system of circulation management which permits of the liminal spaces that enable (lesbian) encounter. For this reason and as Meaghan Morris suggests, it is important that in this paper we move away from morphological accounts of *the* prison to an historical account of *these* prisons. Equally, we must work away from the idea of a pre-existing grammar of carceral architecture towards an analysis which admits that space is practised and which re-inscribes users in that space. In this sense, we support Michel de Certeau's distinction between '*opérations* spatialisantes' and '[les] systèmes spatiaux'; between 'parcours' and 'carte',[3] for the evidence in these prison narratives leads us necessarily to reinscribe the user within (and as constitutive of) space. This, of course, is what Meaghan Morris means when she writes: 'space is not a prior condition of something else ("place"), but rather an outcome, the *product* of an activity, and so it necessarily has a temporal

---

[3]   Michel de Certeau, *L'Invention du quotidien* (Paris: Gallimard, 1990), I: *Arts de faire*, 172.

dimension.'[4] Our examination of the prison space in which lesbian identities and practices are performed, hidden, enabled and yet prohibited will therefore, of necessity, be historical. It will also be grounded in the premise that the kind of binary geometrism described by Gaston Bachelard[5] is performed by users (rather than inscribed in plastic form by the designers and architects), and emerges, surprisingly perhaps, in and against the openness and flow of the carceral environment. Equally, if we accept Judith Butler's premise that (gendered and sexual) identities are performed symmetrically, that is to say as an 'act of differentiating the two oppositional moments of the binary [which] results in a consolidation of each term [and] the respective internal coherence of sex, gender and desire';[6] and if we bear in mind also that hegemonic sexual identity is a 'spatially constituted discourse',[7] then we can also begin to understand how the dissolution of geometric carceral space has a profoundly destabilising effect on its already destabilised inhabitants. An attention to carceral spatiality is particularly necessary in that in the works of both Sarrazin and Cons, lesbians are predominantly described in terms of their irruption in — and disruption of — the normative heterosexual spaces which describe the prison. Lesbian desire opens up 'moral' space; it disrupts the boundaries which inmates attempt to recreate for themselves. Lesbian desire transforms the closeted into open, and inside out; it is treated thus as abject (a term which I borrow from Kristeva) — at once attractive and horrifying — by those for whom hegemonic hetero-sexuality constitutes the very foundation of their 'normality' and identity. In this sense, the paper seeks to show how topographical disruptions

[4]   Meaghan Morris, 'Great Moments in Social Climbing: King Kong and the human fly', in *Sexuality and Space*, ed. Beatriz Colomina (Princeton: Princeton Architectural Press, 1992), 3 (1–52).

[5]   Gaston Bachelard, *La Poétique de l'espace* (Paris: Presses Universitaires de France, 1967), 192.

[6]   Judith Butler, *Gender Trouble: Feminism and the Subversion of Identity* (London: Routledge, 1990), 22–23.

[7]   Gill Valentine, '(Re)negotiating the Heterosexual Street: lesbian productions of space', in *Body Space: Destabilizing Geographies of Gender and Sexuality*, ed. Nancy Duncan (London: Routledge, 1996), 152 (144–55).

mirror and coincide with the turbulence created by lesbian identities and practices within an aggressively normative field.

To think of the prison as a relatively open space of flux and flow goes against received notions of the carceral environment. However, it is only in these terms that we can begin to address any notion of intersubjective — including lesbian — relations between inmates in prison. Michel Foucault's work on the panoptical model in *Surveiller et punir* in many ways set the critical tone. He describes therein a regime of discipline, silence, surveillance and, most importantly in this case, segregation, which he understands as extending beyond the walls of the prison to create a carceral society more generally. It is his work on the prison specifically, rather than his wider sociological study, which concerns us here. Foucault grounds his study of the prison in an analysis of that 'simple idea in Architecture!' — the Panopticon — conceived by Beccaria and Bentham, and in its role as enabler of surveillance and regulation. Within its cellular system, individuals were encouraged to reflect, in solitude and prayer, on their sins. There was minimum contact between prisoners, and when contact was inevitable, inmates were frequently required to maintain absolute silence (a rule enshrined in the French penal code until 1972). Christian Demonchy describes the 'régime de détention' thus:

> Aucune vie sociale n'est envisagée dans ce programme. […] l'administration deploy[ait] toute une panoplie de mesures inhumaines, grotesques et inutiles afin d'empêcher la communication entre détenus et creuser le fossé entre gardiens et gardés. La seule alternative à la promiscuité est devenue très tôt l'isolement. La prison idéale est la prison individuelle. L'urbanisme est interdit intra-muros.[8]

Foucault's belief in the absolute functionality of the Panopticon and 'la pénétration du règlement jusque dans les plus fins détails de l'existence et par une hiérarchie complète'[9] is perhaps as much an 'act of faith' as the

---

[8]   Christian Demonchy, 'Généalogie de la prison moderne', http://www.–insite.fr/interdit/2001aout/prison2b.htm

[9]   Michel Foucault, *Surveiller et punir: naissance de la prison* (1975; Paris: Gallimard, 1994), 231.

many attempted plastic translations of its principles. Foucault's model presupposes the relative immobility and sedentarism of the inmate; it positions her in a series of visible grid references and, as such, is ill-suited to the task of describing the modern carceral space. The spaces in-between are under-theorised, under-represented; the conceptual tool weakens when subjects move and in its presumption that movement can be undertaken without any fluctuation in the conditions associated with immobility. It posits a disciplinarian gaze as a fixed centre to a delimited sphere; it relies on the *possibility* of visibility as a means of (self-) regulation. Thomas Markus makes the point that although the idea of the Panopticon was 'deeply influential', and although many centric institutions were built and claimed to be Panopticons, 'with one exception [the Edinburgh Bridewell built in 1791], none were. They lacked that total asymmetry of power which was an essential feature. Inmates could see and hear each other, or they could see their keepers, or there were periods when they escaped surveillance'.[10]

In fact, the set of ideas which governed the construction of 'panoptical' models was to change radically in the twentieth century. We suggested earlier that space must be understood in its temporal aspect. In this sense, an historical examination of the carceral space inhabited by Cons and Sarrazin is necessary if we are to be attuned, in Morris' words, to 'the socio-economic contexts and to the individuating local intensities' of *this* prison (not *the* prison).[11] Only then can we understand the specificities of the selves which practise *this* space. Petit, Faugeron and Pierre describe the introduction in the second half of the 1940s of a four-stage 'progressive regime' in French prison: 'observation à l'isolement total, répartition dans des groupes en fonction du degré d'"amendabilité" (isolement la nuit, détention en commun le jour), phase de confiance puis semi-liberté.'[12] Fears of moral contagion amongst prisoners and economies of total surveillance gave way, to a certain extent at least, to an ideological scheme

---

[10] Thomas A. Markus, *Buildings and Power: freedom and control in the origin of modern building types* (London: Routledge, 1993), 123.

[11] Morris (1992), 4.

[12] Jacques-Guy Petit, Claude Faugeron and Michel Pierre, *Histoire des prisons en France, 1789–2000* (Toulouse: Éditions Privat, 2002), 184.

which permitted communication between prisoners, created communal spaces, allowed mobility in varying degrees and conferred semi-autonomy upon the most 'reformed' inmates. Even those prisons which had been designed architecturally to implement the cellular — or 'separate' — regime were, in 1955, 'modernised', a process which allowed for the creation of communal spaces such as sports grounds, the introduction of radios (an important link with the world beyond the cell) and the relaxation of rules governing visits.[13]

This period of transition in prison ideology, aggravated by changing staffing policies and the rapid expansion of the prison population in the 1950s (in no small part due to the claims for independence and eventual war in Algeria), led to what Petit *et al* have described as 'une situation ingérable qui tient du bricolage sous un habillage scientifique'.[14] Certainly, there is a great sense of ideological and spatial perturbation in the writings of Sarrazin, whose incarceration spanned some of the most turbulent years in recent French prison history. She describes the overcrowding ('une arrivante, nous voilà 6 [dans la cellule]!!');[15] the enforced proximity between inmates ('je suis contente, car leur poste marche du matin au soir, et comme nous sommes pratiquement fenêtre à fenêtre et que la leur reste ouverte... je repasse en piétinant des cha-cha-cha sans oublier les "ris et les jeux" de leurs mouflets');[16] the lack or failure of surveillance ('[la matonne] est pas revenue avant 14 heures et je, à poil dans la cour... et vadrouillant par le quartier en costume d'Eve !!! Ça faisait très "at home"!');[17] '[la matonne] ne pigeait pas grand-chose à nos bavardages, ou [...] elle s'en foutait';[18] and the disruption — with all its intendent security-related consequences — of the prisoner-warder hierarchy:

[13] Ibid., 186, 188.
[14] Ibid., 186.
[15] Albertine Sarrazin, *Biftons de Prison* (Paris: Jean-Jacques Pauvert, 1977), 41.
[16] Ibid., 37.
[17] Ibid., 36.
[18] Ibid., 34.

> Dire que l'an dernier, avec Hivo [a warder], je m'amusais à la boucler chez
> Mauduit [another inmate] en hurlant: 'Ha! ha ! et maintenant, bye ! bye!'
> qu'elles me suppliaient mi-anxieuses, mi-rigolardes, de leur rouvrir !¹⁹

Sarrazin's autobiographical narratives, letters and diaries bear testimony
to the changing spatial practices within the prison. The concrete shape of
the prison as it was before the introduction of the progressive regime
becomes a surface on which the inmates trace their own 'parcours'. A
clear example of the changing forms and spaces of the environment, the
creative (mis)use of that space by its users — and, indeed, the
insufficiency of a Foucauldian interpretive framework in this context —
can be found in an illicit letter written by Sarrazin from the prison at
Soissons in 1958:

> en cellote, ici, par contre, je peux cacher n'importe quoi, le quartier a des
> ressources. Même, il y a, entre ma piaule et l'atelier, une espèce de fenêtre
> avec porte à petit verrou, barreau, grillage, etc... ça servait pour surveiller les
> condamnés à muerte, mais actuellement on a mis des planches pour obstruer,
> ce qui fait un spacieux placard. En effet, la grande [the warder], avec sa clé
> d'horloge, n'a jamais pu l'ouvrir !!! J'y puis donc mettre mon arsenal en toute
> quiétude.²⁰

Of course, the effect of these 'perturbations' within the system described
by Foucault can be traced in the inmates' relations with each other. The
Space Syntax group, and in particular Bill Hiller, have applied themselves
to the elaboration of new interpretive tool which enables the study of
combinations of spatial units in larger topographical systems such as
prisons.²¹ Changing carceral topographies have enabled inmates to be together, and to communicate with each other along more or less prescribed
lines. If lesbian relations in prison are structurally precluded in Foucault's

---

19 Ibid., 35.
20 Ibid., 28.
21 Hillier's work is discussed in detail by T. Markus in *Buildings and
    Power* (1993). See also Bill Hillier and J. Hanson, *The Social Logic of
    Space* (Cambridge: Cambridge University Press, 1984) and Bill Hillier,
    Space is the Machine: a configurational theory of architecture
    (Cambridge: Cambridge University Press, 1999).

analysis, it will be useful to replace the interpretive paradigms of segregation and visibility with Hillier's model of controlled interfaces between prisoners, and between prisoners and warders. Hillier's basic model, which is a diagrammatic mapping of the kind of prison described by Foucault, describes a tree-like structure, the trunk of which represents the locus of power (and along which communication is channelled), comprising the prison gate, outer courtyard, warder spaces and control rooms. The branches of this tree — deeper within the structure and therefore further removed from power — represent supervised communal spaces: the chapel, washrooms, and so on. Individual cells, or the tips of the branches, are the furthest removed from the *loci* of power and control, and there is no communication between them. Thus, for the inmate there is no possibility of a freely chosen relationship in a private space. The 'rings' — or the powerful outer peripheries — of the prison buildings allow their habitual users (in other words, the inhabitants / warders) free circulation and association. Overall, then, this structure enfolds within itself encounter-generating and encounter-prohibiting possibilities. The subject's positioning either in deep or shallow spaces of the overall structure will govern the frequency and potential of her mobility between spaces, as well as her communication and encounter with others.

The same principles can be applied when schematising more recent, progressive carceral models. According to Sarrazin's narratives, 'ringy' — or liminal — spaces are no longer confined to the external peripheries of the prison, but have proliferated in and between the branches and tips of the model. Inmates benefit from the possibilities of (intimate) encounter and circulation. Multiple occupancy cells and dormitories enable the women to engage in relations that remain (at least partially) invisible to the authorities: 'Aïe! C'est bien ma chance: la tôle est de régime collectif, voilà un dortoir, ce qui implique, demain, l'atelier. Un peu abstrait de supposer qu'on ne couche ensemble que pour se retrouver seule au réveil !'[22] Sarrazin describes not only the formal spatial and organisational consequences of the progressive regime (for example, the unsupervised periods in the workshops), but the manner in which these are

[22]   Sarrazin (1967), 143.

exploited by the inmates (during these unsupervised periods the inmates can prepare their own coffee, stoke the fire, gossip or take a nap...). She describes, for example, the 'bed-hopping' which has become commonplace under the new regime: 'Mauricette a l'air d'un garçon [...]; j'ai pensé au pire lorsqu'elle a abordé mon lit, mais je permets quand même.'[23] In fact, the younger woman is the 'post woman', charged with collecting and delivering 'biftons' (illicit notes) by means of a wire and line which she swings between the dormitory windows, across the external surface of the prison — another transgressive use, this time of the 'architecture terrible' of the prison façade.

The rings deep within the carceral structure are irregularly positioned and inmates benefit to varying degrees from the encounter-generating possibilities they offer. For example, in *La Cavale* we are told that women in the workshops are allowed unlimited access to 'la salle d'eau'. Perversely, only one designated inmate at a time is allowed to move there from the laundry, and that inmate is accompanied by a warder and the doors are firmly locked behind her. This is because the laundry also serves the men's prison, and as such the laundress potentially represents an illegitimate intermediary or surface between two disconnected rings. Rings occur in Sarrazin's prison — a multi-storey 'pigeonnier' — most frequently at the level of the uppermost floors, which house the dormitories. Unlike Hillier's basic model which precludes contact between the tips of the branches, the inmates in *La Cavale* benefit from a certain number of freedoms and enhanced possibilities of encounter. For example, they sit on the rooftop and sunbathe, or observe what is going on in the courtyard down below (traditionally a powerful place, which the inmates have no right to inhabit). There are still restrictions, for example: 'pas de contact entre les dortoirs', although the fact that there are ten women in each dormitory, that they are for the most part unsupervised during the night, and that each of them meet women from other dormitories in their various places of work and occupation during the day undermine rather these notional attempts at segregation and spatial control. A case in point is the night-time encounter described by Sarrazin:

[23] Ibid., 44.

> Mona est de réputation accueillante, et lorsqu'elle se baguenaude d'un lit à l'autre, en slip et en haut de pyjama, les cheveux insolemment longs et épais coulant jusqu'à la taille, on se sent des envies d'hospitalité en retour. On se sent vibro-masseur.[24]

There are other, sanctioned ways of exploiting the existence of these liminal spaces which, in their turn, contribute further to the spatio-hier-archical disruption of the carceral organisation. For example, Anick — the narrator of *La Cavale* — decides to 'faire garde-manger commun' with a new friend, Jane. Jane has previously enjoyed a privileged relation-ship with a senior warder (another indication of a changing regime), who bestows gifts and privileges upon her. Now that Jane shares these with Anick, the latter gleefully notes that 'la matonne est dépitée de voir que je profite de ses bienfaits sans avoir à l'en remercier ni à la servir en retour, puisque c'est Jane qui me les offre.'[25] Further intimate relations develop in the conducive spaces of the softly lit dormitory and the open, fre-quently unsupervised space of the courtyard. Anick experiences a 'coup de foudre'[26] and begins to spend long hours whispering and dreaming with another inmate, Maria. She also engages in an intimate — although ambiguous — relationship with Mona, whose sexual ambivalence and relations with other women in the prison are well documented:

> Je fais auprès d'elle de minuscules actes de présence, je fabrique avec ses longs cheveux des coiffures étranges et haut épinglées, je la laque d'esthétique et de délicat, et chaque semaine j'agrémente au Bic, avec des roses et des pen-sées, la lettre qu'elle taille en soupirant pour son mari, son mari de Fresnes.[27]

This quotation is significant in terms of our understanding of lesbian practices in the prison described by Sarrazin. It seems that despite the possibilities offered by the increasingly 'ringy' spaces of the progressive prison, lesbian practices and desires exist under erasure. The legitimacy of the women's relationship is guaranteed by its male axis; their attention

---

[24]   Ibid., 205.
[25]   Ibid., 267.
[26]   Ibid., 217.
[27]   Ibid., 183.

to each other is transformed into — or, at least, articulated as being that of the female retinue to the bride. The pattern repeats itself elsewhere. The 'coup de foudre' which binds Anick to Maria is legitimised (and thus facilitated) when the narrator offers to draw her friend's son from a photograph. The intimate, sexualised encounter between Anick and Fatima again has a man (this time, Julien — Anick's lover) at its core:

> je dus m'étendre à même le ciment crasseux, la gorge nue, appuyée en travers des cuisses de Fatima, qui s'était accroupie commodément à la mode de son pays et me serrait le kiki d'un bras pour m'empêcher de gigoter, tandis que de l'autre elle piquait, piquait selon le tracé, marmonnant lorsque perlait le sang et essuyant mon nichon sans douceur avec son torchon.[28]

Other inmates use their male lovers, husbands and 'straight' friends as a normalising shield behind which they can ironise their lesbian relationships and desires. Anick notes, for example: 'Gina ne veut se "faire" personne (et Tony, alors ?) mais ça l'amuse de brancher les lesbiennes: à coups de "ma poule" et de cigarettes, elle a amené Mona à amener une couverture entre le lit de Nadine et le sien'; 'à présent elles la font s'exhiber.'[29]

Of course, it is possible to present a pragmatic view of this pattern of disavowal: heavy penalties are incurred by those who engage in same-sex relations in prison. But equally, we have shown that it is possible within the space we have just described for such relations to remain *unseen* by the authorities. The key to this polemic (and here, we return perhaps to Foucault) is the role of others in the process of self-regulation. The narrator states: 'Personne ne doit savoir, personne ne doit pouvoir balancer combien j'aime Maria. Dans une tôle collective, il faut cacher ses amitiés plus soigneusement que ses haines.'[30] Again, we might be pragmatic. To reveal the presence of a lover in the frequently violent carceral community is to create an additional point of vulnerability, another surface for attack, another pawn for others to play. While Anick makes a point of

---

[28] Ibid., 213.
[29] Ibid., 205.
[30] Ibid., 223.

stating that lesbian presences in the prison do not disturb her — indeed, that she prefers the lesbian community to 'mes petites sœurs tôlardes, qui, à leur manière, savent recréer la société',[31] she remains unable to come out. Her desire for Mona, for example, is — with an enormous degree of self-restraint — censored; the relationship she has with Maria is cast in terms of an asexual intimacy — despite evidence in the text of frequent slippages between 'Mona' (sexually active, an exhibitionist) and 'Maria' (the virgin mother). Equally revealing, of course, is Anick's remark: 'Ce n'est pas que j'aie l'intention de me *remettre* lesbienne.'[32] In fact, relations with other women are presented as a temptation furnished by the nature of the (open) space of the prison. It is for this reason Anick that states: 'J'aurais aimé, je crois, les tôles d'autrefois.'[33] It is also the reason why she addresses her male lover thus: 'Zizi... fais-toi mon maître.'[34] The (historical) liminal nature of Sarrazin's carceral environment creates within her a sense of destabilisation and disruption which, she believes, would be occluded by the rigid binary geometrism of the 'old' prisons. The anxiety-provoking freedom and encounters facilitated by and within this newly liminal space challenge the heterosexual hegemony which has been imported, *intra muros*, with intensified and aggressive fervour from the outside. It is to this spatio-sexual hegemony to which we must now turn our attention.

Recently, feminist geographers and cultural theorists have drawn attention to the links between space and (sexual) identity. According to Judith Butler, identities are performed — an idea which is corroborated by Sarrazin when she speaks of being able to choose one of many identities, rather as an actor might choose their costume, depending on the requirements of the space or setting in which she finds herself.[35] The idea of identity as an 'abiding substance' is 'a fictive construction' which derives from 'the compulsory ordering of attributes into coherent gender

---

31   Ibid., 197
32   Ibid., 176; my emphasis.
33   Ibid., 475.
34   Ibid., 291.
35   Amanda Crawley, 'Grammatical Fictions: reading and writing the self in prison', *French Cultural Studies*, 12: 3/36 (October 2001), 303–18.

sequences'; it is a 'doing' rather than a 'being', 'constituted by the very "expressions" that are said to be its results'.[36] Gill Valentine states that 'the heterosexing of space is a performative act naturalised through repetition and regulation.'[37] It is bound up with the performance of straight desires and, inevitably, hetero-normative identities. To perform desire differently is therefore to 'cut into and disrupt the "normality" of heterosexual space.'[38] It is also to threaten that which is jealously guarded and zealously defended, for the apparent rigidity and naturalness of heterosexual space hide a brittleness and vulnerability born of — and manifest in — worried glances, inconsistencies, anxious repeat performances and defensive-aggressive security measures. Valentine continues: '[r]ather than merely trespassing in heterosexual public space with the political intention of staking out or gaining a share of it, queer is also about confronting and contesting the very production of public space'.[39] In other words, to perform alternative identities and desires in a heterosexual public space is to produce an *other* space in which all identities are necessarily re-thought and re-negotiated.

Erving Goffman has argued that the infantilisation of the prisoner represents one of the means by which the authority of the prison is asserted.[40] Deprived of adult executive agency, inmates find themselves in a situation in which even the most basic decisions regarding the self are made by another. This infantilisation takes a particular form when it is applied to the female subject, and creates a particular tension in terms of the women's relation to, and production of, models of femininity. In the sense that female inmates were expected to neat, clean and tidy, chaste, pious and devoted to domestic issues, there was little to distinguish gender expectations on the inside and outside. Equally, the evidence found in prison narratives of Cons and Sarrazin supports importationist views that external cultures, hierarchies and patterns of behaviour are recreated

[36]   Butler (1990), 24–25.
[37]   Valentine (1996), 146.
[38]   Ibid., 148.
[39]   Ibid., 152.
[40]   Erving Goffman, *Asylums: essays on the social situation of mental patients and other inmates* (Harmondsworth: Penguin, 1961).

inside the prison. When Sarrazin describes the women around her as representing 'l'image, multipliée par dix, de l'Éternel Féminin',[41] she is articulating her ambivalence towards the model of femininity — grounded in industriousness, physical and moral cleanliness, prurience and chastity — advocated and tolerated within the prison. She is also aware that in this most unnatural of environments, there is a grotesque attempt on the women's part to smuggle their transgressive behaviours and identities into the wooden horse of naturalised heterosexual economies: for example, she notes that her fellow inmates discuss her escape plans as they would a recipe and deem her as interesting as 'une femme enceinte'.[42]

It is also important to note that the infantilisation of female inmates requires them to surrender culturally recognisable aspects of their adult, sexed femininity, a process which Cons has described as 'le travail incessant de dépersonnalisation'.[43] Certainly, in the period in which Sarrazin was writing, it was mandatory for married female inmates to reassume their maiden names;[44] visits with children and partners were strictly limited and dependent on the good behaviour of the inmate; cosmetics and personal clothing were removed, and toiletries limited; matters of personal hygiene were regulated and made public; privacy was invaded and ornamentation expressly forbidden. In short, the external and relational markers which — particularly in the 1950s — marked a successful ascension to adult heterosexual femininity were effectively removed. In this environment, a violently defended recourse to those markers by illicit means represented a kind of rebellion against a system designed to refashion identities, but also a means of preserving something of the self which existed before prison. (It is significant, then, that Gina, an inmate on Sarrazin's block, almost escapes the prison by means of the nets — '[le] crochetage' — that she so diligently creates in the prison

---

[41]   Sarrazin (1967), 151.

[42]   Ibid., 185.

[43]   Elisabeth Cons, *La Boîte à oubli: dix ans à Fleury-Mérogis* (Paris: Lattès, 2000), 43.

[44]   Albertine Sazzarin, *Lettres à Julien*, ed. Josane Duranteau (Paris: Jean-Jacques Pauvert, 1971), 78.

workshops.)[45] For this reason, the political and subversive resonance of acts such as writing secret letters to husbands and partners; the assumption of married names; the wearing of home-made eyeliner and the tattooing of lover's names on the body; the importance attached to being allowed to own a pair of tweezers, all of which tend to be read in an unproblematic way on the outside, needs to be more fully recognised.

According to Valentine, the hegemony of heterosexuality is secured only through a series of 'regulatory regimes that constrain the possible performances of gender and sexual identities, in order to maintain [its] "naturalness".'[46] Valentine's argument intersects here with that of Michel Foucault in *Surveiller et punir*, from which she goes on to cite: 'processes, of different origin and scattered location, regulat[e] the most intimate and minute elements of the construction of space, time, desire and embodiment.'[47] I have shown elsewhere how, in the work of Sarrazin, inmates to a large extent regulate their own behaviours, preferring the mantle of anonymity which comes from sameness within the group to the incendiary dangers of the visibility that comes with difference.[48] Here, however, I would like to suggest that this self-regulation (which takes the form of a kind of hyper-femininity) derives also from the desire to maintain an identity which allows the female inmate to conform to penal codes and pass unnoticed through the system. Embracing this identity, being a 'good girl', brings its own rewards. Secondly, in its recreation of external structures, it permits a sense of continuity with the outside world. This model of femininity is a kind of subversion which enables the inmate to maintain an important link with a sense of self that penal technologies seek to obliterate. Heterosexual femininity is performed against the infantilising and desexualising processes of the prison; to be 'feminine' is not to be an inmate. For this reason, there is significant investment on the part of inmates in the production of femininity and heterosexual desire.

---

[45]   Sarrazin (1967), 185.
[46]   Valentine (1996), 148.
[47]   Ibid.
[48]   Crawley (2001).

Albertine Sarrazin was incarcerated during the 1950s and 60s and her writings bear witness to the profound changes which were taking place in prison architecture and organisation around the 1940s. Elisabeth Cons' incriminatory autobiography, *La Boîte à oubli*, was published in 2000 and describes life in a French women's prison in the 1990s. In this sense, Sarrazin and Cons' respective internments fall either side of the prison reforms (social, technological, architectural) which took place in France in the latter part of the twentieth century, and which intensified following the prison riots between 1971 and 1974. The radial prison in which Cons was detained, Fleury-Mérogis, was built in 1968 with an emphasis 'entirely on control, security and economy and the processing of prisoners in the most convenient way'.[49] One of the earliest of the 'new prisons', Cons encounters it thus: 'C'est le dépaysement total: une maison d'arrêt tentaculaire, des kilomètres de couloirs … le gigantisme anonyme.'[50] In fact, in many ways, the material environment of Fleury-Mérogis is grounded in the same principles as the panopticon. Long wings, extending from a central observation hub, are designed to separate inmates and manage their activity and communication. Equally, there is an emphasis on visibility: 'même seule en cellule, on est violée constamment par cet œilleton que les gardiennes ouvrent et par lequel elles voient pratiquement toute la cellule.'[51] However, Cons' experiential — as opposed to the initially visual — encounter with Fleury-Mérogis reveals the same kind of interfaces and liminal spaces — more or less supervised — as Sarrazin's 'pigeonnier'.

Some aspects of the interface are positive. Within the carceral 'bunker', she is able to find 'des plages de détente, où règne un climat plus humain'.[52] For example, spaces such as the library dissolve the internal boundaries which separate and divide categories of inmates and warder: 'Toute la détention s'y retrouvait. Les primaires côtoyaient les ré-

---

[49]   Leslie Fairweather, 'Prison Design in the Twentieth Century', in *Prison Architecture: policy, design and experience*, eds Leslie Fairweather and Seán McConville (Oxford: Architectural Press, 2002), 34 (24–39).

[50]   Cons (2000), 21.

[51]   Ibid., 41.

[52]   Ibid., 191.

cidivistes, les mamans de la nursery et les détenues du service psy.'[53] Like Sarrazin, however, Cons has an ambivalent attitude towards spaces which are conducive to encounter, but therefore open to 'transgression' and miscegenation. To her chagrin, the library is also used for the trafficking of drugs; the exercise yard — in which she is able to converse with others — is also 'une jungle', 'un grand marché', governed by 'le troc et la taxation des plus fortes sur les plus faibles'.[54] Because the cell windows on the ground floor give onto the exercise yard, Cons is able to run a kind of canteen from her window and in this way, engage in communication with others. However, trafficking and illicit communications also take place at this interface, eventually causing the prison authorities to erect a wire fence at some distance from the windows in order to prevent this kind of activity.[55] Cons is shocked by the levels of intimacy and contact which are facilitated by the material and organisational aspects of the prison space. Not only are 'primaires' and 'récidivistes' allowed to frequent each other (thus encouraging the feared 'moral contagion'), but there are no means of separating even those who are involved in the same case, and for legal reasons are not allowed to communicate with each other: 'On se voit par les fenêtres, dans les escaliers et dans la salle d'attente du cabinet médical.'[56] Even when they are held in their cells, the women — to Cons' disgust — are able to send each other messages by 'yo-yo' — 'au nez et à la barbe des gardiennes'.[57]

The contact which takes place in the 'public' spaces of the prison is less disturbing to Cons that that which occurs in the 'private' (or *unseen* — and therefore *unmanageable*) spaces which, in themselves, undermine the definition and function of the carceral space. At the tip of each of the very long, radial wings of the prison, she discovers cells which house up to six inmates, rather than the two or three for which they were designed: 'Ces cellules étaient si loin au fond du couloir que les gardiens

---

[53]   Ibid., 203.
[54]   Ibid., 44.
[55]   Ibid., 50–51.
[56]   Ibid., 44.
[57]   Ibid., 45.

s'en désintéressaient complètement.'[58] These women, usually 'Noires ou Maghrébines', live virtually independently of the prison, cooking their own food and living in an intimacy which appalls the conservative Cons. Like these distant cells, the prison courtyard is poorly supervised and consequently promotes 'inappropriate' contact. In particular, it is a space in which lesbian desires can be enacted and couples formed.[59] While the fear of being seen — and therefore punished — by a warder is still, to an extent, an inhibiting factor, the fact for Cons remains that lesbian desire spills over, from its normally constrained and invisible spaces, into the visible and public arena which she herself inhabits: 'Au demeurant, les lesbiennes se montraient au grand jour et s'affichaient sans vergogne au mépris de la pudeur la plus élémentaire et du respect des autres. Leur principal souci était de ne pas être surprises par la gardienne.'[60] Even worse: 'parmi les gardiennes, il y avait un nombre respectable de "gardiennes-mecs" au crâne rasé selon l'expression employée par les détenues. Les amis et la famille m'en avaient fait la réflexion de même que mon avocat.'[61] The existence of lesbian warders dissolves the thin, defensive line behind which lesbian desire and order more generally in the prison are normally maintained:

> Souvent j'ai entendu les détenues mourir de rire en parlant d'une gardienne lesbienne qui était, disaient-elles, follement amoureuse d'une jeune détenue de la division 3R. Le matin, la gardienne en question lui apportait des croissants pour son petit déjeuner. Or, certaines de ses collègues avaient remarqué le manège et s'arrangeaient à tour de rôle pour arpenter le couloir afin d'empêcher leur collègue d'apporter son petit cadeau à sa chouchoute.[62]

In this situation, even the 'normal' delimitations of age are thrown off kilter. Cons remembers an inmate in her forties who had an affair with a

---

[58] Ibid., 31.
[59] Ibid., 187.
[60] Ibid., 189.
[61] Ibid.
[62] Ibid.

young warder and notes, 'C'était pathétique'; these lovers are simply 'pseudo-couples'.[63]

Cons's violent rejection of what she sees as the inappropriate miscegenation of women is not simply a response to the enforced intimacy and lack of privacy within the prison, although this is a significant factor. Rather, we might trace her denunciation back through the abundance of spatial metaphors of openness within her text. For example, she reacts with disgust as letters are slipped through cracks in the cell doors and are read by whoever gets them first; when lavatories are open to view, and when inmates operate metal fishing lines from one cell window to burgle another.[64] Her corporeal boundaries are equally opened: she is forced to sleep on mattresses which bear the stains of their previous occupants; there are traces of grease and hair on the walls behind her bed.[65] Structural fluidity (in terms of spatial organisation and identity) and porosity eventually overwhelm all sense of boundedness; of separately incarcerated and carefully hierarchised, discrete, autonomous identities. That which facilitated a certain freedom within the prison becomes a matrix of discomfort and anxiety. Thus, Cons — who in this situation is able to profit from her already ambiguous situation as former lawyer and educated lover of the classical arts — befriends the governor, but is appalled by proliferating inmate-warder relations.

Lesbian desire thus troubles such powerful binaries as: private / public, order / disorder, closed / open, contained / fluid. Lesbian bodies are, like those of the prostitutes described by Jane Rendell, 'out of place and out of control'; they represent the 'encroachment' of disorder, the creeping contamination of 'porosity, flow and openness' in the 'defining boundaries and identifying and thresholds which are permanent, closed and fixed around women'.[66] Maud Marin notes how, in the prison, prostitutes and lesbians are warehoused in the same wings, constituting as they do a

---

[63] Ibid., 187.
[64] Ibid., 30.
[65] Ibid., 42.
[66] Jane Rendell, *The Pursuit of Pleasure: gender, space and architecture in Regency London* (London: Athlone Press, 2002), 132.

comparable threat.[67] Cons is particularly sensitive to the effects of lesbian desire, berating what she perceives as a loss of control, the unfixing of identities and the troubling of a comfortingly regulated spatio-sexual order. The open and interstitial spaces of modern prisons — 'trop laxistes, trop "cools"'[68] — and the same-sex relations which are enabled by them represent, then, the 'fall' of the (imagined) old-style prison; the nadir of 'l'esprit de la Roquette' and the segregationist ideology of the nineteenth-century prison.[69] Certainly, Marin is aware that for the majority, 'l'homosexualité, c'est l'épouvante'.[70] This notion of horror is crucial in terms of our understanding of the stark elision and disavowal of lesbian identities and desires in prison literature. The process of abjection within these prison narratives is spatially performed and grounded in exclusion. However, as Butler reminds us, that which is cast outside is, 'after all, "inside" the subject as its own founding repudiation'.[71] The hegemony of exogenous heterosexual relationships and identities in the prisons described is effectively perpetuated by 'repetitive performances of hegemonic asymmetrical gender identities and heterosexual desires [which] congeal over time to produce the appearance that [public] spaces [...] are normally or naturally heterosexual spaces'.[72] 'Heterosexual' in-mates gather in the public spaces of the prison to work, to gossip, to eat. Much of their conversation and exchange revolves around the men in their lives: they share information, pass on snippets from the letters received from partners, perhaps even discuss their sexual relations and the more intimate details and concerns of their relationships. The illiterate have the literate transcribe their intimacies, in the form of letters to their loved ones. However, prevalent and pervasive fears of contamination (such as those experienced by the 'reformed lesbian', Sarrazin) or disruption reveal to what extent these heterosexual spaces are processual, vulnerable, defended. As such, the heterosexism we see in these two

---

[67]   Maud Marin, *Le Quartier des maudites* (Paris: J'ai lu, 1999), 160.
[68]   Cons (2000), 257.
[69]   Ibid., 196–7.
[70]   Marin (1999), 160.
[71]   Judith Butler, *Bodies that Matter* (London: Routledge, 1993), 3.
[72]   Valentine (1996), 154.

narratives is 'a spatially constituted discourse that can be interrupted and undermined'.[73] The *queering* of space, then, is performed by 'those who cut into and disrupt the "normality" of heterosexual space by performing their desires in a way that produces (an)other space'.[74] This 'other' space — which challenges the *production* of heterosexual spaces and identities, is abjected by those for whom the disruption of (imagined) borders represents a threat to already fragile identities and spaces.

In this paper I have described how the 'new' prisons of the twentieth century have sought to regulate inmates through both 'architectural layout and the permissible use of space'.[75] However, this emergent space syntax admits of and enables the production of liminal spaces, which in turn enable movement, encounter and exchange. Both Sarrazin and Cons mobilise in their narratives a hegemonic femininity, the binarism of which reflects the stasis and imaginary binarism of the old, panoptical model. We have seen that the normative heterosexual practices intensify, and that these are not imposed externally; they are performed and re-inforced, in all their insecurity, anxiety and inconsistency, internally. 'Issues of mobility and morality'[76] conflate as lesbian desires and ident-ities disrupt (and are abjected by) the hetero-normative spaces of the prison. Heterosexual femininity is reclaimed with virulence not only in response to the processes of infantilisation, the enforced 'intimité dégradante'[77] and the surfeit of 'straight' (pornographic) mythologies which — as the opening quote from Sarrazin revealed — over-signify and constrain the female inmate, but also as a means of circumscribing dissolved and fearful, re-nascent selves. It remains to be seen if the openness of carceral bodies and architectural spaces — what Certeau might call '[les] procédures [...] multiformes, résistantes, rusées et têtues

---

[73]   Ibid., 152.

[74]   Ibid., 148.

[75]   Annie E.A. Bartlett, 'Spatial Order and Psychiatric Disorder', in *Architecture and Order: approaches to social space*, eds Michael Parker Pearson and Colin Richards (London: Routledge, 1994), 192 (178–95).

[76]   Rendell (2002), 56.

[77]   Cons (2000), 18.

[...] qui échappent à la discipline sans être pour autant hors du champ où elle s'exerce'[78] — can be written differently in the future.

Bibliography

Archer, Jeffrey, *A Prison Diary* (Basingstoke and Oxford: Macmillan, 2002), I: *Belmarsh: Hell.*

Bachelard, Gaston, *La Poétique de l'espace* (Paris: Presses Universitaires de France, 1967).

Bartlett, Annie E.A., 'Spatial Order and Psychiatric Disorder', in *Architecture and Order: Approaches to Social Space*, eds Michael Parker Pearson and Colin Richards (London: Routledge, 1994), 178–95.

Butler, Judith, *Bodies that Matter* (London: Routledge, 1993).

——, *Gender Trouble: feminism and the subversion of identity* (London: Routledge, 1990).

Certeau, Michel de, *L'Invention du quotidien* (Paris: Gallimard, 1990), I: *Arts de faire.*

Cons, Elisabeth, *La Boîte à oubli: dix ans à Fleury-Mérogis* (Paris: Lattès, 2000).

Crawley, Amanda, 'Grammatical Fictions: Reading and Writing the Self in Prison', *French Cultural Studies*, Vol. 12, Part 3: 36 (October 2001), 303–18.

Demonchy, Christian, 'Généalogie de la prison moderne', http://www.insite.fr/interdit/2001aout/prison2b.htm.

Fairweather, Leslie, 'Prison Design in the Twentieth Century', in *Prison Architecture: policy, design and experience*, eds Leslie Fairweather and Seán McConville (Oxford: Architectural Press, 2002), 24–39.

Foucault, Michel, *Surveiller et punir: naissance de la prison* (1975; Paris: Gallimard, 1994).

Goffman, Erving, *Asylums: essays on the social situation of mental patients and other inmates* (Harmondsworth: Penguin, 1961).

---

[78]   Certeau (1991), 146.

Hillier, Bill, *Space is the Machine: a configurational theory of architecture* (Cambridge: Cambridge University Press, 1999).

Hillier, Bill and J. Hanson, *The Social Logic of Space* (Cambridge: Cambridge University Press, 1984)

Markus, Thomas A., *Buildings and Power: freedom and control in the origin of modern building types* (London: Routledge, 1993).

Morris, Meaghan, 'Great Moments in Social Climbing: King Kong and the human fly', in *Sexuality and Space*, ed. Beatriz Colomina (Princeton: Princeton Architectural Press, 1992).

Petit, Jacques-Guy, Claude Faugeron and Michel Pierre, *Histoire des prisons en France, 1789–2000* (Toulouse: Éditions Privat, 2002).

Rendell, Jane, *The Pursuit of Pleasure: gender, space and architecture in Regency London* (London: Athlone Press, 2002).

Sarrazin, Albertine, *Romans, lettres et poèmes : L'Astragale, la Cavale, la Traversière* (Paris: Jean-Jacques Pauvert, 1967).

——, *La Cavale*, in *Romans, lettres et poèmes* (Paris: Jean-Jacques Pauvert, 1967).

——, *Biftons de prison* (Paris: Jean-Jacques Pauvert, 1977).

Valentine, Gill, '(Re)negotiating the Heterosexual Street: Lesbian productions of space', in *BodySpace: destabilizing geographies of gender and sexuality*, ed. Nancy Duncan (London: Routledge, 1996).

The Pleasures of Discovery: Representations of Queer Space by Brassaï and Colette

Frances E. Hutchins
Northwestern University, USA

From the time that Diderot's Suzanne was subjected to the convent, jail, and, finally, death, proto-lesbian figures in French literature followed suit, putting on sensationalistic displays of excessive sexuality and dying tragically in novel after novel. As a literary character, the lesbian remained, for the most part, flat, two-dimensional, enclosed in a world of her own, described in pornography and cautionary tales. By the 1930s, however, new modes of representing queer female sexuality were added to this familiar trope, ones in which the aesthetic distance traditionally employed in the construction of lesbians was rejected by writers and artists such as Colette and Brassaï, who sought to represent the lesbian both through and from within her own world, that is to say, in three-dimensional queer space.

In this chapter, I compare photographs by Brassaï of lesbian bars and Colette's novel *Le Pur et l'Impur*, both of which treat queer space, specifically interior spaces such as bars and other meeting points, as secret places that warrant discovery and explanation for the outside world. They consider the spaces as sites of ethnographic interest and their inhabitants as foreign species and in doing so produce what resembles a literary ethnography of their contemporary lesbian culture. My comparison endeavours to determine the significance of this kind of narration of queer space to the evolution of the trope of the lesbian and consider the problematic position of the participant observer as embodied by Colette and Brassaï.

In 1932, Colette first published *Ces plaisirs*, a novel that includes sketches of lesbian life in Paris around the turn of the century, a scene that Colette was part of for a few years. In the same year, Hungarian photographer Brassaï documented his vision of queer nightlife in Paris, taking photographs at women's bars and queer dancehalls. These examples of cultural production not only provide compelling evidence of the way representation of lesbians was beginning to shift in the 1930s, but also the way such representations continued to resonate for years to come. Colette revised and added to *Ces plasirs*, publishing the results as *Le Pur et l'Impur* in 1941. Several of Brassaï's Monocle photographs were published in 1934 in a provocatively titled edition *Voluptés de Paris*. These, along with several more were reissued in the 1976 retrospective collection *Le Paris secret des années 30*.

As a photographer, Brassaï's position as spectator and outsider would have been conspicuous, especially in the age of the cumbersome camera and indiscreet magnesium flash. Colette, however, had the writer's privilege of unobtrusiveness, in addition to the fact that she was a woman among women and the lover of a known lesbian. However, Brassaï the photographer's or Colette the writer's literal intrusion into queer space is of less concern than the textual embodiment of that intrusion, which is complicated by the autobiographical element in the writings in both cases. In the case of Brassaï, queer subjects are exoticised but at the same time made legible through hetero-normative frameworks, a structure that I refer to as queer exoticism. In the case of Brassaï, the anxieties of the outsider make this contradiction in representation not only possible but also necessary. The Colette of *Le Pur et l'Impur* inscribes herself as a native informant in a way that Brassaï could not. Her privileged status as a former insider compromises her status as outside observer. Reading these two texts together allows for an examination of the shift in lesbian representation from the inside and the outside. Some of the questions that I attempt to answer are: Why and how does Brassaï use the trope of queer exoticism and why and how does Colette use and / or resist the use of it? How does Brassaï inscribe himself inside queer space (in which he did not belong), and how does Colette inscribe herself inside queer space (in which she did, perhaps, belong)? And finally, how do Brassaï and Colette's respective self-inscriptions inform their narration of queer subjects? From their specific positions, what parts of queer culture are visible to them, what do they choose to narrate, and what do they ignore?

Brassaï: 'the eye of Paris'

Brassaï's representation of lesbian subjects is twofold: photographic and textual. I will therefore consider the technology of photography as a representational art, particularly Brassaï's belief in photography as a truth-telling art, as well as his narration of the images he produced. Brassaï's interest in representing Paris through photography prompted Henry Miller to write an essay portraying Brassaï as 'the eye of Paris.'[1] This moniker, which would follow Brassaï for the rest of his career, describes Brassaï's role as an artist as that of an observer.[2] Brassaï's photographs were often thought to be candid, but were actually posed. To create convincing photographs, Brassaï relied upon the complicity of the subject. Many of the situational photographs were staged scenes in which the subject, according to Anne Tucker, 'knew *that* he or she was being photographed, but not exactly *when.*'[3] This complicity was not a given. Tucker quotes Brassaï as saying, 'I had to make friends — buy drinks. Technically, also, it was difficult. I couldn't become invisible.'[4] Once he made it inside, his presence did not go unnoticed. Magnesium flash powder, a wooden tripod, and a photographic assistant made it hard for Brassaï to blend in to his surroundings.[5] For Tucker, the staging of these photographs was not only a technical necessity, but also a part of Brassaï's larger project as an artist: 'Brassaï had a particular picture, or a particular type of picture, in mind for his grand survey of Parisian life.'[6] Part of that grand survey was queer nightlife, which he considered to be perverted but fascinating. In documenting this life, Brassaï perpetrated the trope of queer exoticism and by the same token opened the door to a different kind of lesbian representation.

---

[1] Anne Wilkes Tucker, *The Eye of Paris* (Houston: The Museum of Fine Arts, Houston, 1999), 43.

[2] For example, the 1999 retrospective curated by Anne Wilkes Tucker, of the Houston Museum of Fine Arts, entitled 'Brassaï: The Eye of Paris', focused on the perception that Brassaï had a privileged view of the city.

[3] Ibid., 39.

[4] Ibid., 40.

[5] Ibid., 39.

[6] Ibid., 40.

Brassaï photographs and describes two specifically queer female spaces: *Le Monocle*, a women's bar, and the *bal musette*[7] at Montagne Sainte-Geneviève, which was for queers of all genders. In this section of the chapter, I examine the text and the photos for the Monocle and then comment on one photo from the *bal musette*. I will focus on Brassaï's interpretations of the photos he took and consider his interest in the *premier regard*.

As in the other chapters of *Paris secret*, Brassaï freely admits his status as intruder in the queer nightclubs and cabarets that he visits, but he wants readers to feel that he is a credible source. In the accompanying text, he indicates that he is still well informed so many years later, identifying lesbian bars that were popular at the time of publication. In 1932, Brassaï entered the Monocle under the protection of 'la grosse Claude, une habituée'.[8] This characterises his usual way of penetrating off-limits spaces—gaining a friend on the inside and being introduced as 'un ami'. In some cases, this masquerade would have been more believable, but at the Monocle, there is no chance that Brassaï will be mistaken for 'une amie'. At *Le Monocle* and the *bal musette*, the contradiction inherent in Brassaï's belief in photography as a truth recording mechanism, coupled with his willingness to construct seemingly candid scenarios, comes to the fore.

In several books on the subject of photography, Brassaï expresses his idea of the position of the photographer. 'L'œil photographique enregistre tout ce qui est vrai', begins his *Images de Caméra*.[9] At some points in his writing, Brassaï characterises the photographer as 'an impartial witness and faithful chronicler', renouncing his 'je', while at other times he recognises the way the artist implicates himself in his art.[10] Especially when photographing human subjects, he notes:

---

[7]   'popular dance hall'.
[8]   Brassaï, *Le Paris secret des années 30* (Paris: Gallimard, 1976), 152 (hereafter *Paris secret*).
[9]   'The photographic eye records all that is true'. *Brassaï présente images de caméra* (Paris: Hachette, 1964), epigraph.
[10]   Ibid, 19. Brassaï, *Camera in Paris* (London: The Focal Press, 1949), 7 (hereafter *Camera*).

> For something strange has happened to him [the photographer]: the more scrupulously he has respected the independence and autonomy of his subject, and the closer he has gone towards it instead of bringing it nearer to himself, the more completely has his own personality become incorporated in his pictures.[11]

Thinking about the imbrications of photographer and subject and the notion of constructed realism leads me to question Brassaï's position as intruder. At the time of its taking, the photograph is evidence of lived experience or of existence. Later the photograph serves as artefact—a durable proof of what happened or what was, but one that is open to infinite interpretations. In the case of his queer subjects, Brassaï proffers a Paris that was unknown even to most Parisians of the time the photographs were taken. In regards to Brassaï's photographs from the 1930s, something Brassaï wrote in *Camera in Paris* now seems appropriate. The photographer, he says, '*gives semblance of durability* to the brief moments captured in the flight of time.'[12] The durability of these moments helps construct a framing fiction around their social relevance. The frame of constructed social reality is furthered by the descriptive narrative that Brassaï wrote to accompany these photographs forty years after they were taken.

Le Paris secret des années 30 was published by Gallimard in 1976 with the cooperation of Brassaï, who provided the introduction and accompanying text for the photographs. In the introduction to this collection, Brassaï claims that he was drawn to photography out of 'le désir de traduire en images tout ce qui m'émerveillait dans ce Paris nocturne.'[13] Brassaï's process of moving from desire to document and later to description is framed by his concept of translation (*traduire en images*), not representation. This conception complicates the question of the possibility of representation by implying that Brassaï recognises from the outset that there is something illegible or unreadable in his subjects. In

---

[11]   *Camera*, 19.
[12]   Ibid., emphasis mine.
[13]   *Paris Secret*, 5.

the case of the photographs of queer nightlife, Brassaï's explicit textual framing of the photographs highlights his concern about illegibility.

In *Paris secret*, there are fourteen photographs of queer nightlife, and they are grouped into a section called 'Sodome et Gomorrhe', a reference not to the biblical account of these cities but to Marcel Proust's adoption of them as references to male and female homosexuality, respectively.[14] The photographs are not explicated individually; instead they are accompanied by six pages of anecdotes about Brassaï's experiences (as an outside observer, of course) in gay and lesbian bars of the 1930s. Both the arrangement of the photographs and the text that he wrote to accompany them are of interest to me. Of the fourteen photographs, the five from the Monocle are first. They are admittedly some of the more striking of the photographs, as they feature closely cropped portraits as well as bar and dance floor shots. These photographs are first in the series and get the most lines of text. They require a little more explanation, and in looking at both the pictures and the text we see why. The central problem with Brassaï's concept of translation into images is that he does not let the images alone function as translation, as his initial statement suggests. He fears that without an explanatory metatext, the photographs are likely to be misread, a point that he repeatedly stresses throughout the book. In the case of his individual portraits of butches, Brassaï was concerned about misreading. He uses the narrative to correct this.

Brassaï's narration is characterised by a tendency to focus on the exotic nature of the spaces he photographed. Exoticisation is his primary method of translation; he tries to make the subject matter more approachable by pointing out how different it is from what the readers will be used to seeing. The kind of translation, it turns out, that Brassaï did in the case of the photographs in 'Sodome et Gomorrhe' deploys queer exoticism exactly as his predecessors did — attempting to make sense of the illegible nature of queerness by underlining the very differ-

---

[14]   Many of these photographs had appeared before in various formats, most notably in the 1934 collection *Voluptés de Paris*, in which two photographs from the *Le Monocle* appear. Never before had these fourteen photographs been grouped together.

ence that makes it illegible. In his tidy glossing of his own photographs, Brassaï often creates more questions than he answers.

By directing the reading, Brassaï attempts to control the misreading of the *premier regard*. This kind of misreading is ultimately allowed because it is correctable. From Brassaï's point of view, a less desirable misreading might be to find familiarity in the photographs. The potential for misreading is illustrated by the break between text and photographs in the first part of this chapter. Brassaï's textual introduction that builds up to the first photographs in 'Sodome et Gomorrhe' begins on a page with no photograph. The sentence beginning just before the page break describes the inhabitants of *Le Monocle*: 'si parfaitement masculine qu'on.'[15]

The page turn reveals not the completion of that sentence but two full-page photographs—one of people dancing and the second a portrait of two people seated at a bar table. The next two pages are portraits of individuals, both so perfectly masculine. A final turn of the page reveals the completion of the phrase 'si parfaitement masculine qu'on' to be 'les prenait au premier regard pour des jeunes gens.'[16] Brassaï's use of the gender neutral *gens* here is interesting. He doesn't have to say *what* they are, just that your first reading will be incorrect. It is true that at first glance these subjects *could* be read as young men. The titles are not revealing, either. In the case of the first two photographs, the titles *Au Monocle, blvd. Edgar Quinet, à Montparnasse (vers 1932)* and *Au Monocle, Un couple (vers 1932)*, do not reveal the gender of the subjects. The titles of the second two, *Jeune invertie,* invokes the medico-sexological discourse of the era, revealing the 'true' gender of the subjects, but these would not be taken in at first glance, because all the titles are found in the back matter of the book, not in the accompanying text. Both in the seemingly arbitrary page break and the deliberate exclusion of descriptive titles from immediate context, Brassaï invites readers to take part in the misreading of the *premier regard*. This tactic, if

[15]   *Paris Secret*, 157.
[16]   Ibid., 162.

it works, reinforces Brassaï's position as informant, for in the following text, he reveals himself to be the bearer of the truth about these women.

The language that Brassaï uses to describe the Monocle exemplifies his model of translation through exoticisation. Brassaï romanticises these sites of transgression, calling them 'haut lieu(x) de Gomorrhe', 'temples d'amour saphique', and 'somptueuses boîtes'.[17] This exaggerated tribute may describe the salons of Renée Vivien (which Brassaï did not photograph) but not the simple bars or dance halls that he did infiltrate.

For Brassaï, the Monocle held the allure of the imaginary, even the legendary. In the *premier regard,* he sees only the exterior of these 'femmes en garçonnes, en cheftaines, en hommasses, en gendarmes'.[18] The hairstyles worn by the patrons are not merely short; they have sacrificed their hair to the altar of Sappho and now look like Titus or Joan of Arc.[19] Brassaï's anxious desire to set queer spaces and their inhabitants apart, to exoticise them, is crucial to his ability to direct his reader's interaction with the photographs. He attributes to the subjects of his photographs a sense of mourning for incomplete masculinity. As Judith Halberstam pointed out in a 2003 conference paper, what Brassaï misses in the first look is that his subjects are not mourning at all.[20]

A more serious misreading is Brassaï's incorrect assertion that at the Monocle, 'toutes étaient habillées en homme', when his own photographs show several women wearing dresses.[21] Brassaï focuses his text and his camera on the outward masculine trappings that, for him, belie a lack of masculine interiority in the women he photographs. So fixed is his gaze on what he finds exotic that he ignores, both textually and photographically, many potential queer subjects, and guides the reader to do so as well.

At this point I will move away from Brassaï's misreadings of his own photographs and examine the photographs themselves. The first, 'Au

17 Ibid., 157.
18 Ibid., 162.
19 Ibid.
20 Judith Halberstam, 'Hidden Worlds: photography and subcultural lives', MLA Convention, San Diego, California (29 December 2003).
21 *Paris Secret,* 157.

monocle, Un couple, vers 1932' is a portrait of two people sitting at a table. The subject on the left is wearing a dress that dips in the front. She rests her chin in her right hand and gazes out of the frame. Her mouth is matte and her eyebrows are drawn on long and thin. Her pin-curled hair frames her face in soft waves. Beside her, her companion looks more sombre in a coat and tie, but a rumpled pocket square, loosened tie, and unbuttoned top button tell of a night of dancing (or other strenuous activity). The heavily pomaded hair, however, has managed to stay in place. Her gaze, for this is, presumably, a woman (in context) is also directed out of the frame. From the way that this photograph is positioned in the 1976 collection, they appear to be watching the dancers to the left, but this is revealed as fiction by the fact that the woman wearing the dress is in both pictures. The two women's bodies overlap slightly, an intimate pose. But a pose it is, a construction by Brassaï of what a lesbian couple looks like.

In *Paris Secret*, individual portraits of two women in suits follow the photograph of the couple, what I will call butch portraits. These are not daintily masculine suits like the one Colette wore when she played the *garçon*. These are not the women who cut their hair short like those in Victor Margueritte's *La Garçonne*. These are two women who look like men, enough so that they are often mistaken for men upon first glance, a fact that Brassaï himself notes in his accompanying text. This, and nothing else, makes them worthy of being photographed for individual portraits. If Susan Sontag's assertion that 'to photograph is to confer importance' is true, then it is to these women that Brassaï gives the most queer currency.[22] The most important thing about these two photos is evident, but not obvious. In choosing these women as individual subjects, he chose *not* to take individual portraits of the women in dresses who were also at the bar. For Brassaï, it is the exotic nature of butch masculinity that makes the subject worth photographing.[23]

The subject of the first photograph lifts a glass of Lanson Brut champagne to her unsmiling, bare lips. She wears a large metal ring on

---

[22]   Susan Sontag, *On Photography* (New York: Picador, 1973), 28.

[23]   It is of note, perhaps, that the only other individual portraits of women in *Paris secret* are of prostitutes.

her ring finger and a wristwatch peeks through the sleeve of her tuxedo jacket. Her other hand holds a cigarette. She peers intensely out of the frame. The second subject is young and has the appearance of an adolescnt boy playing dress up. Her tux jacket features pointed lapels and a floppy bow tie. With a cigarette in her right hand, her left casually in her pocket, her pose is cocky and cavalier. She, too, looks out of the frame. To look out of frame is to pose, to acknowledge the photographer and / or audience, but not to engage. Were these two Monocle patrons chosen for their ability to create an illusion of true masculinity, to create gender confusion, thereby coding the picture as queer? This tactic lays bare the way in which femme invisibility is a key element of queer exoticism.

I suggest that Brassaï's misreading of his own work is rooted in his inability to see the women who do not appear exotic, that is, who are not dressed *en homme*. The exotic and strange for him are the 'inverties' who attempt to replicate masculinity, and as he sees it, fail. Leaving the patrons of the Monocle who are dressed in a 'feminine' way out of his narrative allows Brassaï to take another important step toward making queerness legible through its very illegibility.

In the end, Brassaï does seem to return to his earlier awareness of his status as outsider and the impossibility of his desire, even his desire to know and interpret, the problems inherent in translation. He relates that sometimes women will come into the bar and pose as lesbians in order to make a little extra money. This never works, he says, because the regulars can always see through the act. Only the authentic inhabitants of the space have the power to 'démasques... fausses lesbiennes au premier regard'.[24] Unlike the assumed blindness of the outsider's *premier regard*, the insider's first look reveals everything. By assigning the power of being able to read identity to the insider, Brassaï again brings to the fore his position as an outsider, without directly admitting to it. His reluctance to candidly transcribe his status at the Monocle is interesting, considering certain signifiers of his position, including his 'true' masculinity (real or perceived), his demeanour (non-participation in dancing, for example), and, of course, his camera.

---

[24]   '...unmask fake lesbians at first glance'. *Paris Secret,* 162.

It is with his camera that he attempts to capture the *premier regard*. In this way, the first look can be relived infinitely, open to infinite interpretations and understandings, and he, as well as his readers, can be spared the blindness of the first look. This is his point of intrusion, or as he says numerous times in the text, penetration. It is not just curiosity that brings him to the Monocle, but, as Colette would say, 'devoir profess-ionnel'.

At the Monocle, Brassaï seems quite assured of both his own masculinity and the lack of masculinity in the women *en homme*. He reads these pictures, this experience, with no apparent complication and is comfortable, if not over-confident, writing about these women. I propose that this is because, although focusing on the exotic nature of the *femme en homme*, he finds such normalcy in the butch / femme binary that he does not even mention the women who are very obviously dressed *en femme*.

At *Le bal de la Sainte-Geneviève*, he does not find this same kind of familiarity. Missing from this working-class venue are the smartly dressed butches with their smoking noirs, cigarettes, and champagne. At this venue Brassaï's method of exoticising and then familiarising will not work. Still intent on translating for his audience, he instead reads familiarity onto this scene by comparing it to every other *bal musette* that he has visited, apart from the fact that women were dancing with women and men with men. In this section there are no references to the mythical past: no Sappho, Joan of Arc, or Titus. This is no 'haut lieu de Gomorrhe'. The two women stare unabashedly, almost blankly, into the camera, as do the men dancing behind them. This photograph is not a portrait; it is not framed like the others. It is cropped just to show these women. About this fascinating picture, these two women dressed as women, he says nothing. It is called simply, 'Le bal des invertis au bal de la Montagne-Sainte-Geneviève.' In this case, I believe Brassaï has succeeded in 'translating into images' his amazement by saying nothing at all, while at the same time conceding the potential for failure in translation.

Colette: 'professional obligation'

In the case of Colette, the problem of lesbian representation lies not in her outsider status, as is the case with Brassaï. Her narration is complicated by her position inside queer space, which she equivocates from the outset. In the opening pages of *Le Pur et l'Impur*, Colette literally builds the space with her language, creating the image of an opium den that she visits. The opium den is often invoked as a romanticised site of transgression in the Orientalist imagination, but even in the very first sentence of her novel, Colette will not allow it to remain as such. 'En haut d'une maison neuve, on m'ouvrit un atelier vaste comme une halle, pourvu d'une large galerie mi-hauteur, tendu de ces broderies de Chine que la Chine exécute pour l'Occident.'[25] The house is new, not old or romantically falling into disrepair. The wall hangings are oriental, but not authentic. The made-for-export Orientalism condemns the *fumerie* as a space of false exoticism.

In using this space as the opening of the novel that is an exploration of queer space and its inhabitants, Colette acknowledges the history of the making legible of queerness through the trope of exoticism. She is neither abandoning nor rejecting the trope, but is instead using it on her own terms. I argue that Colette is quoting the trope of queer exoticism, not employing it in earnest. Colette's acknowledgement of authenticity manqué draws a distinction between her appropriation of the trope of exoticism and that of her literary predecessors, and also of Brassaï. This moment allows me to draw an important distinction between Colette and Brassaï, who, as I have shown, employs the trope of queer exoticism without irony.

Colette's visit to the opium den functions as a kind of *apologia* for the rest of the work. Just as Brassaï does in his introduction, Colette attempts to justify her intrusions and set herself apart from the *habitués*. She tells a writer she meets there that she has come to the *fumerie* not 'en curieuse' but instead 'par devoir professionnel'. To her acquaintance, this means that she is unable to simply be there for the experience; she cannot

---

[25]   Colette, *Le Pur et l'Impur* (Paris: Hachette, 1979), 9.

'goûter ce luxe'.[26] Coming 'en curieuse' would indicate that Colette entered the space out of a pure, specific desire for it. Instead, she represents her coming as already mitigated by an intended end product.

This excuse for being present works well enough for the opium den, where the narrator does not smoke opium, but it becomes more complicated when Colette forays into specifically queer space—the women's bars that so fascinated Brassaï. Unlike Brassaï, Colette's position of the participant-observer shifts when she enters. She is no longer there *par devoir professionnel.* Her place in these spaces is instead, as a friend tells her, 'une place de spectateur, une de ces places de choix d'où le spectateur, s'il s'enivre, a le droit de s'élancer pour rejoindre [...] la figuration active.'[27]

This is not to say that the narrator accepts or acknowledges this shift, or that she always participates. In fact, she begins this section by asserting that queer female sexuality of her époque was not the feminine equivalent of queer male sexuality, a durable institution. What she sees, especially in the women of the clubs and bars, is not a durable institution, but women groping at fictional group identities. Especially objectionable to her are the women who (almost) dress and act as men, even herself. She mocks the photographs of her former self, 'Elles ne m'abusèrent pas longtemps, ces images photographiques où je porte col droit, régate, un petit veston sur une jupe plate, une cigarette fumante entre deux doigts'.[28] In these photos of herself *en garçonne,* (or as she says, 'singeant le garçon') Colette sees none of her interiority.[29] The clothes and accessories that make her seem masculine are not the root of the masculine streak that she strongly believes she has. Her discourse closely resembles that of Brassaï when she speaks of her 'chevelure sacrifiée', but unlike Brassaï, who sees only masculinity *manqué* behind the clothes, Colette sees the outer trappings of masculinity as so much artifice.

She spares only one member of this circle from her disdain, and it is here that her position clearly shifts from observer to participant. When

26   Ibid., 10.
27   Ibid., 54–55.
28   Ibid., 55.
29   Ibid., 56.

she writes about the woman she calls 'la Chevalière', a character generally assumed to be her former lover, Missy, she takes an almost mournful tone. Is her assessment of 'la plus connue — la plus méconnue — d'entre elles', wrapped up in the specificity of intimate knowledge?[30] Is 'la Chevalière' set apart from the rest of these 'femmes-hommes', or is the distinction Colette makes an imagined, desired difference? To begin to answer this question I argue that at this moment in the text Colette is very much inside queer space. While writing about this woman, Colette becomes actively queer: 'La séduction qui émane d'un être au sexe incertain ou dissimulé est puissante.'[31] Colette is seduced. In this case she is not invading queer space—she is being invaded by one of its inhabitants.

At this place in the text, she reluctantly hints at a kind of interiority that Brassaï does not look for in his queer subjects, or which, even if he did, he would not be able to find. Colette relates an encounter la Chevalière had with a presumptuous young woman who told her 'Viens, je vais te découvrir à toi-même', to which la Chevalière replies: 'Je ne suis ni cela, ni, hélas ! autre chose [...] Ce qui me manque ne se trouve pas en le cherchant.'[32]

For Colette, the *premier regard* is not the only site of misreading. Even from her position as participant-observer, Colette acknowledges the impossibility of representation. For her, this impossibility lies in an essentialist notion of gender and sexuality, which in her mind is often taken for granted as presented in superficial manifestations such as manner of dress. In her position as desired and desiring in queer space, especially in the passages on 'la Chevalière', Colette compromises her *devoir professionnel*. In doing so she moves toward conscious self-inscription.

It is in a final acknowledgement of the impossibility of representation that Colette's work intersects with Brassaï's. Their projects are different in that Brassaï exoticises while simultaneously attempting to read the exotic through frameworks of familiarity; Colette notes the exotic, but

30   Ibid., 57.
31   Ibid., 62.
32   Ibid., 63.

exposes its falseness. She eschews the familiar for the interior, and in the end, admits that even that cannot be found by searching for it. Colette, in rejecting the exoticisation of queerness, valorises the normalcy of gender variation. Brassaï employs the trope of queer exoticism to code his queer subjects as exotic, that is, outside of the sphere of the normal, and by the same token, asserts the power of the observer as interpreter. This tactic is used with the intention of reinforcing the observer's position of normalcy, but often unwittingly undermines the paradigm of the normal. Brassaï's use of queer exoticism assures the reader that he sees certain kinds of queerness, and that queerness that is potentially more subversive, such as queer female expressions of femininity, remains hidden in plain sight.

Bibliography

Brassaï, *Camera in Paris* (London: The Focal Press, 1949).

——, *Le Paris secret des années 30* (Paris: Gallimard, 1976).

Colette, *Le Pur et l'impur* (Paris: Hachette, 1979).

Diderot, Denis, *La Religieuse*, ed. Heather Lloyd (London: Bristol Classical Press, 2000).

Sontag, Susan, *On Photography* (New York: Picador, 1973).

Tucker, Anne Wilkes, *The Eye of Paris* (Houston: The Museum of Fine Arts, 1999).

Elsie de Wolfe, Natalie Clifford Barney, and the Lure of Versailles: Picturesque Spectres and Conservative Aesthetics of Female Homoeroticism

Sheila Crane
University of California, Santa Cruz

> After all, that is the secret of Europe's fascination for us Americans– the ever-present suggestion of permanence. We feel that houses and gardens were planned and built for centuries, not for the passing pleasure of one brief lifetime. We people them with ghosts that please us, and make histories for them that are always romantic and filled with happiness.
>
> (Elsie de Wolfe, *The House in Good Taste*, 293)

Although the work of interior designer Elsie de Wolfe has only recently begun to receive sustained, critical attention, the literary salon that Natalie Clifford Barney orchestrated in Paris in the 1920s and 1930s has become a standard point of reference for histories of lesbian culture, Francophone or otherwise. Whereas de Wolfe migrated between high society circles in France and New York around the turn of the century, Barney set up permanent residence in Paris. While Barney self-consciously fashioned her salon at 20, rue Jacob, as a key site within the literary and artistic topography of the Left Bank, de Wolfe chose a dramatically different location for her French sojourn, rejecting the capital in favour of Versailles where she extensively renovated her shared residence, the Villa Trianon. French society allowed both de Wolfe and Barney to distance themselves somewhat from family and familiar social conventions. At the same time, French culture provided legible signs of distinction that might sufficiently cloak their projects in the guise of acceptability. In this context, de Wolfe and Barney's status as American expatriates and their ample personal wealth gave them unusual latitude to pursue their creative interests.

Recent work on women artists and writers in early twentieth-century Paris has productively analysed how modern lesbian identities were variously consolidated through literary production, visual representation, and performance.[1] However, these studies have largely overlooked the ways in which buildings and landscape were actively employed to imagine and enact individual and communal identities. Both Elsie de Wolfe and Natalie Clifford Barney explicitly understood their living environments as direct expressions of self and as ideal visions of communal identity. As Elsie de Wolfe observed in the opening pages of the handbook to interior design she published in 1913, *The House in Good Taste*, 'you will express yourself in your home, whether you want to or not.'[2] By examining how de Wolfe and Barney manipulated and re-imagined their surroundings, I aim here to shift the frame of analysis to specifically spatial practices.

The aesthetic investments de Wolfe and Barney articulated through the manipulation of their own residences provided an effective language through which to imagine alternative conceptions of domesticity and identity. Despite the geographical distance between their residences, de Wolfe and Barney embraced elements of the picturesque aesthetic linked

---

[1]   Shari Benstock's ground breaking study, *Women of the Left Bank: Paris, 1900–1940* (Austin: University of Texas Press, 1986) has been followed by numerous studies, including Whitney Chadwick and Tirza True Latimer, *The Modern Woman Revisited: Paris between the wars* (New Brunswick, NJ and London: Rutgers University Press, 2003); Laura Doan, *Fashioning Sapphism: the origins of a modern English lesbian culture* (New York: Columbia University Press, 2001); Whitney Chadwick, *Amazons in the Drawing Room: the art of Romaine Brooks* (Berkeley: University of California Press; Washington D.C.: National Museum of Women in the Arts, 2000); and Bridget Elliot, 'Performing the Picture or Painting the Other: Romaine Brooks, Gluck, and the question of decadence in 1923', in *Women Artists and Modernism*, ed. Katy Deepwell (Manchester and New York: Manchester University Press, 1998).

[2]   Elsie de Wolfe, *The House in Good Taste* (New York: The Century Co., 1913); reprint with preface by Hutton Wilkinson (New York: Rizzoli, 2004), 15. I am grateful to Gabrielle Esperdy who first suggested there might be a connection between the aesthetics of Barney's salon and the Versailles obsession of de Wolfe.

more or less overtly to Versailles and to the figure of Marie-Antoinette. For both women, overt revivals of seventeenth and eighteenth-century aesthetics as well as fantasies about their associated social structures encouraged their investment in imagined pasts linked to the French court and aristocracy. Such identifications with *ancien régime* culture have alternatively been embraced as potentially libratory strategies for constructing modern lesbian identity or criticised as excessively reactionary forms of elitism.[3] I want to emphasise instead the intersecting conservative implications and erotic possibilities that were simultaneously embedded in de Wolfe and Barney's re-articulations of their living environments.

Housing Ideals

In a fresco painted by the French illustrator and artist Étienne Drian in the library of the Villa Trianon, Elsie de Wolfe was depicted leaping across the Atlantic, her coat tails flying and her trusty dog in tow behind her.[4]

[3] Terry Castle, for one, argued that 'there is something bizarrely liberating, if not revolutionary, about the transmogrification of Marie-Antoinette into lesbian heroine.' Terry Castle, *The Apparitional Lesbian: female homosexuality and modern culture* (New York: Columbia University Press, 1993), 148. By contrast, accounts of de Wolfe and Barney have emphasised the elitist assumptions of their social, literary, and decorative projects. See Penny Sparke, 'The "Ideal" and the "Real" Interior in Elsie de Wolfe's *The House in Good Taste* of 1913', *Journal of Design History* 16: 1 (2003), 63–76; Chadwick (2000), 10–39; Karla Jay, 'Introduction', in Natalie Clifford Barney, *A Perilous Advantage: the best of Natalie Clifford Barney*, tr. Anna Livia (Norwich, VT: New Victoria Publishers, 1992).

[4] Étienne Drian worked as an illustrator for women's fashion magazines in France, including the *Journal des Dames et des Modes*. His contributions to the renovation of the Villa Trianon thus underscored the intimate connections between fashion, style, decoration, and identity that de Wolfe was interested in asserting in her own house and in promoting through her writings on interior decoration. For discussion of Drian's work, see Laura Casalis, *Parisian fashion, from the Journal des Dames et des Modes*, 1913–1914 (New York: Rizzoli, 1980). De Wolfe herself later observed that 'Drian, the French painter, has told in fresco what

Floating on the ceiling of the library, this image vividly dramatised de Wolfe's active appropriation of French culture. Suspended between North American and European continents, de Wolfe appeared to link two worlds even as she was caught between them. When de Wolfe and Elisabeth Marbury purchased the Villa Trianon in 1906, both women were in fact part of an elite circle of Americans living in New York who spent significant time abroad. In this context, direct knowledge of French culture was an essential marker of social status. Known to their contemporaries as 'the Bachelors', de Wolfe and Marbury established their first residence together in 1887, in New York City in the fashionable neighbourhood of Irving Park.[5] At that time, de Wolfe and Marbury were prominent figures in the theatrical scene and active members of New York high society, de Wolfe a fashionable actress and Marbury a powerful theatrical agent representing American and European authors as a pioneering liaison between stages on either side of the Atlantic. Around the turn of the century, de Wolfe abandoned her theatrical career, redirecting her investments in fashion and drama towards interior design.[6]

By adopting this new role, de Wolfe seemed to uncritically absorb a conventional equation of femininity with domesticity and the interior. In fact, the mural on the library ceiling was a product of de Wolfe's active reclaiming of the interior as a distinctly female space. In this respect, the design of the library in the Villa Trianon, like elements of de Wolfe's experiments in interior design more broadly speaking, was directly influenced by Edith Wharton's interventions at The Mount, her residence

---

[the Villa Trianon] has meant to me.' Elsie de Wolfe, *After All* (New York and London: Harper and Brothers, 1935), 148.

[5] Their residence on East 17th Street and Irving Place had formerly been the home of Washington Irving. See de Wolfe (1935), 83–97; and Elsie de Wolfe (2004), 21–27.

[6] During her acting career, de Wolfe was known as much for the striking gowns she wore as for the roles that she performed. Throughout her life, as photographs formerly in the collections of the Elsie de Wolfe Foundation attest, de Wolfe sat for portraits that echoed the conventions of fashion and celebrity photography. I am grateful to Hutton Wilkinson, President of the Elsie de Wolfe Foundation, for giving me access to these and other images from the Foundation's collection.

in Lennox, Massachusetts, and by her 1897 publication, *The Decoration of Houses*.[7] Vanessa Chase has argued that Wharton's library at the Mount, modelled on Louis XVI's library at Versailles, attempted to neutralise the conventional coding of the library in the late nineteenth century as a masculine space in order to create a model of domesticity predicated on greater equality between the sexes.[8] By contrast, de Wolfe's own portrait emblazoned on the ceiling of the library announced her bold insertion of self into a space habitually perceived as a male bastion and thus signalled de Wolfe's more radical engendering of the house as a specifically female province devoid of masculine referents.

In her reminiscences of their acquisition of the Villa Trianon, Elisabeth Marbury recounted that she and de Wolfe 'had decided that Versailles was the one spot on earth where [they] desired to locate.'[9] In the 1890s, the sleepy town of Versailles had once again become fashionable, thanks in part to several high-profile new residents who had relocated there, including Robert de Montesquiou. The artistic gatherings de Montesquiou and Gabriel Yturri hosted there not only encouraged rival events but also signalled a broader elite retreat from Paris, particularly among wealthy Americans, and an accompanying embrace of Versailles' royal past.[10]

---

[7]   Edith Wharton and Ogden Codman, Jr., *The Decoration of Houses* (New York: Charles Scribner's Sons, 1897). De Wolfe not only used this publication as a template for her 1913 *The House in Good Taste*, but she was also inspired by Wharton and Boston architect Codman's interest in eighteenth-century furnishings. In 1910 De Wolfe collaborated with Codman on the renovation of a brownstone row house on East Seventy-first Street in New York City into a model showroom. See Jane S. Smith, *Elsie de Wolfe: a life in the high style* (New York: Atheneum, 1982), 131–32; de Wolfe (1935), 124–6.

[8]   Vanessa Chase, 'Edith Wharton, the Decoration of Houses, and Gender in Turn-of-the-Century America', in *Architecture and Feminism*, eds Debra Coleman, *et al.* (New York: Princeton Architectural Press, 1996), 149. In this respect, Chase suggests that the library was part of Wharton's broader desire to create 'an opening for a new equality between men and women' within the domestic environment. Ibid., 132, 154.

[9]   Elizabeth Marbury, *My Crystal Ball, Reminiscences* (New York: Boni and Liveright, 1923), 149.

[10] See Franck Ferrand, *Ils ont sauvé Versailles: de 1789 à nos jours*

With concerted effort narrated in detail in their respective memoirs and with the aid of their close friend, the novelist and playwright Victorien Sardou, Elsie de Wolfe and Elisabeth Marbury purchased the Villa Trianon as a permanent summer residence. The property stood on the edge of the palace gardens in Versailles and had once been home to the daughters of Louis XV. While its location suggested an indissoluble link with the neighbouring palace grounds, the main building had been erected in the early nineteenth century.[11]

The nineteenth-century origins of the Villa Trianon did not prevent de Wolfe from transforming it in direct reference to the neighbouring palace. In the 1890s, Pierre de Nolhac, the conservator of Versailles, had initiated an extensive restoration project that aimed to erase changes made there during the nineteenth century, particularly under Louis-Philippe.[12] Introduced to Nolhac by their mutual friend Sardou, De Wolfe's discussions with him and knowledge of his nearby renovation served to further reinforce her existing preference for seventeenth and eighteenth century furnishings and her decision 'to restore the rooms [in the Villa Trianon] to a Louis XV scheme of decoration.'[13] In particular she went to great lengths to find appropriate cladding for the salon, eventually installing a suite of wood panelling painted white with blue highlights salvaged from a friend's house. Outfitted with eighteenth-century furniture, the forms and colour of this central reception space echoed the

(Perrin, 2003), 219–22; Pascale Richard, *Versailles: the American story*, tr. Barbara Mellor (Paris: Alain de Gourcuff, 1999), 110–18; and Robert Pageard, *Mémoires de Versailles: témoignages, souvenirs, évocations* (Paris: Éditions Hervas, 1984), 148–9.

[11] Located at 47 boulevard Saint-Antoine, the so-called Villa Trianon was built for the son of Louis-Philippe, the Duc de Nemours. When Marbury purchased the house, it had been left unoccupied for several decades and required extensive repairs.

[12] Pierre de Nolhac was the director of the château and gardens of Versailles from 1887 to 1920. See Ferrand, 199–218; and Pierre de Nolhac, *La Resurrection de Versailles: souvenirs d'un conservateur, 1887-1920*, ed. Christophe Pincemaille (Paris: Perrin; Versailles: Société des Amis de Versailles, 2002).

[13] De Wolfe (2004), 182.

so-called white salon that Nolhac had recently recreated, amidst a storm of public debate and interest, at Versailles.

As with her previous projects, de Wolfe installed an eclectic mixture of elements at the Villa Trianon, blending modern amenities (most notably individual bathroom suites for each of the five bedrooms in the villa) with eighteenth-century furnishings. One guest room featured a slightly miniaturised rendition of the king's bed, while a collection of eighteenth-century prints distinguished de Wolfe's own bedroom. Penny Sparke has analysed the rhetoric of taste and ideology of class articulated by the interior designs of Elsie de Wolfe, suggesting that her emphasis on French aristocratic traditions provided a ready vocabulary through which the American nouveau riche who comprised de Wolfe's clientele might clearly communicate their cultural and political aspirations.[14] Through their conscientious efforts to underscore the proximity of the Villa Trianon to the original referent of Versailles and the aesthetic forms associated with it, de Wolfe and Marbury inserted themselves even more directly into such a conservative fantasy of aristocratic privilege than was possible in their living spaces in New York.

The neighbouring palace was most overtly mimicked in the miniaturised hall of mirrors that de Wolfe created at the Villa Trianon (Figure 1).

---

[14]   Penny Sparke, 'Always in Good Taste', *Harvard Design Magazine*, 11 (Summer 2000), 16–20. Sparke's work is extremely valuable in charting the ideological contradictions embedded in de Wolfe's efforts to popularise her design programme. While this is an important line of inquiry, here I am interested in examining what these references meant for de Wolfe and her intimates, whom Sparke described in passing as 'a homosexual circle', Sparke (2003), 74.

Figure 1: Interior view of Elsie de Wolfe's renovation of the Villa Trianon,
Versailles, *ca*. 1920s.
© Elsie de Wolfe Foundation, Santa Monica.

The narrow space of the hall with its repeated chandeliers featured a series of French doors opening onto the garden. Two frescos by Drian representing the Versailles gardens were painted on the opposite wall, flanking an elaborate marble mantle that was surmounted by a large, unframed mirror. Mirrors were, in fact, found throughout the Villa Trianon, particularly in its expansive bathrooms where corner mirrors were echoed by small mirrors, including one in de Wolfe's bathroom attached to a tray that sat across the bathtub. Aaron Betsky has suggested that de Wolfe repeatedly used mirrors 'to open up the enclosed space of femininity'.[15] To the contrary, I would argue that far from opening the interior enclosure, de Wolfe's use of mirrors staged an even more insistent interiority; the repeated mirroring refracted décor and inhabitants back onto themselves through the artifice of display and reflection. At the same time, the association of mirrors with narcissism and the repeated slippage in the early twentieth century between images of female narcissism and those of female homoeroticism suggests a rather different reading.[16] The Villa Trianon was an environment organised around the repeated display of representations of de Wolfe and Marbury, whether in Drian's frescos or in their reflected images in the villa's many mirrors. As much de Wolfe's renovation of the Villa Trianon seemed to create a site of narcissistic representation modelled on the self-referential royal splendour of Versailles, the active redoubling of these two women's bodies within these spaces might also be seen to raise the spectre of female homoeroticism through their virtual superimposition.[17]

While de Wolfe and Marbury self-consciously turned away from the capital city, Natalie Barney migrated in the opposite direction. In October 1909, when Barney moved from the suburbs of Neuilly to Paris, she

[15]   Aaron Betsky, *Queer Space* (New York: William Morrow, 1997), 101.
[16]   Tirza True Latimer's discussion of the significance of mirrors in the collaborative 'self-portraits' of Claude Cahun and Marcel Moore is suggestive in this context: 'Looking Like a Lesbian: portraiture and sexual identity in 1920s Paris', in Chadwick and Latimer, 134–7. See also Havelock Ellis, 'Auto-Eroticism, a Psychological Study', *Studies in the Psychology of Sex* (Philadelphia: F.A. Davis & Co., 1910), I.
[17]   For a related treatment of lesbian desire as narcissistic fusion, see Lucille Cairns's chapter in this volume.

positioned herself in the heart of the literary and artistic topography of the Latin Quarter. In the midst of the city, at 20, rue Jacob, Barney discovered a protected refuge that would nonetheless allow her to insert herself more directly into the contemporary literary world.[18] Barney's dwelling stood at the far end of a cobblestone courtyard behind the four-story apartment building that fronted the street. This seventeenth-century *pavilion* was a two-story, semi-detached residence, with its own private gardens. According to Barney, the miniature Greek temple, known as the Temple de l'Amitié (Temple of Friendship), that stood in the rear garden made her particularly interested in moving there. As with de Wolfe and Marbury's acquisition of the Villa Trianon, Barney's investment in this place was motivated by the desire to inhabit a suitably evocative environment that might simultaneously confer the social distinction she sought.

Barney's architectural interventions at 20, rue Jacob were much less elaborate than those of de Wolfe at the Villa Trianon, but she did make one key structural modification to the property. Although her house and gardens were set back and protected from the main street, Barney erected a garage at the end of the rear alley that further restricted visual and physical access to the Temple de l'Amitié.[19] With this addition, the garden and its folly were even more clearly distinguished as a space apart from the surrounding city and from contemporary social norms. In a letter to Isabelle Gardner, Elsie de Wolfe expressed a similar desire to turn away from external realities, writing, 'I shut my eyes close to shut in all

[18]   Unlike de Wolfe and Marbury, Barney lived permanently in France, self-consciously distancing herself from the United States and adopting an identity of cosmopolitan expatriate. Not only did she become an active part of Francophone and Anglophone literary and artistic communities in Paris, but she also published most of her writings in French. Sandra M. Gilbert and Susan Gubar have argued that the expatriate identity of Barney and her circle was critical to their conception of lesbianism 'as a perpetual, ontological expatriation' in '"She Meant What I Said": Lesbian Double-Talk', in *No-Man's Land: the place of the woman writer in the twentieth century* (New Haven and London: Yale University Press, 1989), II, 219.

[19]   Jean Chalon, *Chère Natalie Barney: portrait d'une séductrice* (Paris: Flammarion, 1992), 6.

the beauty of [...] your wonderful things and shut out all the *banalité* and sordidness of our incredible present.'[20] Both Barney and de Wolfe worked to emphatically separate their living environments from the modern urban landscape, either by creating an enclosed oasis at once embedded in and detached from Paris or by retreating to Versailles. The white linen curtains Natalie Barney installed in her bedroom expressed such a desire in no uncertain terms as they were embroidered with the phrase, 'May our closed curtains separate us from the world.'[21] By self-consciously immersing themselves in a carefully designed interiority oriented towards earlier historical traditions, de Wolfe and Barney created controlled environments in which to stage alternative visions for the present by way of imaginative fantasies of the past.

Barney's seemingly haphazard accumulation of objects and furnishings at 20, rue Jacob would seem to bear little resemblance to de Wolfe's concerted orchestration of a coordinated aesthetic at the Villa Trianon. In contrast to the representational strategies of de Wolfe's eighteenth-century furnishings as markers of privilege, the interior spaces of 20 rue Jacob were transformed by Barney's weekly salon gatherings. On Fridays, she invited writers, scholars, artists, and friends to afternoon gatherings that included such figures as Gertrude Stein, Robert de Montesquiou, Isadora Duncan, Radclyffe Hall, André Gide, Ezra Pound, and Dolly Wilde.[22] Following the seventeenth and eighteenth-century tradition of the salon, Barney conceived these events as private gatherings of selected guests and simultaneously as interventions into the broader

---

20 Elsie de Wolfe, cited in David Park Curry, *Cultural Leadership in America: art matronage and patronage* (Boston: Trustees of the Isabella Stewart Gardner Museum, 1997).

21 'Aux fenêtres, des rideaux de linon blanc où est brodée cette phrase: "Que nos rideaux fermés nous séparent du monde."' Chalon (1992), 125.

22 While Barney's salon was most active in the 1910s and 1920s, it continued to meet during the following decade, until Barney left Paris in 1940, near the beginning of the Second World War. Although in 1949 Barney resumed her gatherings, they were held on a much smaller scale. See Michèle Causse, *Berthe, ou un demi-siècle auprès de l'amazone* (Paris: Editions Tierce, 1980).

literary sphere. Historically, the salon provided a space in which aristocratic women were allowed unusual latitude to both orchestrate and participate in literary, artistic, and political circles.[23] In this way, the eighteenth-century identifications of Barney's interiors were constituted less through the revival of a particular style of furnishings than through reference to the model of sociability provided by famed *salonnières*.

Through the performative ritual of her salon, Barney actively remapped the symbolic significance of her surroundings, as was suggested by an unusual drawing she included as the frontispiece to her 1929 collection of literary portraits, *Aventures de l'esprit* (Figure 2).[24] At the top of the drawing, the Temple de l'Amitié that stood in her rear garden hovers above the outlines of the interior spaces and the scrawled names of salon habitués to form an iconic architectural figurehead for the salon. However, it is the imagined movements of Barney herself, represented by the meandering line that winds through the salon and up the steps of the Temple de l'Amitié, inscribed at various points with her literary moniker 'the Amazon', that activates the imagined community of the salon.[25] Barney's pseudonym might also be seen to connect her salon

[23]   See Erica Harth, 'The Salon Woman Goes Public...Or Does She?', in *Going Public: women and publishing in early modern France*, eds Elizabeth C. Goldsmith and Dena Goodman (Ithaca and London: Cornell University Press, 1995); and Dena Goodman, 'Public Sphere and Private Life: toward a synthesis of current historiographical approaches to the old regime', *History and Theory*, 31: 1 (1992), 1–20.

[24]   Natalie Clifford Barney, *Aventures de l'esprit* (Paris: Émile-Paul Frères, 1929); *Adventures of the Mind*, tr. John Spalding Gatton (New York and London: New York University Press, 1992). This drawing and its relationship to the performative aesthetics of Barney's salon is explored more fully in Sheila Crane, 'Mapping the Amazon's Salon : symbolic landscapes and topographics of identity in Natile Clifford barney's salon, in *Gender and Landscape: renegotiating the moral landscape, ed. Lorraine Dowler, et. al* (London and New York : Routledge, 2005).

[25]   Barney was first introduced to a broad Parisian literary public by way of her moniker, 'the Amazon', when Rémy de Gourmont published of his correspondence with Barney in 1914 in *Lettres à L'Amazone* (Paris: Crès, 1914). Although Barney's intimates had long known her by this nickname, Gourmont's publication solidified her literary identity in these terms even as they helped to further her own writing career.

and her embrace of the role of *salonnière* to the tradition of the *précieuses*, a group of seventeenth-century literary women who overtly rejected traditional feminine roles of wife and mother.[26]

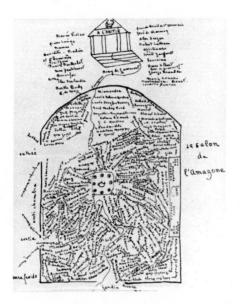

Figure 2: Natalie Clifford Barney, 'Le Salon de l'Amazone', frontispiece to N.C. Barney, *Aventures de l'esprit* (Paris: Émile Frères, 1929). © Bancroft Library, University of California, Berkeley.

Barney's pseudonym referred not only to her penchant for horseback riding but also to her own identification with a historical tradition of actively independent women.

[26] See Harth, 183; Jolanta Pekacz, *Conservative Tradition in Pre-Revolutionary France: Parisian salon women* (New York: Peter Lang, 1999), 85–97; and Donna Stanton, 'The Fiction of Préciosité and the Fear of Women', *Yale French Studies*, 62 (1981), 107–34. Barney's friend, Magdeleine Wauthier, described her precisely in these terms, recalling her habit of dressing in the guise of Mlle Montpensier, as an Amazon of the seventeenth century: 'Portrait de Natalie Barney', in Natalie Clifford Barney, *Traits et portraits* (Paris: Mercure de France, 1963), 13.

As much as the salon tradition provided Barney with a means of articulating her own individual literary identity, it also offered a ready vocabulary for imagining alternative forms of sociability. The repeated term, 'the Amazon', scrawled along the meandering line in the drawing, depicted multiple sites of encounters between Barney and her guests. At her weekly gatherings, Barney actively brought people together, in the same way that in the drawing the line of her suggested movement organised the individuals assembled in these spaces and united them into an imagined community. The drawing thus functioned neither simply as a self-portrait of a single individual nor merely as a group portrait. Instead, Barney drew herself in relationship to others, constructing her own identity in terms of the people she gathered around her in the vein of earlier *salonnières*. Through the repeated experience of her Friday gatherings, the spaces of 20, rue Jacob were activated as sites for an ideal community inspired by the mythic vision of female autonomy, inter-subjective exchange, and shared creativity that Barney saw in the historical model of the salon.

Garden Follies

As much as the interiors of the Villa Trianon and 20, rue Jacob served as important sites for imaginative reoccupations, the suggestive qualities of their gardens encouraged de Wolfe and Barney to focus particular attention on exterior spaces. In the case of both the Villa Trianon and 20, rue Jacob, the existing landscapes were significantly fragmentary. In particular, an outlying building at the Villa Trianon appeared to be a vestige of the infamous *hameau* (hamlet) that Marie-Antoinette constructed in the gardens of Versailles. In her memoirs, de Wolfe lamented the presence of a wall separating this building from its pendants, noting that it was the sight of this rustic lodge that had 'worked upon our imaginations until we were bound to have [the Villa Trianon] as our own.'[27] One of the property's only extant physical traces of this site's

27   De Wolfe (1935), 152.

former contiguity with Versailles, this structure was incorporated into de Wolfe's renovation and transformed into a guesthouse.

In consultation with period plans of this site provided by Pierre de Nolhac, de Wolfe restored the formal garden area known as *la salle de verdure*, an open, grassy area encircled by trees with a marble nymph by the eighteenth-century sculptor Clodion at its centre.[28] Another section of the garden was organised around a small domed garden folly, known as the Music Pavilion, erected by de Wolfe at one end of a reflecting pool.[29] Both gardens were created as outdoor rooms, with the walls surrounding the property imagined as extensions of the main building's facades. Although these boundaries separated this site from the château and grounds of Versailles, their imagined connection was expressed anew through the construction of a broad, covered terrace along the rear façade of the Villa Trianon. Enclosed by walls at either end, the terrace oriented the gaze of its inhabitants towards the garden where de Wolfe had erected an elaborate trellis structure (Figure 3). Above it, through an opening in the trees, the palace could be glimpsed in the distance. De Wolfe thus drew upon the strategies of the English picturesque tradition in which the composition of landscapes repeatedly 'focused on organising experience into a series of framed picture planes deployed for their associative value.'[30] In this way, de Wolfe's physical and spatial manipulations of the Villa Trianon made visible her understanding of Versailles as its essential point of orientation and symbolic origin.

[28]   De Wolfe (2004), 179.
[29]   This structure was designed in collaboration with the architect M. du Chêne; 'Villa Trianon, Versailles', *Architectural Record*, 53 (March 1923), 224–7.
[30]   Sylvia Lavin, 'Sacrifice and the Garden: Watelet's "Essai sur les jardins" and the Space of the Picturesque', *Assemblage*, 28 (December 1995), 18. Also see Stephanie Ross's description of Thomas Duncombe's construction in 1758 of a terrace at his Yorkshire estate at Rievaulx in 'The Picturesque: an eighteenth-century debate', *The Journal of Aesthetics and Art Criticism*, 46: 2 (Winter 1987), 271–72.

Figure 3: Elsie de Wolfe, Garden treillage, Villa Trianon, Versailles, 1923.
© Architectural Record, 53 (March 1923)

In contrast to de Wolfe's Music Pavilion, Natalie Barney's garden folly
was not a new construction, but seemed to have been erected in the early
nineteenth century (Figure 4).[31] Like the vestiges of Marie-Antoinette's
hameau at the Villa Trianon, the Temple de l'Amitié gestured towards the
past, particularly given its legendary origins as a tomb for the eighteenth-
century actress, Adrienne Lecouvreur. At the same time, however, the
temporal detachment of the temple from its romantic beginnings was
underscored by the fact that it was no longer a prominent marker within a
coordinated landscape, but simply an overlooked remnant crowded into
one corner of an extremely condensed garden. While the temple became a
focal point of Barney's salon activities, the surrounding garden was never
transformed into carefully orchestrated, formal assemblages like those de

---

[31]   See Pierre Champion, 'Le Temple de l'Amitié', in *Mon Vieux Quartier*
       (Paris: Éditions Bernard Grasset, 1932), 388–400; and M. Melicourt, 'Le
       Temple de l'Amitié à Paris', *Vieilles Maisons Françaises*, 66 (October
       1975), 28–29.

Wolfe created, but was maintained instead as a somewhat overgrown, verdant enclosure.

Figure 4: Temple de l'Amitié (Temple of Friendship) in Natalie Barney's rear garden at 20, rue Jacob, Paris, ca. 1920. Arch Phot. Coll. MAP © Caisse National des Monuments, Paris.

Despite their differences, the garden follies of de Wolfe and Barney were both inspired by the picturesque garden tradition. Beginning in the early eighteenth century, English gardens incorporated varied constructions (*fabriques*) that were 'included to diversify the scene, promote associations, and interact with the natural forms' of their surroundings.[32] During this period, structures dedicated either to friendship or to love became familiar elements of such pleasure gardens. One of the earliest versions was designed by William Kent for Lord Burlington's gardens at Chiswick in 1729. By mid century, variants on this theme were necessary components of aristocratic gardens in France, including Watelet's garden at Moulin Joli.[33] However, the most immediate reference known to both de Wolfe and Barney was the Temple de l'Amour constructed by Charles Mique for Marie-Antoinette as part of her renovation of the gardens surrounding the Petit Trianon in the late 1770s. A new focal point of Marie-Antoinette's expanded pleasure garden, this structure was repeatedly transformed by night-time illumination and fireworks into a spectacular backdrop and stage for concerts, plays, costume balls, and others of the queen's famous *divertissements*.

At once the architectural figurehead of the garden's libertine pleasures, the Temple de l'Amour dramatically recreated nature as elaborate, excessive artifice, pushing the structural logic of Versailles to new and expressly eroticised heights.

---

[32]   John Dixon Hunt, *The Picturesque Garden Tradition in Europe* (London: Thames and Hudson, 2002), 32. See also David Watkin, *The English Vision: the picturesque in architecture, landscape and garden design* (New York: Harper and Row, 1982); Dora Wiebenson, *The Picturesque Garden in France* (Princeton: Princeton University Press, 1978); Eleanor P. DeLorme, *Garden Pavilions and the Eighteenth-Century French Court* (Woodbridge, Suffolk: Antique Collectors' Club, 1996).

[33]   Watelet's garden at Moulin Joli is an important reference in this context, since it served as the meeting place for his salon where Marie-Antoinette was a frequent visitor. Lavin, 19–20; Claude-Henri Watelet, *Essai sur les jardins* (Paris: Prault, 1774); *Essay on Gardens*, tr. Samuel Denon (Philadelphia: University of Philadelphia Press, 2003). See also Bernd Dams, 'Betz: le temple à l'amitié', in *La Folie de Bâtir: pavillons d'agrément et folies sous l'Ancien Régime* (Paris: Flammarion, 1995).

According to de Wolfe, the Music Pavilion was designed to recreate the eighteenth-century garden follies in *treillage* (trellis work) that once populated the park of Versailles, but which had been largely destroyed.[34] For the inaugural party de Wolfe and Marbury hosted in honour of this new structure, the reflecting pool was stocked with a pair of swans and illuminated for the occasion, while the sounds of distant trumpet players stationed behind the walls on the palace grounds heightened the evocative atmosphere. After dinner, musical entertainment in the Pavilion featured works by Lully and Mozart, Marie-Antoinette's favourite composers, to further create an appropriate mood. The Music Pavilion thus marked de Wolfe's desire to reclaim her garden and its follies as sites where natural elements were transformed by theatrical artifice, following the model of Marie-Antoinette's interventions at Versailles.

Although de Wolfe first used *treillage* in her interior designs for the Colony Club, the first private club for women that opened in New York in 1907, she claimed Marie-Antoinette's Temple de l'Amour in Versailles as the inspiration for this device.[35] Similar elements were common in earlier gardens in France, including the one Louis XIV created in Marly-le-Roi in the late 1670s and Watelet's later Moulin Joli.[36] In de Wolfe's hands, however, *treillage* became the dominant motif of the Villa Trianon's landscape. Both exterior and interior walls of the Music Pavilion were submerged beneath green strips of wood arranged in crisscrossed latticework, and their patterns were echoed in the upholstery of its furnishings. The glass dome brought light into the interior, casting shifting shadows through the latticework forms of hollow columns arrayed along its walls. As much as de Wolfe's attempt to recreate the garden as a series of outdoor rooms inverted the usual relationship between interior and exterior, the trellises covering the Music Pavilion

---

[34]   See Dixon, 115.
[35]   The building itself was designed by the architect Stanford White. See Smith, 102–12; de Wolfe (1935), 49–65; 'The Work of McKim, Mead and White: Colony Club', *New York Architect*, 2 (November 1908), 251, 285–95, 307; and 'Colony Club, New York', *Architectural Record*, 54 (July 1923), 30–31.
[36]   De Wolfe (2004), 170.

seemed to dematerialise its solid, architectural structure, notionally dissolving it into the surrounding landscape.

The *treillage* element erected opposite the outdoor terrace pushed these dynamics to an even further extreme, as this freestanding structure became a permeable screen, punctuated by the series of marble sculptures of cupids and two old benches placed in front of it. Here de Wolfe claimed to replicate the entrance arch and doors to the famous labyrinth in the gardens of Versailles, although the fact that these structures had long been destroyed allowed her free reign to exercise her fantasy.[37] In a photo of this structure published in 1923 (see Figure 3 above), the surrounding vegetation had grown through many of the perforated openings, to the point where the landscape threatened to completely absorb the trellis wall. De Wolfe played with these screens' ability to obscure from view as much as they seemed at first to reveal. As she later explained, 'Always in the garden I think one must feel one has not come to the end, one must go on and on in search of new beauties and the hidden delights we feel sure must be behind the clipped hedges or the trellis walls.'[38] Through such theatrical mediation of nature and artifice, de Wolfe staged perceptual tricks in the garden akin to the duplicitous reflections in the Villa Trianon's numerous mirrors. At some point, de Wolfe herself concretised this connection by incorporating mirrors into her outdoor *treillage* structures.

Although Versailles was less a direct reference, Natalie Barney understood her garden folly in similar terms to Marie-Antoinette's Temple de l'Amour as a site of and symbol for erotic attachments. For Barney, the picturesque provided a vocabulary for celebrating friendship and love that resonated with the historic culture of the salon even as it drew on classical Epicurean philosophy that identified the garden as a privileged site for ideal friendship.[39] Barney self-consciously appropriated

---

[37]   Ibid., 171.

[38]   Ibid.

[39]   For a provocative discussion of this connection, see Lavin, 20–21 where she notes that Watelet dedicated his treatise on gardens to friendship (*l'amitié*). For an examination of the eighteenth-century iconography initiated by Madame de Pompadour, see Katherine K. Gordon, 'Madame

and redirected such traditions in direct relation to the Temple de l'Amitié in her garden. Indeed, Barney effectively reconsecrated the temple to her own conception of *l'amitié*. Inspired by Epicurean and Platonic philosophies of virtuous love, Barney nevertheless recast their usual masculine focus in her formulation of friendship that focused primarily, although not exclusively, on relationships between women.

For Barney, *l'amitié* was a flexible form combining eighteenth-century ideals of *esprit* and Sapphic eroticism that were understood together as the necessary basis for productive artistic creativity. Barney believed *l'amitié* to be an inter-subjective process, shared and constructed between two people through their creative, intellectual, and potentially erotic exchanges. Ideally, however, this original dyadic structure was not a stable end in itself, but should instead be oriented towards and eventually absorbed into the broader community.[40] Following her interpretation of Sappho's life, Barney rejected conventions of fidelity and monogamy, emphasising instead the importance of constancy, passion, intellectual engagement, and creative exchange to her ideal vision of social, artistic, and erotic relationships. Barney thereby envisioned *l'amitié* as a new form of modern sociability constructed through creative exchange and fluid affective bonds in which female homoeroticism occupied a privileged position.

Thanks to its inscription, the Temple de l'Amitié became the architectural embodiment of Barney's ideal. Although salon gatherings were never held inside Barney's garden folly, its doors were often left open so that visitors could take a brief tour.[41] Select guests might visit the temple's interior to pay homage to the 'cult' of *l'amitié* that the building

---

de Pompadour, Pigalle, and the Iconography of Friendship', *Art Bulletin* 50: 3 (September 1968), 249–62.

[40] As Barney later explained, 'And didn't the great Sappho live in harmony, not with one but with several of her female friends who, in succession, felt those sweet rivalries that were more a subject of inspiration than discordance.' ['Et la grande Sapho ne vécut-elle pas en harmonie, non avec une seule mais plusieurs de ses amies qui, se succèdent, éprouvèrent de ces douces rivalités qui furent plutôt un sujet d'inspiration que de discorde.'] Barney (1963), 173.

[41] Berthe Cleyrergue, quoted in Causse, 133.

evoked. Such an association was further cemented by the fact that Barney only formally used the room inside the temple for small dinner parties limited to her most intimate friends. Barney's ethics of *l'amitié* were intended as a critique of both contemporary social practices and institutional structures. In response to the masculine bias of the Académie Française, Barney created her own Académie des Femmes that brought together Francophone and Anglophone writers, poets, and artists. In the early months of 1927, each new member was honoured at an induction ceremony held on the steps of Barney's prized garden folly.[42] As the physical stage for these events, the Temple de l'Amitié and the garden that surrounded it framed a site where such an ideal of female creativity and lesbian desire might not merely be imagined but finally actualised.

Spectral Presences

In the eyes of their residents, the Villa Trianon and 20, rue Jacob were houses haunted by phantoms. Echoes of imagined histories seemed to continually intrude on the present. In her memoirs, Elsie de Wolfe nostalgically characterised the early stages of her occupation of the Villa Trianon with Elisabeth Marbury as a quest for absent presences:

> We often wondered about this house, about the kind of people who had lived there, and about the lives they led. We used to make up stories about them, peopling the gardens and empty rooms with all sorts of fanciful figures of a bygone day. Sometimes on moonlit nights we surely saw them–bewitching ghosts, glamorous in their patches and paints and powder. It was easy to create fantasies in surroundings so romantic that anything might have happened in them. Especially this was so with me, as I never felt a stranger in Versailles.[43]

De Wolfe's project of recreating the Villa Trianon was undertaken not simply as an architectural renovation, but even more importantly as a

---

42 Although other performances had taken place in front of the Temple de l'Amitié, Barney called the Academy of Women 'one of its most sacred missions'. Barney (1992), 129.

43 De Wolfe (1935), 151.

constructive fantasy. As de Wolfe remarked, 'there were several old stone benches under the trees that must have known the secrets of the famous ladies of the eighteenth-century courts.'[44] Theatrical artifice thus merged with imaginative speculation in the shadows of the garden. Uncanny disturbances were frequently revealed in the filtered light and protected recesses of gardens, whether in the carefully restored landscape of the Villa Trianon or in Barney's relatively unkempt and overgrown enclosure behind her house.

At 20, rue Jacob, the rear garden likewise formed the setting for imaginative séances orchestrated by Natalie Barney. In her 1929 drawing, her garden and its folly were clearly distinguished as memorial sites visited by familiar ghosts. The outlined façade of the Temple de l'Amitié at the top of the drawing was flanked by the names of people associated with her salon who had died, including such luminaries as Pierre Louÿs, Anatole France, Rainer Maria Rilke, and Marcel Proust. Here Renée Vivien, a poet and Barney's lover who committed suicide in 1909, held a primary position. The separation of this register in the drawing from the outlined interior spaces below distinguished the Temple de l'Amitié as a monument to the deceased at the same time that it positioned Barney as the active connection between these two sites. In at least one salon meeting, the temple functioned as a commemorative space where the ghosts of the dead were directly invoked. Six years after Renée Vivien's death, a special memorial program was held in her honour that began with a reading of one of her poems in front of the temple before moving inside to the salon's usual quarters.[45] In this way, the Temple de l'Amitié became a symbolic link within both the drawing and the topography of salon performances between the living salon and its deceased members.

---

[44] De Wolfe (2004), 184. Elsewhere, however, de Wolfe wistfully regretted that the Villa Trianon was directly linked to Louis XV's daughters rather than more romantic figures like Madame du Berry or Madame de Pompadour. Ibid., 177.

[45] Programme reprinted in Jean-Paul Goujon (éd.), *Correspondances Croisées: Pierre Louÿs, Natalie Clifford Barney, Renée Vivien* (Muizon: À l'Ecart, 1983).

As a key fulcrum, the temple forged an imagined continuity between past and present communities that might be conjured together in its shadows.

Terry Castle has argued that lesbianism constitutes a ghostly presence within modern culture, one most readily recognised through its negation and disavowal. Since the nineteenth century, literary texts repeatedly transformed women who desired other women into apparitions, effectively de-realising their sexual desire at the very moment it threatened finally to appear.[46] While the ghostly metaphor was a means of denying female homoeroticism, beginning in the early twentieth century, lesbian writers used this figure to their own ends.[47] Such evocations of phantom visitors thus provided a productive poetics through which to articulate unconventional longings in narrative form. I would suggest that de Wolfe and Barney charted similar aesthetics through the imaginative recreation of their living environments.

While waiting for the sale of the Villa Trianon to be approved in 1906, de Wolfe and Marbury voraciously read accounts of court life at Versailles, immersing themselves in the vanished world suggested by their surroundings.[48] The previous year, de Wolfe and Marbury had attended a costume ball in New York where they donned dresses inspired by Marie-Antoinette and courtly ladies of the eighteenth century. Through her recreation of the Villa Trianon, Elsie de Wolfe attempted to bring such associations to life within these spaces. In this setting, she and Marbury could more easily transport themselves to another time and place. Pierre de Nolac, the consummate narrator of Versailles's mythic past, affirmed this vision, telling de Wolfe, 'you are not a modern woman. You are a ghost who has come back from the court of Louis XVI.'[49] At Versailles, rather than a temporary travesty, the fantasy of

---

[46]   Castle, 2–5, 28–45.
[47]   Ibid., 46–60.
[48]   De Wolfe (1935), 154.
[49]   Pierre de Nolhac, quoted in de Wolfe (1935), 151. Nolhac's extensive series, *Études sur la cour de France*, published by Calmann-Lévy (Paris), documented the history of Versailles and its inhabitants, focusing particularly on the lives of its female inhabitants: *La reine Marie-Antoinette* (1900); *Louis XV et Madame de Pompadour d'après des documents inédits* (1906); *Louis XV et Marie Leczinska, d'après de*

stepping into the shoes of Marie-Antoinette or other romantic figures of the royal past, seemed to become a palpable reality.

While de Wolfe and Marbury were clearly seduced by the aura of privilege and refinement that Versailles represented, their re-creation of the Villa Trianon was not simply a revival of historical styles, but an attempt to revivify an idealised, past world. While de Wolfe and Marbury might seemed to have been modelling themselves after the image of Marie-Antoinette as honourable queen stilled in time before the Revolution, their adoption of the guise of court ladies of Versailles might be read as a somewhat more ambiguous gesture. After all, as de Wolfe herself observed, 'Nothing is impossible in this garden.'[50] Might their investment in the romantic secrets and ghostly presences thus seemed to resonate powerfully with rather more transgressive images of aristocratic women and with the illicit pleasures in which Marie-Antoinette was accused of indulging within her garden follies.

During the French Revolution, the Petit Trianon and its extensive gardens at Versailles were specifically satirised as dangerously libidinous spaces in pamphlets criticising Marie-Antoinette's libertine practices, including her supposed affairs with women.[51] As Marie-Antoinette's private retreat, the Petit Trianon functioned as an intimate space insistently detached from the palace where the queen was known to entertain her favourites, including the Princess de Lamballe. Whereas

nouveaux documents (1910); *Le Trianon de Marie-Antoinette* (1924); and *Madame de Pompadour et la politique, d'après des documents nouveaux* (1928).

[50]   De Wolfe (1935), 151.

[51]   Representations of Marie-Antoinette in revolutionary pamphlet literature has been the subject of significant recent historical work: Elizabeth Colwill, 'Pass as a Woman, Act Like a Man: Marie-Antoinette as tribade in the pornography of the French Revolution', in *Marie-Antoinette: writings on the body of the queen*, ed. Dena Goodman (New York and London: Routledge, 2003), 139–69; Chantal Thomas, *The Wicked Queen: the origins of the myth of Marie-Antoinette* (New York: Zone Books, 1999), esp. 119–35; Lynn Hunt, 'The Many Bodies of Marie Antoinette', *The Family Romance of the French Revolution* (Berkeley: University of California Press, 1992), 88–123, repr. in Goodman (2003), 117–38; and Castle, 126–31, repr. in Goodman (2003), 199–238.

Marie-Antoinette's late nineteenth-century biographers, including Pierre de Nolhac, attempted to put to rest rumours of her homosexuality, their defense of her friendships as platonic nevertheless placed renewed focus on her erotic investments.[52] Speculation fuelled by revolutionary pamphlets that depicted Marie-Antoinette as *tribade* thus continued to haunt subsequent representations of the queen to the point where, according to Terry Castle, she was effectively embraced in the early twentieth century as a lesbian heroine.[53]

Castle has suggested that controversy surrounding the sexual proclivities of the queen and the illicit character of her gardens must bear some connection to the publication of an unusual volume, *An Adventure*, in 1911.[54] Written by Charlotte Anne Moberly and Eleanor Jourdain, the principal and vice-principal of St Hugh's College at Oxford University, the book recounted their visit to the gardens of Versailles in 1901. Near the Petit Trianon, they encountered a series of remarkable personages who they later decided must have been apparitions from the court of Marie-Antoinette. Their joint venture to document their shared experience of Versailles through the imaginative reconstruction of the past recalled the concerted attempt by de Wolfe and Marbury to recreate their surroundings following their own similarly speculative immersions. In both cases, this shared project seemed to be a means of negotiating the erotics of their own relationships by way of projected fantasies safely redirected towards the past. While the court ladies that so entranced Moberly and Jourdain, as they did de Wolfe and Marbury, might at first appear to register safely within the bounds of aristrocatic propriety, such

---

[52]   See Nolhac (1900). Libertine pamphlets and the accusations they advanced against the queen were the focus of two publications by Hector Fleischmann that appeared around the time that de Wolfe was undertaking her renovation of the Villa Trianon: *Les Pamphlets libertins contre Marie-Antoinette* (Paris: Les Publications Modernes, 1908) and *Les Maitresses de Marie-Antoinette* (Paris: Éditions des Bibliophiles, 1910).

[53]   Castle, 148.

[54]   Ibid, 112–16, 122–5. See Charlotte Anne Moberly, *An Adventure* (London: Macmillan, 1911).

allusions simultaneously revealed the spectre of female homoeroticism lurking at the murky edges of Versailles' expansive gardens.

By contrast, lesbian sexuality was a more overt structuring device for the ideal community Natalie Barney imagined and orchestrated within the spaces of 20, rue Jacob. The iconographic link between the Temple de l'Amour that Marie-Antoinette commissioned for the gardens of the Petit Trianon and Barney's Temple de l'Amitié is suggestive in this regard. One of the most compelling examples of what Terry Castle describes as 'the Marie Antoinette obsession' is found *The Well of Loneliness*, the novel by Radclyffe Hall, a close friend of Barney's. The protagonist, Stephen Gordon, makes a pilgrimage to the gardens of the Petit Trianon at a key moment in the narrative. The Temple de l'Amour frames the climax of the tour as the site where Gordon references the Princess de Lamballe, in a coded gesture to her own homosexuality. Here the reference to the Temple de l'Amour must also be understood as a gesture to Barney's folly, given Hall's familiarity with this structure through her repeated visits to Barney's salon. Here, Hall was re-reading the Temple de l'Amour by way of Barney's own miniature temple. Rather than simply a product of what Castle describes as a 'Marie-Antoinette obsession', this passage bears witness to Barney's successful reinterpretation of the Temple de l'Amitié to articulate a philosophy and aesthetics of female homoeroticism not simply in the guise of a vanishing phantom, but physically manifest in concrete architectural form and indeed productive of social and erotic liens.

Both Elsie de Wolfe and Natalie Barney so thoroughly identified with and absorbed the landscapes and structures they inhabited that they retrospectively reconstructed their choices to inhabit these places as inevitabilities. As de Wolfe observed, 'even when I first came to [the Villa Trianon] years ago, it was as if I was only returning to something I had known before.'[55] While Barney, for her part, claimed, 'it must not be by chance that I have in my garden a little Temple of Friendship.'[56] Elsie de Wolfe and her companion Elisabeth Marbury variously invoked the

[55]   De Wolfe (1935), 151.
[56]   Barney (1992), 129.

architectural forms, interior elaboration, and landscaping traditions of Versailles in their renovation of the so-called Villa Trianon at the edge of the palace gardens. By contrast, Natalie Barney conjured the ghosts of eighteenth-century salon culture and the picturesque garden tradition to articulate the philosophy of creative friendship and amorous attachments she hoped to encourage in the spaces of 20, rue Jacob. For both women, eighteenth-century models provided an aesthetic vocabulary that cloaked female homoeroticism in the normalising and conservative trappings of an aristocratic tradition.

As Sylvia Lavin has noted, the qualities that defined the eighteenth-century picturesque — including theatricality, the decorative, artifice, pictorialism, and an interest in detail and fragments – seemed at once to rely upon and to be used to effectively contain femininity, particularly in the spaces of aristocratic gardens.[57] Although the particular tactics they embraced were not the same, de Wolfe and Barney attempted to redirect the picturesque and its relation to femininity as the basis for their own productive aesthetic strategies, for recreating and orchestrating the spaces and experiences of buildings and landscape. In this way, the picturesque offered a way of extending aestheticism to one's entire way of life by creating an idealising living environment expressive of the imagined character of its actual and desired inhabitants.[58] Rather than pursuing this aim by adopting the example of the dandy aesthete, as represented for example by de Wolfe and Barney's mutual friend, Robert de Montesquiou, these women conjured phantom female interlocutors from past literary and aristocratic culture — whether famed *salonières*, the court ladies of Versailles, or Marie-Antoinette herself — as models for self-fashioning and for shaping idealised modes of homoerotic sociability. In the process, past objects and sites were redefined with the aim of transforming their meanings into symbolic expressions of contemporary

---

[57] Lavin, 18, 27.

[58] For a related discussion of this phenomenon in early twentieth-century women's fashion, see Ann Bermingham, 'The Picturesque and Ready-to-Wear Femininity', in *The Politics of the Picturesque*, eds Stephen Copley and Peter Garside (Cambridge: Cambridge University Press, 1994), 87–88.

identity. The complicity that de Wolfe and Barney shared with various aspects of courtly and aristocratic culture thus allowed them to transgress social conventions while nonetheless remaining safely ensconced behind the protective walls of their homes, where there was little threat of radically challenging the broader society outside their restricted purview.

Bibliography

Barney, Natalie Clifford, *Aventures de l'esprit* (Paris: Émile-Paul Frères, 1929); *Adventures of the Mind*, tr. John Spalding Gatton (New York and London: New York University Press, 1992).

Benstock, Shari, *Women of the Left Bank: Paris, 1900–1940* (Austin: University of Texas Press, 1986).

Bermingham, Ann, 'The Picturesque and Ready-to-Wear Femininity', in *The Politics of the Picturesque*, eds Stephen Copley and Peter Garside (Cambridge: Cambridge University Press, 1994).

Betsky, Aaron, *Queer Space* (New York: William Morrow, 1997).

Casalis, Laura, *Parisian fashion, from the Journal des Dames et des Modes, 1913–1914* (New York: Rizzoli, 1980).

Castle, Terry, *The Apparitional Lesbian: female homosexuality and modern culture* (New York: Columbia University Press, 1993).

Causse, Michèle, *Berthe, ou un demi-siècle auprès de l'amazone* (Paris: Éditions Tierce, 1980).

Chadwick, Whitney and Tirza True Latimer, *The Modern Woman Revisited: Paris between the wars* (New Brunswick, NJ and London: Rutgers University Press, 2003).

Chadwick, Whitney, *Amazons in the Drawing Room: the art of Romaine Brooks* (Berkeley: University of California Press; Washington D.C.: National Museum of Women in the Arts, 2000).

Chalon, Jean, *Chère Natalie Barney: portrait d'une séductrice* (Paris: Flammarion, 1992).

Champion, Pierre, 'Le Temple de l'Amitié', in *Mon Vieux Quartier* (Paris: Éditions Bernard Grasset, 1932), 388–400.

Chase, Vanessa, 'Edith Wharton, the Decoration of Houses, and Gender in Turn-of-the-Century America', in *Architecture and Feminism*, ed. Debra Coleman, *et al.* (New York: Princeton Architectural Press, 1996).

Chêne, M. du, 'Villa Trianon, Versailles', *Architectural Record*, 53 (March 1923), 224–27.

Colwill, Elizabeth, 'Pass as a Woman, Act Like a Man: Marie-Antoinette as tribade in the pornography of the French Revolution', in *Marie-Antoinette: writings on the body of the queen*, ed. Dena Goodman (New York and London: Routledge, 2003).

Crane, Sheila, 'Mapping the Amazon's salon: symbolic landscapes and topographies of identity in Natalie Clifford Barney's literary salon', *Gender and Landscape: renegotiating the moral landscape*, ed. Lorraine Dowler, *et. al.* (London and New York: Routledge, 2005).

Curry, David Park, *Cultural Leadership in America: art matronage and patronage* (Boston: Trustees of the Isabella Stewart Gardner Museum, 1997).

Dams, Bernd, 'Betz: le temple à l'amitié', in *La Folie de Bâtir: pavillons d'agrément et folies sous l'Ancien Régime* (Paris: Flammarion, 1995).

DeLorme, Eleanor P., *Garden Pavilions and the Eighteenth-Century French Court* (Antique Collectors' Club, 1996).

Doan, Laura, *Fashioning Sapphism: the origins of a modern English lesbian culture* (New York: Columbia University Press, 2001).

Elliot, Bridget, 'Performing the Picture or Painting the Other: Romaine Brooks, Gluck, and the question of decadence in 1923', in *Women Artists and Modernism*, ed. Katy Deepwell (Manchester and New York: Manchester University Press, 1998).

Ellis, Havelock, 'Auto-Eroticism, a Psychological Study', *Studies in the Psychology of Sex* (Philadelphia: F. A. Davis Co., 1910), volume 1.

Ferrand, Franck, *Ils ont sauvé Versailles: de 1789 à nos jours* (Perrin, 2003).

Fleischmann, Hector, *Les Maitresses de Marie-Antoinette* (Paris: Éditions des Bibliophiles, 1910).

——, *Les Pamphlets libertins contre Marie-Antoinette* (Paris: Les Publications Modernes, 1908).

Gilbert, Sandra M. and Susan Gubar, '"She Meant What I Said": Lesbian Double-Talk', in *No-Man's Land: the place of the woman writer in the twentieth century* (New Haven and London: Yale University Press, 1989), II.

Goodman, Dena, 'Public Sphere and Private Life: toward a synthesis of current historiographical approaches to the old regime', *History and Theory* 31: 1 (1992), 1–20.

Gordon, Katherine K., 'Madame de Pompadour, Pigalle, and the Iconography of Friendship', *Art Bulletin*, 50: 3 (September 1968), 249–62.

Goujon, Jean-Paul, ed., *Correspondances Croisées: Pierre Louÿs, Natalie Clifford Barney, Renée Vivien* (Muizon: A l'Ecart, 1983).

Gourmont, Rémy de, *Lettres à l'amazone* (Paris: Crès, 1914).

Harth, Erica, 'The Salon Woman Goes Public...Or Does She?', in *Going Public: Women and Publishing in Early Modern France*, eds Elizabeth C. Goldsmith and Dena Goodman (Ithaca and London: Cornell University Press, 1995).

Hunt, John Dixon, *The Picturesque Garden Tradition in Europe* (London: Thames and Hudson, 2002).

Hunt, Lynn, 'The Many Bodies of Marie Antoinette', *The Family Romance of the French Revolution* (Berkeley: University of California Press, 1992).

Jay, Karla, 'Introduction', in Natalie Clifford Barney, *A Perilous Advantage: the best of Natalie Clifford Barney*, tr. Anna Livia (Norwich, VT: New Victoria Publishers, 1992).

Lavin, Sylvia, 'Sacrifice and the Garden: Watelet's 'Essai sur les jardins' and the Space of the Picturesque', *Assemblage*, 28 (December 1995), 16–33.

Marbury, Elizabeth, *My Crystal Ball, Reminiscences* (New York: Boni and Liveright, 1923).

Melicourt, M., 'Le temple de l'amitié à Paris', *Vieilles Maisons Françaises*, 66 (October 1975), 28–29.

Moberly, Charlotte Anne, *An Adventure* (London: Macmillan, 1911).

Nolhac, Pierre de, *La Résurrection de Versailles: souvenirs d'un conservateur, 1887–1920*, ed. Christophe Pincemaille (Paris: Perrin; Versailles: Société des Amis de Versailles, 2002).

Pageard, Robert, *Mémoires de Versailles: témoignages, souvenirs, évocations* (Paris: Éditions Hervas, 1984).

Pekacz, Jolanta, *Conservative Tradition in Pre-Revolutionary France: Parisian salon women* (New York: Peter Lang, 1999).

Richard, Pascale, *Versailles: the American story*, tr. Barbara Mellor (Paris: Alain de Gourcuff, 1999).

Ross, Stephanie, 'The Picturesque: an eighteenth-century debate', *The Journal of Aesthetics and Art Criticism*, 46: 2 (Winter 1987), 271–9.

Smith, Jane S., *Elsie de Wolfe: a life in the high style* (New York: Atheneum, 1982), 131–32.

Sparke, Penny, 'Always in Good Taste', *Harvard Design Magazine*, 11 (Summer 2000), 16–20.

——, 'The "Ideal" and the "Real" Interior in Elsie de Wolfe's *The House in Good Taste* of 1913', *Journal of Design History*, 16: 1 (2003), 63–76.

Stanton, Donna, 'The Fiction of Préciosité and the Fear of Women', *Yale French Studies*, 62 (1981), 107–34.

Thomas, Chantal, *The Wicked Queen: the origins of the myth of Marie-Antoinette* (New York: Zone Books, 1999).

Watelet, Claude-Henri, *Essai sur les jardins* (Paris: Prault, 1774); *Essay on Gardens*, tr. Samuel Denon (Philadelphia: University of Philadelphia Press, 2003).

Watkin, David, *The English Vision: the picturesque in architecture, landscape and garden design* (New York: Harper and Row, 1982).

Wauthier, Magdeleine, 'Portrait de Natalie Barney', in *Traits et portraits*, ed. Natalie Clifford Barney (Paris: Mercure de France, 1963).

Wharton, Edith and Ogden Codman, Jr., *The Decoration of Houses* (New York: Charles Scribner's Sons, 1897).

Wiebenson, Dora, *The Picturesque Garden in France* (Princeton: Princeton University Press, 1978).

Wolfe, Elsie de, *After All* (New York and London: Harper and Brothers, 1935).

——, *The House in Good Taste* (New York: The Century Co., 1913); reprint with preface by Hutton Wilkinson (New York: Rizzoli, 2004).

Notes on Contributors

Sophie Bélot coordinates and lectures on the part-time degree in French Language and Cultures at the University of Sheffield. She has published a number of articles on contemporary French cinema and most particularly on the issue of women's film-making in present-day France. She is currently completing a monograph on the director and scriptwriter Catherine Breillat for Rodopi.

Mireille Brioude teaches in secondary education and lectures on literature and cinema at the University of Paris III. She is an independent scholar who published her thesis *Violette Leduc: la mise en scène du je* with Rodopi in 2000. She has written numerous articles on Violette Leduc and has created the first web site dedicated to Leduc (http://www.violette leduc.com). More recently her work has focused on women's cinema in particular the work of Agnès Varda and she published an article on Varda in *Création au féminin* published by Éditions Universitaires de Dijon in 2006.

Lucille Cairns is Professor of French at Durham University. She has published numerous articles and chapters both on French women's writing and on male and female homosexuality in French literature and film; four single-authored monographs: *Marie Cardinal: motherhood and creativity* (Glasgow: University of Glasgow French and German Publications, 1992), *Privileged Pariahdom: homosexuality in the novels of Dominique Fernandez* (Berne: Peter Lang, 1996), *Lesbian Desire in Post-1968 French Literature* (New York/ Ontario/ Lampeter: The Edwin Mellen Press, 2002), and *Sapphism on Screen: lesbian desire in French and Francophone cinema* (Edinburgh: Edinburgh University Press, 2006); and one sole-edited volume, *Gay and Lesbian Cultures in France* (Oxford, Bern, Berlin, Brussels, Frankfurt, New York, Vienna: Peter Lang, 2002). Her new project centres on Jewish women's writing in French. She is also President of AUPHF (Association of University Professors and Heads of French).

Sheila Crane is an Assistant Professor in the History of Art and Visual Culture at the University of California, Santa Cruz. Her research focuses on architecture, visual cultures and urban histories of modern Europe and the Mediterranean Basin, with a particular interest in France and North

Africa. She is currently completing a book entitled *Mediterranean Cross-roads: Marseille and the remaking of modern architecture.* The essay on Elsie de Wolfe and Natalie Clifford Barney is part of an on-going project examining the spatial practices and performative aesthetics of Natalie Clifford Barney, Romaine Brooks and Elsie de Wolfe.

Amanda Crawley Jackson is Lecturer in French at the University of Shef-field. Her first book is on the early writings of Jean-Paul Sartre and she has written extensively on Simone de Beauvoir and Albertine Sarrazin. Her recent research focuses on the representation and theorisation of space in twentieth-century autobiography and fiction and the contemporary visual arts. The impact of a recently curated exhibition forms part of her current research into cultural policy and strategy in the visual arts and the representation of urban spaces in new art from France.

David Evans is Lecturer in French at the University of St Andrews. His research, which deals with rhythm and music in nineteenth- and twentieth-century French poetry, includes *Rhythm, Illusion and the Poetic Idea: Baudelaire, Rimbaud and Mallarmé* (Amsterdam: Rodopi, 2004) and a series of articles on Théodore de Banville and Michel Houellebecq.

Owen Heathcote is an Honorary Visiting Reader in Modern French Studies at the University of Bradford. He researches on the relationship between violence, gender and representation in French literature and film and has published widely on such authors as Balzac, Cardinal, Duras, Guibert, Guyotat, Jourdan and Wittig. He has recently edited or co-edited special issues of *South Central Review* (on gendered violence) and *Modern and Contemporary France* (on gays and lesbians in contemporary France). He is currently co-editing a volume, *Negotiating Boundaries: identities, sexualities, diversities* for Cambridge Scholars' Press and preparing a monograph on violence in Balzac.

Fran Hutchins is a doctoral candidate at Northwestern University in Evanston, Illinois and is completing a dissertation on the subject of queer exoticism in French novels and performance.

Brigitte Rollet is Senior Lecturer in French Cultural Studies at the University of London Institute in Paris (ULIP). She is the author of *Coline Serreau* (Manchester University Press, 1998) and co-author of *Cinema and the Second Sex: women's filmmaking in France in the 1980s and 1990s* (New York, London: Continuum, 2001). She has published widely on French cinema and television from a gender perspective. She has co-directed *Television in Europe* (Exeter: Intellect, 1997) and *Genre et légitimité culturelle* (Paris: L'Harmattan, 2007). Her last book *Télévision et homosexualité: 10 ans de fictions françaises (1995-2005)* is forthcoming.

Stephanie Schechner is Associate Professor of French and Assistant Dean of the College of Arts and Sciences at Widener University. Her work on nineteenth- and twentieth-century women authors has been published in *Dalhousie French Studies*, *Women in French Studies*, and *Excavatio*. She is currently working on a manuscript devoted to the representation of lesbians in contemporary French cinema.

Ursula Tidd is Senior Lecturer in French Studies at the University of Manchester, UK. Her research interests are the literature and philosophy of Simone de Beauvoir; post-war French culture and thought, with a current focus on the representation of Holocaust experience in French literature and film. She has published two monographs on Simone de Beauvoir: *Simone de Beauvoir, Gender and Testimony*, in the Cambridge Studies in French series (Cambridge: Cambridge University Press, 1999) and *Simone de Beauvoir*, an introduction to Beauvoir's thought in the Routledge 'Critical Thinkers' series (London and New York: Routledge, 2004). She has also recently authored articles and chapters on Beauvoir's *Les Mandarins* and *Les belles images,* Sartre's *La Nausée* and the Holocaust testimonies of Jorge Semprún. Her current projects include a critical biography of Simone de Beauvoir, to be published in the 'Critical Lives' series for Reaktion Books.